Nepal : Land and People
Custom, Tradition and Cultural Values

NEPAL

Land and People

Custom, Tradition and Cultural Values

Dr. Krishna Kumari

PRASHANT PUBLISHING HOUSE
DELHI-110094

Published by :
Prashant Publishing House
C-34, 28 Foota Road, Gali-3,
West Karwal Nagar, Delhi-110094
Phone : 011-22963970, Mob. : 9810396373
e-mail.: prashantpublishinghouse@gmail.com

Nepal : Land and People
Custom, Tradition and Cultural Values
Reserved
First Published 2017

ISBN 978-81-934253-12

PRINTED IN INDIA
Published by Mr. R.K. Jha M/s Prashant Publishing House and Published at H.S. Offset House Press, Delhi.

Contents

Preface

Nepal is named for the Kathmandu Valley, where the nation's founder established a capital in the late eighteenth century. Nepali culture represents a fusion of Indo-Aryan and Tibeto-Mongolian influences, the result of a long history of migration, conquest, and trade.

A landlocked country, Nepal was sandwiched between two giant neighbours—China and India. To the north, the Himalayas constituted a natural and mostly impassible frontier, and beyond that was the border with China. To the south, east, and west, Nepal was hemmed in by India. Without an outlet to the sea, Nepal was dependent on India for international trade and transit facilities.

Nepal is landlocked by India on three sides and China's Tibet Autonomous Region to the north. West Bengal's narrow Siliguri Corridor or Chicken's Neck separate Nepal and Bangladesh. To the east are India and Bhutan. Nepal depends on India for goods transport facilities and access to the sea, even for most goods imported from China.

Nepal, long under the rule of hereditary prime ministers favouring a policy of isolation, remained closed to the outside world until a palace revolt in 1950 restored the crown's authority in 1951; the country gained admission to the United Nations in 1955. In 1991 the kingdom established a multiparty parliamentary system. In 2008, however, after a decadelong period of violence and turbulent negotiation with a strong Maoist insurgency, the monarchy was dissolved, and Nepal was declared a democratic republic.

The culture of Nepal is rich and unique. The cultural heritage of Nepal has evolved over the centuries. This multi-dimensional heritage encompasses the diversities of Nepal's ethnic, tribal, and social groups, and it manifests in music and dance; art and craft; folklore andfolktales; languages and literature; philosophy and religion; festivals and celebration; foods and drinks.

Nepalese society was ethnically diverse and complex in the early 1990s, ranging in phenotype (physical characteristics) and culture from the Indian to the Tibetan. EPeople in Nepalxcept for the sizable population of those of Indian birth or ancestry concentrated in the Tarai bordering India, the varied ethnic groups had evolved into distinct patterns over time. The two major groups in Nepalese society are Tibeto-Burmans, or Mongoloids from the north, and Indo-Aryans from the south. Many customs are inherited from both sides and have been developed by the influences of the land, climate and available resources. The varied ethnic groups of nepal had evolved into distinct patterns over time.

This book has been carefully edited and structured, to allow flexibility in use to match a variety of course needs and requirements and this makes it an essential reading for the students taking courses on Nepal : Land and People.

—*Editor*

1

Nepal : An Introduction

After centuries of petty rivalry between the three kingdoms, in the mid-18th century, Prithvi Narayan Shah, a Gorkha King, set out to unify the kingdoms. Seeking arms and aid from India, and buying the neutrality of bordering Indian kingdoms, he embarked on his mission in 1765. After several bloody battles and sieges, he managed to unify the Kathmandu Valley three years later in 1768.

However, an actual battle never took place to conquer the Kathmandu valley; it was taken over by Prithvi Narayan and his troops without any effort, during Indra Jatra, a festival of Newars, when all the valley's citizens were celebrating the festival. This event marked the birth of the modern nation of Nepal. In 1788 the Nepalese overran Sikkim and sent a punitive raid into Tibet. Kangra in northern India was also occupied by the Nepalese. In 1809, Ranjit Singh the ruler of the Sikh state in the Punjab, had intervened and drove the Nepalese army east of the Satluj river.

At its maximum extent, Greater Nepal extended from the Tista River in the east, to Kangara, across the Sutlej River in the west as well as further south into the Terai plains and north of the Himalayas than at present. A dispute and subsequent war with Tibet over the control of mountain passes forced the Nepalese to retreat and pay heavy reparations to China.

Rivalry between Nepal and the British East India Company over the annexation of minor states bordering Nepal eventually led to the Anglo-Nepalese War (1815–16). At first the British underestimated the Nepalese and were badly defeated until committing more military resources than they had anticipated needing. They were greatly impressed by the valour and competence of their adversaries. Thus began the reputation of "Gurkhas" as fierce and ruthless soldiers. The war ended in the Treaty of Sugauli, under which Nepal ceded recently captured portions of Sikkim and lands in Terai as well as the right to recruit soldiers.

Factionalism inside the royal family had led to a period of instability. In 1846 a plot was discovered revealing that the reigning queen had planned to overthrow Jung Bahadur Rana, a fast-rising military leader. This led to the Kot Massacre; armed clashes between military personnel and administrators loyal to the queen led to the execution of several hundred princes and chieftains around the country. Jung Bahadur Rana emerged victorious and founded the Rana lineage.

The king was made a titular figure, and the post of Prime Minister was made powerful and hereditary. The Ranas were staunchly pro-British and assisted them during the Indian Sepoy Rebellion in 1857 (and later in both World Wars). Some parts of the Terai Region were given back to Nepal by the British as a friendly gesture, because of her military help to sustain British control in India during the Sepoy Rebellion. In 1923, the United Kingdom and Nepal formally signed an agreement of friendship, in which Nepal's independence was recognized by the UK.

Slavery was abolished in Nepal in 1924. Nevertheless debt bondage even involving debtors' children has been a persistent social problem in the Terai.

In the late 1940s, newly emerging pro-democracy movements and political parties in Nepal were critical of the Rana autocracy. Meanwhile, with the assertion of Chinese control in Tibet in the 1950s, India sought to counterbalance the perceived military threat from its northern neighbour by taking pre-emptive steps to assert more influence in Nepal. India sponsored both King Tribhuvan (ruled 1911-55) as Nepal's new ruler in 1951 and a new government, mostly comprising the Nepali Congress Party, thus terminating Rana hegemony in the kingdom.

After years of power wrangling between the king and the government, King Mahendra (ruled 1955-72) scrapped the democratic experiment in 1959, and a "partyless" panchayat system was made to govern Nepal until 1989, when the "Jan Andolan" (People's Movement) forced King Birendra (ruled 1972-2001) to accept constitutional reforms and to establish a multiparty parliament that took seat in May 1991. In 1991–92, Bhutan expelled roughly 100,000 ethnic Nepalis, most of whom have been living in seven refugee camps in eastern Nepal ever since.

In 1996, the Communist Party of Nepal (Maoist) started a bid to replace the royal parliamentary system with a people's socialist republic by violent means. This led to the long Nepal Civil War and more than 12,000 deaths. On June 1, 2001, there was a massacre in the royal palace. King Birendra, Queen Aiswarya, Crown Prince Dipendra and seven other members of the royal family were killed. Dipendra was accused of patricide and of committing suicide thereafter. This outburst was alleged to have been Dipendra's response to his parents' refusal to accept his choice of wife. Nevertheless there are speculation and doubts among Nepalese citizens about who was responsible.

Following the carnage, Birendra's brother Gyanendra inherited the throne. On February 1, 2005, Gyanendra dismissed the entire government and assumed full executive powers to quash the violent Maoist movement, but this initiative was unsuccessful because a stalemate had developed where the Maoists were firmly entrenched in large expanses of countryside yet could not dislodge the military numerous towns and the largest cities. In September 2005, the Maoists declared a three-month unilateral ceasefire in order to negotiate.

In response to the 2006 democracy movement King Gyanendra agreed to relinquish sovereign power to the people. On April 24, 2006 the dissolved House of Representatives was reinstated. Using its newly acquired sovereign authority, on

May 18, 2006 the House of Representatives unanimously voted to curtail the power of the king and declared Nepal a secular state, ending its time-honoured official status as a Hindu Kingdom. On December 28, 2007, a bill was passed in parliament to amend Article 159 of the constitution — replacing "Provisions regarding the King" by "Provisions of the Head of the State"-declaring Nepal a federal republic, and thereby abolishing the monarchy. The bill came into force on May 28, 2008, as the constituent assembly overwhelmingly voted to abolish royal rule.

Republic

The Communist Party of Nepal (Maoist) won the largest number of seats in the Constituent Assembly election held on April 10, 2008, and formed a coalition government which included most of the parties in the CA. Although acts of violence occurred during the pre-electoral period, election observers noted that the elections themselves were markedly peaceful and "well-carried out."

The newly elected Assembly met in Kathmandu on May 28, 2008, and, after a polling of 564 constituent Assembly members, 560 voted to form a new government, with the monarchist Rastriya Prajatantra Party, which had four members in the assembly, registering a dissent note.

At that point, it was declared that Nepal had become a secular and inclusive democratic republic, with the government announcing a three-day public holiday from May 28 to 30. The King was thereafter given 15 days to vacate the Narayanhiti Royal Palace, in order to re-open it as a public museum.

Nonetheless, political tensions and consequent power-sharing battles have continued in Nepal. In May 2009, the Maoist-led government was toppled and another coalition government with all major political parties barring the Maoists was formed. Madhav Kumar Nepal of the Communist Party of Nepal (Unified Marxist-Leninist) was made the Prime Minister of the coalition government.

FEDERAL DEMOCRATIC REPUBLIC

On May 28, 2008 the newly elected Constituent Assembly declared Nepal a Federal Democratic Republic, abolishing the 240-year-old monarchy. The motion for abolition of monarchy was carried by a huge majority; out of 564 members present in the assembly, 560 voted for the motion while 4 members voted against it.

Finally, on June 11, 2008 ex-king Gyanendra left the palace. Ram Baran Yadav of the Nepali Congress became the first president of the Federal Democratic Republic of Nepal on July 23, 2008. Similarly, Pushpa Kamal Dahal, popularly known as Prachanda, of the Unified Communist Party of Nepal (Maoist) was elected as the first Prime Minister on August 15, 2008, defeating Sher Bahadur Deuba of the Nepali Congress Party.

After failure to draft a constitution with deadline, the existing constitution constituent assembly was dissolved and new interim government was formed under prime-ministership of Supreme Court judge. The election was held and Nepali Congress won the election largest votes but still failed to get majority. A conclusion was reached to form coalition government between UML and Nepali Congress and Sushil Koirala of Nepali Congress was elected as Prime-minister with support from UML.

THE KIRATIS & BUDDHIST BEGINNINGS

Nepal's recorded history kicks off with the Hindu Kiratis. Arriving from the east around the 7th or 8th century BC, these Mongoloid people are the first known rulers of the Kathmandu Valley. King Yalambar (the first of their 29 kings) is mentioned in the Mahabharata, the Hindu epic, but little more is known about them. In the 6th century BC, Prince Siddhartha Gautama was born into the Sakya royal family of Kapilavastu, near Lumbini, later embarking on a path of meditation and thought that led him to enlightenment as the Buddha. The religion that grew up around him continues to shape the face of Asia.

Around the 2nd century BC, the great Indian Buddhist emperor Ashoka (c 272-236 BC) visited Lumbini and erected a pillar at the birthplace of the Buddha. Popular legend recounts how he then visited the Kathmandu Valley and erected four stupas (pagodas) around Patan, but there is no evidence that he actually made it there in person. In either event, his Mauryan empire (321-184 BC) played a major role in popularising Buddhism in the region, a role continued by the north Indian Buddhist Kushan empire (1st to 3rd centuries AD).

Over the centuries Buddhism gradually lost ground to a resurgent Hinduism and by the time the Chinese Buddhist pilgrims Fa Xian (Fa Hsien) and Xuan Zang (Hsuan Tsang) passed through the region in the 5th and 7th centuries the site of Lumbini was already in ruins.

Licchavis, Thakuris, then Darkness

Buddhism faded and Hinduism reasserted itself with the arrival from northern India of the Licchavis. In AD 300 they overthrew the Kiratis, who resettled in the east and are the ancestors of today's Rai and Limbu people.

Between the 4th and 8th centuries, the Licchavis ushered in a golden age of cultural brilliance. The chaityas (stupas) and monuments of this era can still be seen at the Changu Narayan Temple, north of Bhaktapur, and in the backstreets of Kathmandu's old town. Their strategic position allowed them to prosper from trade between India and China. It's believed that the original stupas at Chabahil, Bodhnath and Swayambhunath date from the Licchavi era.

Amsuvarman, the first Thakuri king, came to power in 602, succeeding his Licchavi father-in-law. He consolidated his power to the north and south by marrying his sister to an Indian prince and his daughter Bhrikuti to the great Tibetan king Songsten Gompo. Together with the Gompo's Chinese wife Wencheng, Bhrikuti managed to convert the king to Buddhism around 640, changing the face of both Tibet and, later, Nepal.

From the late 7th century until the 13th century Nepal slipped into its 'dark ages', of which little is known. Tibet invaded in 705 and Kashmir invaded in 782. The Kathmandu Valley's strategic location, however, ensured the kingdom's growth and survival. King Gunakamadeva is credited with founding Kantipur, today's Kathmandu, around the 10th century. During the 9th century a new lunar calendar was introduced, one that is still used by Newars to this day.

The Golden Age of the Mallas

The first of the Malla kings came to power in the Kathmandu Valley around 1200. The Mallas (literally 'wrestlers' in Sanskrit) had been forced out of India and their name can be found in the Mahabharata and in Buddhist literature. This period was a golden one that stretched over 550 years, though it was peppered with fighting over the valuable trade routes to Tibet.

The first Malla rulers had to cope with several disasters. A huge earthquake in 1255 killed around one-third of Nepal's population. A devastating Muslim invasion by Sultan Shams-ud-din of Bengal less than a century later left plundered Hindu and Buddhist shrines in its wake, though the invasion did not leave a lasting cultural effect here (unlike in the Kashmir Valley which remains Muslim to this day). InIndia the damage was more widespread and many Hindus were driven into the hills and mountains of Nepal, where they established small Rajput principalities.

Apart from this, the earlier Malla years (1220-1482) were largely stable, reaching a high point under the third Malla dynasty of Jayashithi Malla (1382-1395), who united the valley and codified its laws, including the caste system. The mid-13th century saw the de facto rule of Queen Devaladevi, the most powerful woman in Nepal's history.

After the death of Jayashithi Malla's grandson Yaksha Malla in 1482, the Kathmandu Valley was divided up among his sons into the three kingdoms of Bhaktapur (Bhadgaon), Kathmandu (Kantipur) and Patan (Lalitpur). They proceeded to fight with each other over the right to control the rich trading routes with Tibet.

The rest of what we today call Nepal consisted of a fragmented patchwork of almost 50 independent states, from Palpa to Jumla, and the semi-independent states of Banepa and Pharping, most of them minting their own coins and maintaining standing armies.

One of the most important of these was the Nepali-speaking Khasa empire (Western Mallas), based in the far west in the Karnali basin around Sinja and Jumla. The kingdom peaked in the 13th and 14th centuries, only to fragment in the 15th century. Its lasting contribution was the Nepali language that is spoken today as the unifying national language.

Nepal's most profound export was perhaps its architecture; in the 13th century the Nepali architect Arniko travelled to Lhasa and the Mongol capital in Beijing, bringing with him the design of the pagoda, thus changing the face of religious temples across Asia.

The rivalry between the three kingdoms of the Kathmandu Valley found its expression in the arts and culture, which flourished in the competitive climate. The outstanding collections of exquisite temples and buildings in each city's Durbar Square are testament to the huge amounts of money spent by the rulers to outdo each other.

The building boom was financed by trade, in everything from musk and wool to salt, Chinese silk and even yak tails. The Kathmandu Valley stood at the departure point for two separate routes into Tibet, via Banepa to the northeast and via Rasuwa and the Kyirong Valley near Langtang in the northwest. Traders would cross the jungle-infested Terai during winter to avoid the virulent malaria and then wait in Kathmandu for the mountain passes to open later that summer. Kathmandu grew rich and its rulers converted their wealth into gilded pagodas and ornately carved royal palaces. In the mid-17th century Nepal gained the right to mint Tibet's coins using Tibetan silver, further enriching the kingdom's coffers.

In Kathmandu King Pratap Malla (1641-74) oversaw that city's cultural highpoint with the construction of the Hanuman

Dhoka Palace, the Rani Pokhari pond and the first of several subsequent pillars that featured a statue of the king facing the protective Temple of Taleju, who the Mallas had by that point adopted as their protective deity. The mid-17th century also saw a highpoint of building in Patan.

Around 1750 King Jaya Prakash Malla built Kathmandu's Kumari Temple. Not long afterwards came the Nyatapola Temple in Bhakatapur, the literal highpoint of pagoda-style architecture in Nepal.

The Malla era shaped the religious as well as artistic landscape, introducing the dramatic chariot festivals of Indra Jatra and Machhendranath. The Malla kings shored up their position by claiming to be reincarnations of the Hindu god Vishnu and establishing the cult of the kumari, a living goddess whose role it was to bless the Malla's rule during an annual celebration.

The cosmopolitan Mallas also absorbed foreign influences. The Indian Mughal court influenced Malla dress and painting, presented the Nepalis with firearms and introduced the system of land grants for military service, a system which would have a profound effect in later years. Persian terminology was introduced to the court administration and in 1729 the three kingdoms sent presents to the Qing court in Beijing, which from then on viewed Nepal as a tributary state. In the early 18th century Capuchin missionaries passed through Nepal to Tibet, giving the West its first descriptions of exotic Kathmandu.

But change didn't only come from abroad. A storm was brewing inside Nepal, just 100km to the east of Kathmandu.

Unification under the Shahs

It took more than a quarter of a century of conquest and consolidation, but by 1768 Prithvi Narayan Shah, ruler of the tiny hilltop kingdom of Gorkha (halfway between Pokhara and Kathmandu), stood poised on the edge of the Kathmandu Valley, about to realise his dream of a unified Nepal.

Prithvi Narayan had taken the strategic hilltop fort of Nuwakot in 1744 and had blockaded the valley, after fighting off reinforcements from the British East India Company. In 1768 Shah took Kathmandu, sneaking in while everyone was drunk during the Indra Jatra festival. A year later he took Kirtipur, finally, after three lengthy failed attempts. In terrible retribution his troops hacked 120 pounds of noses and lips off Kirtipur's residents; unsurprisingly, resistance throughout the valley quickly crumbled. In 1769 he advanced on the three Malla kings, who were quivering in Bhaktapur, ending the Malla rule and unifying Nepal.

Shah moved his capital from Gorkha to Kathmandu, establishing the Shah dynasty, which rules to this day, with its roots in the Rajput kings of Chittor. Shah died just six years later in Nuwakot but is revered to this day as the founder of the nation.

Shah had built his empire on conquest and his insatiable army needed ever more booty and land to keep it satisfied. Within six years the Gurkhas had conquered eastern Nepal and Sikkim. The expansion then turned westwards into Kumaon and Garhwal, only halted on the borders of the Punjab by the armies of the powerful one-eyed ruler Ranjit Singh.

The kingdom's power continued to grow until a 1792 clash with the Chinese in Tibet led to an ignominious defeat, during which Chinese troops advanced down the Kyirong Valley to within 35km of Kathmandu. As part of the ensuing treaty the Nepalis had to cease their attacks on Tibet and pay tribute to the Chinese emperor in Beijing; the payments continued until 1912.

The expanding Nepali boundaries, by this time stretching all the way from Kashmir to Sikkim, eventually put it on a collision course with the world's most powerful empire, the British Raj. Despite early treaties with the British, disputes over the Terai led to the first Anglo-Nepali war, which the British won after a two-year fight. The British were so impressed by their enemy that they decided to incorporate Gurkha mercenaries into their own army.

The 1816 Sugauli treaty called a halt to Nepal's expansion and laid down its modern boundaries. Nepal lost Sikkim,

Kumaon, Garhwal and much of the Terai, though some of this land was restored to Nepal in 1858 in return for support given to the British during the Indian Mutiny (Indian War of Independence). A British resident was sent to Kathmandu to keep an eye on things but the Raj knew that it would be too difficult to colonise the impossible hill terrain, preferring to keep Nepal as a buffer state. Nepalis to this day are proud that their country was never colonised by the British, unlike the neighbouring hill states of India.

Following its humiliating defeat, Nepal cut itself off from all foreign contact from 1816 until 1951. The British residents in Kathmandu were the only Westerners to set eyes on Nepal for more than a century.

On the cultural front, temple construction continued impressively, though perhaps of more import to ordinary people was the introduction, via India, of chillis, potatoes, tobacco and other New World crops.

The Shah rulers, meanwhile, swung from ineffectual to seriously deranged. At one point the kingdom was governed by a twelve-year-old female regent, in charge of a nine-year-old king! One particularly sadistic ruler, Crown Prince Surendra, expanded the horizons of human suffering by ordering subjects to jump down wells or ride off cliffs, just to see whether they would die.

The Ranocracy

The death of Prithvi Narayan Shah in 1775 set in motion a string of succession struggles, infighting, assassinations, feuding and intrigue that culminated in the Kot Massacre in 1846. This bloody night was engineered by the young Chhetri noble, Jung Bahadur; it catapulted his family into power and sidelined the Shah dynasty.

Ambitious and ruthless, Jung Bahadur organised (with the queen's consent) for his soldiers to massacre several hundred of the most important men in the kingdom - noblemen, soldiers and courtiers - while they were assembled in the Kot courtyard adjoining Kathmandu's Durbar Square. He then exiled 6000 members of their familles to prevent revenge attacks. Jung Bahadur took the title of Prime Minister and changed his family name to the more prestigious Rana. He later extended his title to maharajah (king) and decreed it hereditary. The Ranas became a second 'royal family' within the kingdom and held the reins of power - the Shah kings became listless figureheads, requiring permission even to leave their palace.

The hereditary family of Rana prime ministers held power for more than a century, eventually intermarrying with the Shahs. Development in Nepal stagnated, although the country did manage to preserve its independence. Only on rare occasions were visitors allowed into Nepal.

Jung Bahadur Rana travelled to Europe in 1850, attended the opera and the races at Epsom, and brought back a taste for neoclassical architecture, examples of which can be seen in Kathmandu today.

To the Ranas' credit, sati (the Hindu practice of casting a widow on her husband's funeral pyre) was abolished in 1920, 60, 000 slaves were released from bondage and a school and a college were established in Kathmandu. But while the Ranas and their relations lived lives of opulent luxury, the peasants in the hills were locked in a medieval existence.

Modernisation began to dawn on Kathmandu with the opening of the Bir Hospital, Nepal's first, in 1889, the first piped water system, limited electricity and the construction of the huge Singha Durbar palace. In 1923 Britain formally acknowledged Nepal's independence and in 1930 the kingdom of Gorkha was renamed the kingdom of Nepal, reflecting a growing sense of national consciousness.

The arrival of the Indian railway line at the Nepali border greatly aided the transportation of goods but sounded a death knell for the caravan trade that bartered Nepali grain and rice for Tibetan salt. The transborder trade suffered another setback when the British opened a second, more direct trade route with Tibet through Sikkim's Chumbi Valley (the real nail in the coffin came in 1966, when the Chinese closed the border to local trade).

Elsewhere in the region dramatic changes were taking place. The Nepalis supplied logistical help during Britain's invasion of Tibet in 1903, and over 300, 000 Nepalis fought in WWI and WWII, garnering a total of 13 Victoria Crosses - Britain's highest military honour - for their efforts.

After WWII, India gained its independence and the communist revolution took place in China. Tibetan refugees fled into Nepal in the first of several waves when the new People's Republic of China tightened its grip on Tibet, and Nepal became a buffer zone between the two rival Asian giants. At the same time King Tribhuvan, forgotten in his palace, was being primed to overthrow the Ranas.

GEOGRAPHY

Geography of Nepal is uncommonly diverse. Nepal is of roughly trapezoidal shape, 800 kilometres (497 mi) long and 200 kilometres (124 mi) wide, with an area of 147,181 km^2 (56,827 sq mi).

Nepal is commonly divided into three physiographic areas: the Mountain, Hill, Siwalik region and Terai Regions. These ecological belts run east-west and are vertically intersected by Nepal's major, north to south flowing river systems. The southern lowland plains or Terai bordering India are part of the northern rim of the Indo-Gangetic plains. They were formed and are fed by three major Himalayan rivers: the Kosi, the Narayani, and the Karnali as well as smaller rivers rising below the permanent snowline. This region has a subtropical to tropical climate. The outermost range of foothills called Shiwalik or Churia Range cresting at 700 to 1,000 metres (2,297 to 3,281 ft) marks the limit of the Gangetic Plain, however broad, low valleys called Inner Tarai (Bhitri Tarai Uptyaka) lie north of these foothills in several places.

The Hill Region (*Pahad*) abuts the mountains and varies from 800 to 4,000 metres (2,625 to 13,123 ft) in altitude with progression from subtropical climates below 1,200 metres (3,937 ft) to alpine climates above 3,600 metres (11,811 ft). The Mahabharat Lekh reaching 1,500 to 3,000 metres (4,921 to

9,843 ft) is the southern limit of this region, with subtropical river valleys and "hills" alternating to the north of this range. Population density is high in valleys but notably less above 2,000 metres (6,562 ft) and very low above 2,500 metres (8,202 ft) where snow occasionally falls in winter.

The Mountain Region (Parbat), situated in the Great Himalayan Range, makes up the northern part of Nepal. It contains the highest elevations in the world including 8,848 metres (29,029 ft) height Mount Everest (*Sagarmatha* in Nepali) on the border with China. Seven other of the world's eight thousand metre peaks are in Nepal or on its border with China: Lhotse, Makalu, Cho Oyu, Kanchenjunga, Dhaulagiri, Annapurna and Manaslu. Nepal has five climatic zones, broadly corresponding to the altitudes. The tropical and subtropical zones lie below 1,200 metres (3,937 ft), the temperate zone 1,200 to 2,400 metres (3,937 to 7,874 ft), the cold zone 2,400 to 3,600 metres (7,874 to 11,811 ft), the subarctic zone 3,600 to 4,400 metres (11,811 to 14,436 ft), and the Arctic zone above 4,400 metres (14,436 ft).

Nepal experiences five seasons: summer, monsoon, autumn, winter and spring. The Himalaya blocks cold winds from Central Asia in the winter and forms the northern limit of the monsoon wind patterns. In a land once thickly forested, deforestation is a major problem in all regions, with resulting erosion and degradation of ecosystems.

Nepal is popular for mountaineering, containing some of the highest and most challenging mountains in the world, including Mount Everest. Technically, the south-east ridge on the Nepali side of the mountain is easier to climb; so, most climbers prefer to trek to Everest through Nepal. Morever Nepal has 8 of the top 10 highest mountains of the world with postcard beauty.

Environment

The dramatic differences in elevation found in Nepal result in a variety of biomes, from tropical savannas along the Indian border, to subtropical broadleaf and coniferous forests in the

Hill Region, to temperate broadleaf and coniferous forests on the slopes of the Himalaya, to montane grasslands and shrublands and rock and ice at the highest elevations.

At the lowest elevations we find the Terai-Duar savanna and grasslands ecoregion. These form a mosaic with the Himalayan subtropical broadleaf forests, which occur from 500 to 1,000 metres (1,600 to 3,300 ft) and include the Inner Terai Valleys. Himalayan subtropical pine forests occur between 1,000 and 2,000 metres (3,300 and 6,600 ft).

Above these elevations, the biogeography of Nepal is generally divided from east to west by the Gandaki River. Ecoregions to the east tend to receive more precipitation and to be more species-rich. Those to the west are drier with fewer species. From 1,500 to 3,000 metres (4,900 to 9,800 ft), we find temperate broadleaf forests: the eastern and western Himalayan broadleaf forests. From 3,000 to 4,000 metres (9,800 to 13,000 ft) are the eastern and western Himalayan subalpine conifer forests. To 5,500 metres (18,000 ft) are the eastern and western Himalayan alpine shrub and meadows.

Subdivisions

Nepal is divided into 14 zones and 75 districts, grouped into 5 development regions. Each district is headed by a permanent chief district officer responsible for maintaining law and order and coordinating the work of field agencies of the various government ministries. The 5 regions and 14 zones are:

- Eastern Region (Purwanchal)
    - Koshi
    - Mechi
    - Sagarmatha
- Central Region (Madhyamanchal)
    - Bagmati
    - Janakpur
    - Narayani
- Western Region (Pashchimanchal)
    - Dhawalagiri

  - o Gandaki
  - o Lumbini
- Mid-Western Region (Madhya Pashchimanchal)
  - o Bheri
  - o Karnali
  - o Rapti
- Far-Western Region (Sudur Pashchimanchal)
  - o Mahakali
  - o Seti.

GOVERNMENT AND POLITICS

Nepal has seen rapid political changes during the last two decades. Until 1990, Nepal was a monarchy running under the executive control of the king. Faced with a Communist movement against the absolute monarchy, King Birendra, in 1990, agreed to large-scale political reforms by creating a parliamentary monarchy with the king as the head of state and a prime minister as the head of the government.

Nepal has also been noted for its recent speed of development, such as being one of the few countries in Asia to abolish the death penalty and the first country in Asia to rule in favor of same-sex marriage, which the government has a seven-person committee studying after a November 2008 ruling by the nation's Supreme Court, which ordered full rights for LGBT individuals, including the right to marry.

Nepal's legislature was bicameral, consisting of a House of Representatives called the Pratinidhi Sabha and a National Council called the Rastriya Sabha. The House of Representatives consisted of 205 members directly elected by the people. The National Council had 60 members: ten nominated by the king, 35 elected by the House of Representatives, and the remaining 15 elected by an electoral college made up of chairs of villages and towns. The legislature had a five-year term but was dissolvable by the king before its term could end. All Nepali citizens 18 years and older became eligible to vote.

The executive comprised the King and the Council of Ministers (the Cabinet). The leader of the coalition or party securing the maximum seats in an election was appointed as the Prime Minister. The Cabinet was appointed by the king on the recommendation of the Prime Minister. Governments in Nepal tended to be highly unstable, falling either through internal collapse or parliamentary dissolution by the monarch, on the recommendation of the prime minister, according to the constitution; no government has survived for more than two years since 1991.

The movement in April 2006 brought about a change in the nation's governance: an interim constitution was promulgated, with the King giving up power, and an interim House of Representatives was formed with Maoist members after the new government held peace talks with the Maoist rebels. The number of parliamentary seats was also increased to 330. In April 2007, the Communist Party of Nepal (Maoist) joined the interim government of Nepal.

On April 10, 2008, the first election in Nepal for the constitution assembly took place. The Maoist party led the poll results but failed to gain a simple majority in the parliament.

On December 10, 2007, the interim parliament passed a bill that would make Nepal a federal republic, with the Prime Minister becoming head of state. On May 28, 2008, lawmakers in Nepal legally abolished the monarchy and declared the country a republic, ending 239 years of royal rule in the Himalayan nation. The newly elected assembly, led by the former communist rebels, adopted the resolution at its first meeting by an overwhelming majority. King Gyanendra was given 15 days to leave the former Royal Palace in central Kathmandu by the Nepalese Constituent Assembly. He left the former Royal Palace on June 11.

On June 26, 2008, Prime Minister Girija Prasad Koirala tendered his resignation to the Nepalese Constituent Assembly, which is also functioning as the Nepalese Parliament; however, a new Prime Minister has yet to be elected by the Nepalese Constituent Assembly.

On July 19, 2008, the first round of voting for the election of the country's president and vice president took place in the Constituent Assembly. Parmanand Jha became the first vice president of Nepal. However, the two presidential frontrunners, Dr. Ram Baran Yadav of Nepali Congress and the Maoist-backed candidate Ram Raja Prasad Singh, both failed to gain the minimum 298 votes needed to be elected, with Yadav receiving 283 votes and Singh receiving 270. 578 out of 594 CA members registered in the voter list had cast their votes, of which 24 were invalid.

On July 21, 2008, the second round of voting was held. Yadav received 308 of the 590 votes cast, securing his election as president. On August 15, 2008, Maoist leader Prachanda (Pushpa Kamal Dahal) was elected Prime Minister of Nepal, the first since the country's transition from a monarchy to a republic. On May 4, 2009, Mr. Pushpa Kamal Dahal resigned over on-going conflicts over sacking of the Army chief.

MILITARY AND FOREIGN AFFAIRS

Nepal's military consists of the Nepalese Army, which includes the Nepalese Army Air Service (the air force unit under it.) Nepalese Police Force is the civilian police and the Armed Police Force Nepal is the paramilitary force. Service is voluntary and the minimum age for enlistment is 18 years. Nepal spends $99.2 million (2004) on its military—1.5% of its GDP. Many of the equipment and arms are imported from India. Consequently, the USA provided M16s M4s and other Colt weapons to combat communist (Maoist) insurgents. As of now, the standard-issue battle rifle of the Nepalese army is the Colt M16.

Nepal has close ties with both of its neighbours, India and China. In accordance with a long-standing treaty, Indian and Nepalese citizens may travel to each others' countries without a passport or visa. Nepalese citizens may work in India without legal restriction. Although Nepal and India typically have close ties, from time to time Nepal becomes caught up in the problematic Sino-Indian relationship. Recently, China has been asking Nepal to curb protests in Nepal against China's Policy on Tibet, and on April 17, 2008, police arrested over 500 Tibetan protestors citing a need to maintain positive relations with China.

Terai News writes, "*Being a Hindu Nation Nepal has a permanent relation, especially with the important religious places of the northern states of India. Religion has played a great role in the cultural relations between Nepal and India.*"

ECONOMY

Nepal's gross domestic product (GDP) for the year 2008 was estimated at over US$12 billion (adjusted to Nominal GDP), making it the 115th-largest economy in the world. Agriculture accounts for about 40% of Nepal's GDP, services comprise 41% and industry 22%. Agriculture employs 76% of the workforce, services 18% and manufacturing/craft-based industry 6%. Agricultural produce — mostly grown in the Terai region bordering India — includes tea, rice, corn, wheat, sugarcane, root crops, milk, and water buffalo meat. Industry mainly involves the processing of agricultural produce, including jute, sugarcane, tobacco, and grain.

Its workforce of about 10 million suffers from a severe shortage of skilled labour. The spectacular landscape and diverse, exotic cultures of Nepal represent considerable potential for tourism, but growth in this hospitality industry has been stifled by recent political events. The rate of unemployment and underemployment approaches half of the working-age population. Thus many Nepali citizens move to India in search of work; the Gulf countries and Malaysia being new sources of work. Nepal receives US$50 million a year through the Gurkha soldiers who serve in the Indian and British armies and are highly esteemed for their skill and bravery. The total remittance value is worth around US$1 billion, including money sent from the Persian Gulf and Malaysia, who combined employ around 700,000 Nepali citizens.

A long-standing economic agreement underpins a close relationship with India. The country receives foreign aid from

India, Japan, the United Kingdom, the United States, the European Union, China, Switzerland, and Scandinavian countries. Poverty is acute; per-capita income is less than US$470. The distribution of wealth among the Nepalis is consistent with that in many developed and developing countries: the highest 10% of households control 39.1% of the national wealth and the lowest 10% control only 2.6%.

The government's budget is about US$1.153 billion, with expenditures of $1.789 billion (FY05/06). The Nepalese rupee has been tied to the Indian Rupee at an exchange rate of 1.6 for many years. Since the loosening of exchange rate controls in the early 1990s, the black market for foreign exchange has all but disappeared. The inflation rate has dropped to 2.9% after a period of higher inflation during the 1990s.

Nepal's exports of mainly carpets, clothing, leather goods, jute goods and grain total $822 million. Import commodities of mainly gold, machinery and equipment, petroleum products and fertilizer total US$2 bn. India (53.7%), the US (17.4%), and Germany (7.1%) are its main export partners. Nepal's import partners include India (47.5%), the United Arab Emirates (11.2%), China (10.7%), Saudi Arabia (4.9%), and Singapore (4%).

Nepal remains isolated from the world's major land, air and sea transport routes although, within the country, aviation is in a better state, with 48 airports, ten of them with paved runways; flights are frequent and support a sizable traffic. The hilly and mountainous terrain in the northern two-thirds of the country has made the building of roads and other infrastructure difficult and expensive.

There were just over 8,500 km of paved roads, and one 59-km railway line in the south in 2003. There is only one reliable road route from India to the Kathmandu Valley. The only practical seaport of entry for goods bound for Kathmandu is Calcutta in India. Internally, the poor state of development of the road system (22 of 75 administrative districts lack road links) makes volume distribution unrealistic. Besides having landlocked, rugged geography, few tangible natural resources and poor infrastructure, the long-running civil war is also a factor in stunting the economic growth.

There is less than one telephone per 19 people. Landline telephone services are not adequate nationwide but are concentrated in cities and district headquarters. Mobile telephony is in a reasonable state in most parts of the country with increased accessibility and affordability; there were around 175,000 Internet connections in 2005. After the imposition of the "state of emergency", intermittent losses of service-signals were reported, but uninterrupted Internet connections have resumed after Nepal's second major people's revolution to overthrow the King's absolute power.

DEMOGRAPHICS

The Nepalese are descendants of three major migrations from India, Tibet, and North Burma and Yunnan via Assam.

Among the earliest inhabitants were the Kirat of east mid-region, Newar of the Kathmandu Valley and aboriginal Tharu in the southern Terai region. The ancestors of the Brahman and Chetri caste groups came from India's present Kumaon, Garhwal and Kashmir regions, while other ethnic groups trace their origins to North Burma and Yunnan and Tibet, e.g. the Gurung and Magar in the west, Rai and Limbu in the east (from Yunnan and north Burma via Assam), and Sherpa and Bhutia in the north (from Tibet).

In the Terai, a part of the Ganges Basin with 20% of the land, much of the population is physically and culturally similar to the Indo-Aryans of northern India. Indo-Aryan and East Asian looking mixed people live in the hill region. Indo-Aryan ancestry has been a source of prestige in Nepal for centuries, and the ruling families have been of Indo-Aryan and Hindu background. The mountainous highlands are sparsely populated. Kathmandu Valley, in the middle hill region, constitutes a small fraction of the nation's area but is the most densely populated, with almost 5% of the population.

Nepal is a multilingual society. These data are largely derived from Nepal's 2001 census results published in the *Nepal Population Report 2002.*

According to the *World Refugee Survey 2008*, published by the U.S. Committee for Refugees and Immigrants, Nepal hosted a population of refugees and asylum seekers in 2007 numbering approximately 130,000. Of this population, approximately 109,200 persons were from Bhutan and 20,500 from People's Republic of China. The government of Nepal restricted Bhutanese refugees to seven camps in the Jhapa and Morang districts, and refugees were not permitted to work in most professions. At present, the United States is working towards resettling more than 60,000 of these refugees in the US.

Languages Spoken in Nepal.

Population Structure

Data	Size
Population	**28,676,547 (2005)**
Growth Rate	2.2%
Population below 14 Years old	39%
Population of age 15 to 64	57.3%
Population above 65	3.7%
The median age (Average)	20.07
The median age (Male)	19.91
The median age (Females)	20.24
Ratio (Male:Female)	1, 000:1,060
Life expectancy (Average)	59.8 Years
Life expectancy (Male)	60.9
Life expectancy (Female)	59.5
Literacy Rate (Average)	53.74%
Literacy Rate (Male)	68.51%
Literacy Rate (Female)	42.49%

Despite the migration of a significant section of the population to the southern plains or terai in recent years, the majority of the population still lives in the central highlands. The northern mountains are sparsely populated.

Kathmandu, with a population of around 800,000 (metropolitan area: 1.5 million), is the largest city in the country.

Nepal religiosity

Religion	percent
Hinduism	80.6%
Buddhism	10.7%
Islam	4.2%
Mundhum	3.6%
Christianity	0.5%
Other	0.4%

The overwhelming majority in Nepal follow Hinduism. Shiva is regarded as the guardian deity of the country. Nepal is home to the largest Shiva temple in the world, the famous Pashupatinath Temple, where Hindus from all over the world come for pilgrimage. According to mythology, Sita Devi of the epic Ramayana was born in the Mithila Kingdom of King Janaka Raja.

Near the Indian border, Lumbini, is a Buddhist pilgrimage site and UNESCO World Heritage Site site in the Kapilavastu district. It is held to be the birthplace in about 563 B.C. of Siddhartha Gautama, a Kshatriya caste prince of the Sakya clan, who, as the Buddha Gautama, gave birth to the Buddhist tradition. The holy site of Lumbini is bordered by a large monastic zone, in which only monasteries can be built. All three main branches of Buddhism exist in Nepal and the Newar people have their own branch of the faith. Buddhism is the dominant religion of the thinly populated northern areas, which are inhabited by Tibetan-related peoples, such as the Sherpa.

The Buddha, born as a Hindu, is also said to be a descendant of Vedic Sage Angirasa in many Buddhist texts. The Buddha's family surname is associated with Gautama Maharishi. Differences between Hindus and Buddhists have been minimal in Nepal due to the cultural and historical intermingling of Hindu and Buddhist beliefs. Morever traditionally Buddhism and Hinduism were never two distinct religions in western sense of world. In Nepal, the faiths share common temples and worship common deities. Among other natives of Nepal, those more influenced by Hinduism were the Magar, Sunwar, Limbu and Rai and the Gurkhas. Hindu influence is less prominent among the Gurung, Bhutia, and Thakali groups who employ Buddhist monks for their religious ceremonies. Most of the festivals in Nepal are Hindu. The Machendrajatra festival, dedicated to Hindu Shaiva Siddha, is celebrated by many Buddhists in Nepal as a main festival. As it is believed that Ne Muni established Nepal, some important priests in Nepal are called "Tirthaguru Nemuni".

Health

The fertility rate in Nepal was at 3.7 births per woman in the early 2000s. Public expenditure on health was at 1.5 % of the GDP in 2004. Private expenditure on health was 4.1 % in 2004. In the early 2000s, there were 21 physicians per 100,000 people. Infant mortality was 56 per 1000 life births in 2005. Culture

A typical Nepalese meal is *dal-bhat-tarkari*. *Dal* is a spicy lentil soup, served over *bhat* (boiled rice), served with *tarkari* (curried vegetables) together with *achar* (pickles) or *chutni* (spicy condiment made from fresh ingredients).. The Newar community, however, has its own unique cuisine. It consists of non-vegetarian as well as vegetarian items served with alcoholic and non-alcoholic beverages. Mustard oil is the cooking medium and a host of spices, such as cumin, coriander, black peppers, sesame seeds, turmeric, garlic, ginger, methi (fenugreek), bay leaves, cloves, cinnamon, pepper, chillies, mustard seeds, etc., are used in the cooking. The cuisine served on festivals is generally the best.

The Newari Music orchestra consists mainly of percussion instruments, though wind instruments, such as flutes and other similar instruments, are also used. String instruments are very rare. There are songs pertaining to particular seasons and festivals.

Paahan chare music is probably the fastest played music whereas the Dapa the slowest. There are certain musical instruments such as Dhimay and Bhusya which are played as instrumental only and are not accompanied with songs. The dhimay music is the loudest one. In the hills, people enjoy their own kind of music, playing saarangi (a string instrument), madal and flute. They also have many popular folk songs known as *lok geet* and *lok dohari*.

The Newar dances can be broadly classified into masked dances and non-masked dances. The most representative of Newari dances is Lakhey dance. Almost all the settlements of Newaris organise Lakhey dance at least once a year, mostly in the Goonlaa month. So, they are called Goonlaa Lakhey. However, the most famous Lakhey dance is the Majipa Lakhey dance; it is performed by the Ranjitkars of Kathmandu and the celeberation continues for the entire week that contains the full moon of Yenlaa month. The Lakhey are considered to be the saviors of children.

Folklore is an integral part of Nepalese society. Traditional stories are rooted in the reality of day-to-day life, tales of love, affection and battles as well as demons and ghosts and thus reflect local lifestyles, cultures and beliefs. Many Nepalese folktales are enacted through the medium of dance and music. The Nepali year begins in mid-April and is divided into 12 months. Saturday is the official weekly holiday. Main annual holidays include the National Day, celebrated on the birthday of the king (December 28), Prithvi Jayanti (January 11), Martyr's Day (February 18), and a mix of Hindu and Buddhist festivals such as dashain in autumn, and *tihar* in late autumn. During tihar, the Newar community also celebrates its New Year as per their local calendar Nepal Sambat.

Most houses in rural lowland of Nepal are made up of a tight bamboo framework and walls of a mud and cow-dung mix. These dwellings remain cool in summer and retain warmth in winter. Houses in the hills are usually made of unbaked bricks with thatch or tile roofing. At high elevations construction changes to stone masonry and slate may be used on roofs.

Nepal's flag is the only national flag in the world that is non-quadrilateral in shape, and one of only two non-rectangular flags in use (the other being the flag of the U.S. state of Ohio). According to its official description, the red in the flag stands for victory in war or courage, and is also color of the rhododendron, the national flower of Nepal. Red also stands for aggression. The flag's blue border signifies peace. The curved moon on the flag is a symbol of the peaceful and calm nature of Nepalese, while the sun represents the aggressiveness of Nepalese warriors.

Education

About two thirds of female adults and one third of male adults are illiterate. Net primary enrolment rate was 74 % in 2005. It now is at about 90 %. In 2009 the World Bank has decided to contribute a further US$130 million towards meeting Nepal's Education for All goals. Nepal has several universities.

NEPAL: RECENT DEVELOPMENTS

The Communist Party of Nepal - Maoist (CPN-M), the group which waged an armed struggle against the former government of Nepal, won what was a three-way power struggle with the monarchy and a collection of democratic parties with their electoral victory in the April 10, 2008 Constituent Assembly election. Over 60% of Nepali voters cast ballots in the election that had been twice delayed. What was surprising to many observers was that the Maoists won power through the democratic process. The Maoists had previously waged a 10-year insurrection between 1996 and 2006 that claimed an estimated 13,340 lives. During this period their stated aim was to establish a peasant-led revolutionary communist regime.

Now that they are in control of the democratically elected Constituent Assembly, Nepal's legislature, the Maoists are confronted by a number of pressing issues, including the drafting of a new constitution, mounting ethnic demands particularly with the Madhesis of the Terai region, and the need to revitalize Nepal's economy. Some have speculated that the Maoists won the election because many Nepalis viewed that as the best way to keep them from returning to their violent struggle for power. Addressing issues contributing to political instability and achieving a peaceful transition to stable democracy are viewed by observers as key to providing the basis for economic growth. The Maoists will likely focus on how to retain control of the next government as the Constituent Assembly (CA) determines its form. Uncertainty remains over how well Nepal will negotiate this political transition in the months ahead.

Some analysts have expressed concern that the Maoists could once again resort to widespread violence if they view their influence as curtailed too much by democratic political opposition. Although the Maoists have the most seats in parliament, they do not have an outright majority. This makes them to an extent reliant on smaller coalition partners. The fact that the Maoists were not able to place one of their own in the office of the president demonstrates that there are limits to their power in the current configuration of government. The Communist Party of Nepal Maoist (CPN-M) has been supported by the Communist Party of Nepal United Marxist-Leninist (CPN-UML) and the Madhesi Peoples Rights Forum (MPRF) in the CA. The Nepali Congress (NC) is the main opposition party. The Economist Intelligence Unit has described the CPN-M as having "established its political pre-eminence while falling short of outright dominance." The Maoist government has received criticism in Nepal for not having made progress on drafting a new constitution.

HISTORICAL CONTEXT TO THE PRESENT POLITICAL SITUATION

Nepal has been an independent kingdom since 1768. Never colonized, the country was almost totally isolated from outside influence until the early 1950s. A transition from strict rule by the king to constitutional monarchy began in 1959, when then-King Mahendra issued a new constitution and held the country's first democratic elections. In 1960, however, the king declared the parliamentary system a failure, dismissed the fledgling government, suspended the constitution, and established a partyless system of rule under the monarchy. Although officially banned, political parties continued to exist and to agitate for a return to constitutional democracy.

In February 1990, student groups and the major political parties launched the Movement for the Restoration of Democracy. The centrist Nepali Congress (NC) party joined with the leftist parties to hold peaceful demonstrations in Nepal's urban centers. In April 1990, after more than 50 people were killed when police fired on a crowd of demonstrators, then-King Birendra turned power over to an interim government. This government drafted a constitution in November 1990 establishing Nepal as a parliamentary democracy with a constitutional monarch as head of state. The king at that time retained limited powers, including the right to declare a state of emergency with the approval of a two-thirds majority of parliament.

In February 1996, the leaders of the underground CPN-M launched a "People's War" in the mid-western region of Nepal, with the aim of replacing the constitutional monarchy with a one-party Communist regime. The uprising appears to have been fuelled by widespread perceptions of government corruption and failure to improve the quality of life of citizens, including providing access to cultivable land. The Maoists ran a parallel government, established their own tax system, burned land records, and redistributed seized property and food to the poor, in 45 districts. The insurgency was waged, in part, through torture, killings, and bombings targeting police, the military, and public officials. A number of bank robberies, combined with "revolutionary tax" revenue, made the Nepali Maoists one of the wealthiest rebel groups in Asia.

The Kathmandu government faced additional turmoil in June 2001, when Crown Prince Dipendra shot and killed his parents, King Birendra and Queen Aishwarya, seven other members of the royal family, and himself reportedly after a disagreement over whom he should marry. This incident did much to undermine the legitimacy of the monarchy. King Gyanendra, the former king's brother, was crowned on June 4, 2001, and he appointed a commission to investigate the assassinations. By mid-June, the country began returning to normal following rioting and widespread refusal to believe official accounts of the massacre. In July 2001, Prime Minister Girija Prasad Koirala stepped down amid fears of continuing instability and his government's failure to deal with the growing Maoist insurgency. He was replaced by NC leader Sher Bahadur Deuba, who then became the head of Nepal's eleventh government in as many years.

Constitutional Crisis

During the summer of 2002, the government of Nepal was thrown into a constitutional crisis that interfered with its ability to effectively combat the Maoist insurgency. The crisis began in late May, when King Gyanendra, at the request of the prime minister, dissolved parliament and unilaterally declared a three-month extension of emergency rule, which had expired on May 24, 2002. The prime minister, who also scheduled early elections for November 2002, reportedly took such action after his centrist Nepali Congress party refused to support his plan to extend emergency rule. Following the prime minister's actions, 56 former members of parliament filed a lawsuit against him, claiming there was no constitutional precedent for the dissolution of parliament during emergency rule. In August 2002, the Supreme Court rejected this lawsuit. Although opponents of the prime minister agreed to accept the verdict, they emphasized the difficulty of holding free and fair elections two years ahead of schedule when much of the country was under either rebel or army control.

Although the prime minister pledged that there would be no emergency rule during the scheduled November 2002 elections, Maoist attacks and threatened strikes prompted the government to consider various measures to prevent a Maoist disruption of the polls. The government discussed imposing a partial state of emergency in areas most affected by the insurgency. However, opposition parties, which urged the government to open a dialogue with the Maoists, argued that by curbing civil liberties, emergency rule would inhibit free and fair elections.

As an alternative, the government announced in September 2002 that it would hold the elections in six stages over two months, starting in mid-November, so that government troops could be transferred around the country to protect voters and candidates.

After further deliberation, however, Nepal's cabinet concluded that the security situation was too risky to hold elections. On October 3, 2002, the cabinet asked King Gyanendra to postpone the national elections for one year. The next day, the king dismissed the prime minister, disbanded his cabinet, and assumed executive powers.

The King's Takeover

The security situation in Nepal deteriorated after the collapse of the ceasefire between the Maoists and the government on August 27, 2003. The Maoists favoured drafting a new constitution that would abolish the monarchy. The king opposed such a move and wanted the Maoists to relinquish their weapons. Accommodation between the king and opposition democratic elements had been thought to be key to creating the unified front necessary to defeat the Maoists. With his direct assumption of powers, and arrest of opposition democratic elements, the king decided to try to defeat the Maoists on his own. This move proved to be the beginning of the end of the power of the monarchy in Nepal.

After seizing direct power in February 2005, King Gyanendra exerted control over democratic elements, but made little progress in the struggle against the Maoists. The king reportedly thought he could take advantage of a split in the Maoist leadership and disarray amongst democrats to seize control and use the Royal Nepal Army (RNA) to defeat the Maoists. The seizure of power by the king appears to have been aimed as much, if not more so, at asserting the king's control over democratic forces. Many observers felt that a military solution to the conflict with the Maoists was not achievable and that a concerted effort by the king and the democrats was needed to establish a unified front to defeat the Maoists.

When the king assumed power he stated that he would take steps to reinstate a constitutional democracy within 100 days, which he then failed to do.

Although some political prisoners were released by the king, hundreds of others remained under arrest and restrictions on civil liberties, such as public assembly and freedom of the press, remained in place. A U.N. Office of the High Commissioner of Human Rights team was established in Nepal in April 2005 to monitor the observance of human rights and international humanitarian law.

By moving against the democrats, who under different circumstances could have worked with the king against the Maoists, the king strengthened the position of the Maoists. By some estimates almost half of the RNA was occupied with palace security, civil administration, and efforts to restrict communications and civil rights. The king's legitimacy with the people was weakened due to the circumstances under which he assumed the throne, the way he seized direct rule, and due to poor popular perceptions of his son, Prince Paras Shah. The former Crown prince was unpopular with Nepalis "for his drunken antics and playboy lifestyle."

Maoist Reaction. From February 13 to 27, 2005, the Maoists reacted to the king's actions by blockading major highways linking the country's 75 districts, as well as international road links to India and China. This led to clashes between Maoists and the RNA and brought trade by road to a standstill. The army organized armed convoys which allowed limited trade to continue. The Maoists had earlier cut off land routes to Kathmandu in August 2004. During the week-long blockade in 2004, prices of some basic foods more than doubled and fuel was rationed. This increase in food prices reportedly recurred in the 2005 blockade. By blockading Kathmandu, the Maoists successfully increased pressure on the king's government and demonstrated their power.

Democratic Uprising

On April 24, 2006, mounting popular resistance in support of the political parties led King Gyanendra to hand over power to the Seven Party Alliance.

This followed weeks of violent protests and demonstrations against direct royal rule in Nepal.

The Seven Party Alliance that opposed the king in April included the parties as listed below. The Maoists were not part of the Seven Party Alliance, though they worked with the alliance to oppose the monarchy. This was made possible by the king's political crackdown on the democrats.

- The Nepali Congress (NC)
- Communist Party of Nepal Unified Marxist Leninist CPN (UML)
- Nepali Congress (Democratic) or NC (D)
- Nepal Sadbhavana Party (Anandi Devi) or NSP (A)
- Jana Morcha Nepal
- Samyukta Baam Morcha (United Left Front) or ULF
- Nepal Workers and Peasants Party (NWPP).

The seven parties worked together through their alliance to promote a more democratic Nepal in the face of direct rule by the king.

In May 2006, six of the seven political parties formed a coalition government. On November 8, 2006, the Seven Party Alliance and the Maoists reached a peace agreement ending a decade-old insurgency that claimed over 13,000 lives.

In it, the Maoists agreed to put down their arms and postpone a decision on the future disposition of the monarchy until after the election of a Constituent Assembly. Under the peace agreement, Constituent Assembly elections were to be held by the end of June 2007. The June election date slipped but Constituent Assembly elections were eventually held in April 2008.

GOVERNMENT, POLITICS, AND REGIONAL TENSIONS

Structure of Government

The structure of the current 601-seat legislature is a mixed member system with 240 members elected from single member constituencies and 335 members elected on a proportional basis from party lists. A further 26 members are nominated by the cabinet to represent ethnic and indigenous groups. Administratively, the country is divided into 75 districts.

The CPN-M, with 220 seats and 36.6% of seats, is the largest party in the Constituent Assembly. The 110 seats for the NC represent 18.3% of the CA while the 103 seats belonging to the CPN-UML represents 17.1%. The 52 seats of the MPRF represent 8.7% and the 20 seats of the TMDP represent 3.3%. Twenty other parties and independents, all with less than 2% of the CA seats, account for the balance. The current government includes President Ram Baran Yadav of the Nepali Congress Party and Prime Minister Pushpa Kamal Dahal — also known by his Maoist nom de guerre Prachanda — as head of government. The president was elected by the Constituent Assembly on July 21, 2008, while the prime minister was elected on August 18, 2008. In accordance with the interim constitution, legislative powers passed from the previous parliament to the CA after its election in April 2008. The prime minister is selected by a vote of the CA. The CA is to develop a new constitution within a two-and-ahalf- year time-frame during which it will also perform legislative functions. Former Prime Minister and Nepali Congress leader Girija Koirala accused the Maoists of "hatching a conspiracy to end parliamentary democracy." Koirala has stated his concern that the Maoists' communist model of a new socialist political system represents a significant challenge to parliamentary democracy.

The Nepal Army

The Nepal Army, which fought a protracted counter-insurgency war against the Maoists from 1996 to 2006, has remained largely outside politics but could become a key actor should the Maoists once again turn to violence as a means of achieving their objectives.

The NC has opposed Maoist plans to integrate their forces into the Nepali Army. Instead, the NC advocates that they should be placed into an industrial security force, the police, or other sectors. Some estimates place the number of former Maoist fighters in cantonment at 20,000 or more.

The Nepal Army is thought to number approximately 95,000 soldiers that are divided into six regional divisions. NC President Koirala has warned that a movement would be launched if attempts are made to integrate former Maoist fighters into the Nepal Army.

Vice President of the NC Ram Chandra Poudel has stated that "If the rebel army is integrated [into the regular Nepal Army] the country will once again see conflict."

Intercommunal Strife and Regional Tension

As violence associated with the former Maoist insurgency has abated, intercommunal tensions have mounted and at times become violent.

This has been particularly acute in the Terai region where the Madhesi live. An estimated 49% of the country's population live in the Terai region. The Madhesi, or plains folk, seek autonomy to free themselves from what they feel is domination by Pahadis from the more mountainous parts of northern Nepal.

The Madhesis also have closer ties to India than other regions of Nepal. Madhesis have pressed for regional autonomy for the Terai region where most Madhesi live. Other ethnic groups in the Terai have opposed this. By some estimates there are 12 to 14 armed groups fighting a lowintensity struggle for autonomy in the region. It has been estimated that over 200 were killed as the result of Madhesi agitation for autonomy over the past year. In September 2008, fourteen armed groups reportedly met in the neighbouring Indian state of Bihar to discuss forming a unified armed movement to promote Madhesi interests.

The Madhesi have added a new regional dimension to Nepal's struggle for political stability. A new threat to the political stability of Nepal has emerged from a number of groups representing Madhesi in southern Nepal. The MPRF, TMDP, Sadbhavana Party and the Dalit Janajati Party represent Madhesis and command 85 seats in the CA.

The new president and vice president are also Madhesi. Madhesis are culturally and ethnically close to peoples of northern India. There have been allegations from inside Nepal that Hindu radicals may have had a role in the violence in the Terai. Madhesi have complained about their underrepresentation in parliament, the government, police, and army as well as economic discrimination against them.

The Economy

Nepal is one of the poorest countries in the world. Political instability and insurgency-related violence of recent years has undermined the country's economy. Over 76% of its inhabitants earn a living through agriculture while only 16% of the land is arable.

Major crops include rice, wheat, maize, jute, sugarcane, and potatoes. Political uncertainty and continued reliance on subsistence farming could keep Nepal poor for many years to come. Though the industrial base is small, Nepal produces carpets, garments, and, increasingly, textiles, which now account for a majority of merchandise exports. Other major revenue sources are tourism and remittances including those from Nepal's famed Gurkha soldiers serving in the British and Indian armies.

Government efforts to increase foreign trade and investment have been impeded by political instability, corruption, the resistance of vested interests, the small size of the economy, its remote and landlocked location, the lack of technological development, and frequent natural disasters, including floods and landslides. Nepal's infrastructure is poor and it has few commercially exploitable resources other than hydro power and cement grade limestone deposits. Nepal also suffers from low rates of investment and domestic savings. Firewood supplies an estimated 76% of total energy consumed in Nepal and is used for heating and cooking.

Nearly a quarter of the national budget is externally funded through foreign aid. Real economic growth averaged 3.5% between fiscal years 2002/03 and 2005/06. Growth in 2006/07 is estimated by the Economist Intelligence Unit to be 2.6%. Remittances have increased in importance as a source of foreign exchange as tourism has depended on an uncertain political situation in recent years. Nepal's key export partners include most significantly India (70%), the United States (8.9%), and Germany (4.1%).

2

Religion in Nepal

INTRODUCTION

Nepal is a secular state. Prior to the movement for democracy in early 2006 and the sacking of King Gyanendra, the country was officially aHindu state.

History

According to the 2011 census, 84.2% of the Nepalese population was Hindu, 9.0% was Buddhist, 4.4% was Muslim, 3.0% wasKirant/Yumaist, 1.42% was Christian, and 0.9% follow other religions or no religion.

According to the 2001 census, 84.2 percent of Nepalese were Hindu, 10.74 percent Buddhist, 4.20 percent Muslim, 3.60 percent Kirant(an indigenous religion), 0.45 percent Christian, and 0.4 percent were classified as other groups such as Bön religion. In 1971 Hindus were 89.4 percent of the population, Buddhists 7.5 percent, and Kirants statistically 0 percent. However, statistics on religious groups are complicated by the ubiquity of dual faith practices, particularly among Hindus and Buddhists. Moreover, shifts in the population's religious composition also reflect political changes.

The geographical distribution of religious groups in the early 1990s revealed a preponderance of Hindus, accounting for at least 87 percent of the population in every region. The largest concentrations of Buddhists were found in the eastern hills, the Kathmandu Valley, and the central Tarai; in each area about 10 percent of the people were Buddhist. Buddhism was more common among the Newar andTibeto-Nepalese groups. Among the Tibeto-Nepalese, those most influenced by Hinduism were the Magar, Sunwar, and Rai peoples. Hindu influence was less prominent among the Gurung, Limbu, Bhote, Tamang and Thakali groups, who continued to employ Buddhist monks for their religious ceremonies. Since both Hinduism as well as Buddhism are Dharmic religions, they usually accept each other's practices and many people practice a combination of both.

HINDUISM IN NEPALESE CULTURE

It is even believed, according to Nepalese theology that Lord Brahma, Vishnu and Shiva had come to Nepal in the form of deer.

Establishment of Nepal by Ne Muni

He used to perform religious ceremonies at Teku, the confluence of the Bagmati and Bishnumati rivers. He is said by legend to have selected a pious cowherd to be the first of the many kings of the Gopala Dynasty. These rulers are said to have ruled Nepal for over 500 years. He selected Bhuktaman to be the first king in the line of the Gopal (*Cowherd*) Dynasty. The Gopal dynasty ruled for 621 years. Yakshya Gupta was the last king of this dynasty.However,this mythology can be challenged as no such name as Ne exists in Nepali or other Sanskrit-derived languages.

Flag of Nepal

It is believed that Lord Vishnu had organized the Nepali people and given them this flag, with the sun and moon as emblems on it. In a Hindu Purana, it is written that it was Lord Shiva who handed the flag to Lord Vishnu, and then Lord Vishnu to Lord Indra, for the purpose for battling demons.

This type of Flag is seen in all Temples of Nepal and India. This is basically a design of flag that was carried by the Kingdoms since Hinduism was established. India managed to change the shape of its flag into a rectangular flag as it has all types of religions followed,eventhough it has the largest Hindu population of the earth; but Nepal held in the Hindu traditional flag and thus has a unique flag no other country has.

Gorakhnath and Gurkhas

It is said that Gorakhnath came to Nepal in the reign of the 8th Thakuri King.

The Gurkhas of Nepal are the descendants of Gorakhnath of the Nath sect. Gorakhnath was a disciple of Machendranath, a backward-caste saint.

Machendrajatra is a national festival in Nepal to celebrate the birth of the saint. It is said that the Gurkha war-cry to this day is "Guru Gorakhnath ki jai". It is more often said that their war cry is Jaya Mahakali, Ayo Gorkhali.

According to a Terai myth, when the Pandavas were ascending to heaven, they all fell, but Bhima from the Pandava brothers was rescued by Gorakhnath.

One Nepalese myth says that as Gorakhnath arrived in Nepal, the terrible dought in occurring in the period halted!

Buddha's lineage from Vedic Sages

Lord Buddha is said to be a descendant of Sage Angirasa in many Buddhist texts. Scholars like Dr. Eitel too connect the name to the Rishi Gautama.

Placenames from Hindu icons

There are many places in Nepal with names signifying icons in Hindu history.

Janakpur is a city, named after Raja Janak, the father of Sita. The modern-city is the capital of the Janakpur Zone.

The Mahakali Zone is also the name of a collection of districts, named after Kali Maa. Within this zone, there is also the Mahakali River.

The Kapilvastu District is named after Sage Kapila.

The Vyasa Valley is the name given to the Kalapaani (near the Lipu-Lekh pass at the border between India and Tiblet) and Kailash Lake Mansarovar.

BUDDHISM IN NEPAL

Buddha was born in Shakya (Sakya) Kingdom of Kapilvastu at around which lies in present day Rupandehi district, Lumbini zone ofNepal. It has not been possible to assign with certainty the year in which Prince Siddhartha (birth name of the Buddha) was born, it is usually placed at around 623 B.C. 10.74% of Nepal's population practice Buddhism, consisting mainly of Tibeto-Burmanethnicities. In Nepal's hill and mountain regions Hinduism has absorbed Buddhist tenets to such an extent that in many cases they have shared deities as well as temples. For instance, the Muktinath Temple is sacred and a common house of worship for both Hindus and Buddhists.

Overview

In Nepal majority of people identify as Hindu, however, Buddhist influences are pervasive in most aspects of Nepali culture to an extent that Buddhist and Hindu temples are shared places of worship for peoples of both faith so that, unlike, in other countries, the distinction between Hinduism and Buddhism in Nepal is not always clear. During the reign of King ACœuvarman Nepalese princess Bhrikuti played a significant role in spreading and developing Buddhism in Tibet and the Far East. Tibetan Buddhist architecture has long been influenced by Nepalese artists and sculptors like Araniko. The sacred Buddhist texts in Mahayana Buddhism are mainly written inRanjana script (the script of Newars) or scripts like Lantsa which are derived from Ranjana.

In traditional Nepalese Buddhism, there are nine special texts which are called the "Nine Dharma Jewels" (*Navagrantha*), and these are considered the nine books of Buddhism par excellence:

- Astasâhasrikâ Prajnapâramitâ Sûtra
- Gandavyûha Sûtra

- Dasabhûmika Sutra
- Samadhiraja Sutra
- LaEkâvatâra Sûtra
- Saddharma Punarîka Sûtra
- Tathâgataguhya Sûtra
- Lalitavistara Sûtra
- SuvarGaprabhâsa Sûtra

Among the Tibeto-Burman tribes, Tibetan Buddhism is the most widely practised form. Newar practice Newar variant of Vajrayana Buddhism and Theravada Buddhism. Many Buddhist groups are also influenced by Hinduism. Buddhism is the dominant religion of the thinly-populated northern areas, which are inhabited by Tibetan-related peoples, namely the Sherpa, Lopa, Manangi, Thakali, Lhomi, Dolpa and Nyimba. They constitute a small minority of the country's population.

Ethnic groups that live in central Nepal, such as Gurung, Lepcha, Tamang, Magar, Newar, Yakkha, Thami, Chhantyal and Chepang, are also followers of Buddhism. These ethnic groups have larger populations compared to their northern neighbours. They came under the influence of Hinduism due to their close contacts with the Hindu castes. In turn, many of them eventually adopted Hinduism and have been largely integrated into the caste system.

The Kirant tribes, especially the Limbu and the Rai, have also adopted Tibetan Buddhist practises from their Buddhist neighbours. The Jirel, which is considered a Kirata tribe, have also adopted Tibetan Buddhism.

JUDAISM IN NEPAL

In 1986, the Israeli embassy in Katmandu organized a Passover celebration as a service to the 7000 Israelis that visit Nepal annually. The celebration was taken over in 1999 by the Chabad (/'abad/) movement, a Hassidic Jewish movement that specializes in outreach to nonobservant Jews. Prior to 1986, there was no organized practice of Judaism in Nepal, and there is no native Jewish community.

The Nepalese Chabad center has achieved some degree of notability, primarily for the Passover celebration, reputed to be the largest such celebration in the world, with 1500 participants. The couple that runs the center were models for a television series in Israel.

Passover seder

In 1986, the Israeli embassy in the Thamel section of Katmandu started the tradition of holding a Passover Seder for Israeli travelers. In 1999, the Chabad house took over the event.

By 2006, the annual Passover seder sponsored by Chabad hosted 1,500 participants. It has been called the "world's largest seder", requiring 1,100 pounds of Matzo, the ritual unleavened bread of the festival. By 2014 the event drew 1,700 attendees, though the ceremony was threatened by a strike that delayed a shipment of Matzo.

Growth of Chabad house in Nepal

The Chabad movement maintains houses throughout the world, to provide services to the local Jewish communities and to Jewish travellers. The Chabad house in Kathmandu was opened in 1999 by Rabbi Chezki Lifshitz and his wife Chani.

According to Chani, the movement had difficulty finding *shlichim* (emissaries) to go to Nepal. "They couldn't find shluchim [emissaries] willing to go to such a third-world country," she said in an interview. "We were the crazy couple willing to do it."

The house was a success, and the movement opened two satellite houses in Nepal, one in the city of Pokhara in November 2007, and a third in Manang in April 2014.

In May 2012, the Israeli television network *Reshet* launched the miniseries "Kathmandu," starring Israeli actor Michael ("Moni") Moshonov, based on true events from Chabad house Nepal. The series ran for 13 episodes.

Besides being the model for the television series, Chabad house has often made news. In October 2013, Rabbi Lifshitz prevented the cremation of a religious Jewish woman from Australia who was killed in a traffic accident. Cremation, customary in Nepal, is forbidden by orthodox Judaism. The organization was also involved in recovery of the remains of a New Jersey woman killed in a plane crash in the Himalayas. The house has been featured in numerous magazines, including *The Atlantic*, the *Jerusalem Post*, and other media.

Israeli tourism in Nepal

According to the Nepal Ministry of Tourism, 7151 Israelis visited Nepal in 2012, staying an average of 16 days. Although Israelis comprise only about one percent of total tourism in Nepal, their mark is noticeable. "Any visitor to Nepal is guaranteed to hear Hebrew being spoken in the streets and to see Hebrew signs and T-shirts in the main tourist locations," writes Rabbi Ben in his travel blog "The Travelling Rabbi".

Jewish religious leaders have expressed concern that many Israeli and American Jews visit Nepal in a spiritual quest that distances them from their Jewish roots. "The antipathy to religious ritual that many Israeli Jews have inherited from that early generation of founding Zionists, leads many of them to search for spiritual fulfillment in Nepal or India...," writes Rabbi Daniel Gordis. "Ashrams in Nepal and India are filled with young Jewish people, mostly American and Israeli.". In fact, however, very few Israelis go to Nepal for spiritual reasons – 62 in 2012, or less than one percent of all Israeli visitors to the country, and far below the average of 14 percent for all nationalities. It is unknown how many Americans of Jewish extraction visit Nepal for spiritual reasons.

Other Jewish links to Nepal

The French Jewish scholar Sylvain Lévi visited Nepal in 1898 and published a three-volume historical study (*Le Népal: Étude historique d'un royaume hindou*, 1905–1908), considered the authoritative Western account of the country for most of the 20th century. Lévi later wrote a comparative study of the Jewish and Hindu religions, based on his Nepalese researches

The Hong Kong-based Jewish Kadoorie family has been involved with philanthropy in Nepal (as elsewhere in Asia), particularly serving Gurkha communities, and Horace Kadoorie was awarded the Order of Gorkha Dakshina Bahu (First Class) by the Nepalese government.

Security issues

The U.S. State Department has found Anti-Semitism to be "not an issue of any significance" in Nepal, and has reported no Anti-Semitic acts in annual reports on the country.

Haaretz reported in 2013 that an Iranian suspected of planning terror attack on the Israeli embassy was arrested by embassy security personnel and handed over to the police in Katmandu, Nepal.

The Times of India reported in 2014 that Indian security forces had foiled a plot by the Indian Mujahideen to kidnap Jewish tourists in Nepal to be used in exchange for the female Pakistani scientist Aafia Siddiqui held in a US jail, and that the organization had rented a hiding place in the hills of Nepal to hold their hostages captive.

ISLAM IN NEPAL

Islam is a minor religion in Nepal. According to the 2011 Nepal census, 4.4% of the population are Muslim.

Islam is thought to have been introduced by the Indian Muslims settling in Nepal. The 4.2 % of the population being Muslim according to a 2006 Nepalese census. However, more recent estimates indicate that Muslims constitute approximately 5-10% of the population. Islam is generally thought to have been introduced by Indian Muslims that travelled to Nepal and then settled there.

BAHÁ'Í FAITH IN NEPAL

The Bahá'í Faith in Nepal begins after a Nepalese leader encountered the religion in his travels before World War II. Following World War II, the first known Bahá'í to entire Nepal was about 1952 in the person N. P. Sinha who moved to Birganj and the first Nepalese Bahá'í Local Spiritual Assembly elected in 1959, and its National Assembly in 1972. For a period of time, between 1976 and 1981, all assemblies were dissolved due to legal restrictions. The 2001 census reported 1211 Bahá'ís, and since the 1990s the Bahá'í community of Nepal has been involved in a number of interfaith organizations including the Inter-religious Council of Nepal promoting peace in the country. The Association of Religion Data Archives (relying on World Christian Encyclopedia) estimated some 4300 Bahá'ís in 2005.

Early days

In the 1920-1940 period Col. Raja Jai Prithvi Bahadur Singh, Raja Of Bajang, travelled to Europe and the Americas and heard of the Bahá'í Faith through contact with individuals like Lady Blomfield.

The first known entry of members of the Bahá'í Faith to Nepal was about 1952 by N. P. Sinha, an Indian Bahá'í, to Birganj soon followed by Kedarnath Pradhan who was from Sikkim before moving to Kathmandu along with his family. News of the religion also arrived following a United Nations conference in Colombo at which Nepalese delegates expressed interest in the religion. Following conversions and further pioneers the first Local Spiritual Assembly in Nepal was that of Kathmandu city which was elected in 1959. In 1960 there were assemblies in Kathmandu,Dohlka Shahr, and Bhaktapur and smaller groups of Bahá'ís in Dharan, Baklong, Pokhara, and Biratnagar; and over one hundred members of the religion.

Growth

By 1963 the local assemblies of Nepal included: Bhaktapur, Biratnagar, Dharan, Kathmandu, and Pokhara, with small groups of Bahá'ís inBodegaon, Dabeha, Nalar, and Dolkhashahr. Isolated Bahá'ís were in Bakloong, Damdame, Rakhughati, and Rakheshwav and Hand of the Cause John Esslemont's *Bahá'u'lláh and the New Era* was translated into Nepalese. Perhaps the first Hand of the Cause to visit Nepal wasRúhíyyih Khanum in 1964. In 1967 ambassador Ram Prasad Manandhar visited the Bahá'í House of Worship in Wilmette, USA. In 1969 Hand of the Cause Adelbert Mühlschlegel visited a number of central Asian countries including Nepal at the request of the Universal House of Justice. In August 1971 youth from Nepal were among the attendees at a western Asian Bahá'í youth conference in India.

With Hand of the Cause Ali-Akbar Furutan representing the Universal House of Justice, the Bahá'ís of Nepal held their first national convention to elect their National Spiritual Assembly in 1972 during the reign of King Mahendra. The convention had forty delegates. The members of the first national assembly were: Amar Pradhan, Shyam Maherjan, Jujubhai Sakya, Aranda Lal Shrestha, Dinesh Verma, Keith de Folo, W. F. Chaittonalla, P. N. Rai, D. K. Malla - from Buddhist, Hindu, Christian backgrounds. In November 1972 delegates from the local assemblies of the Narayani Zone gathered for a local conference on the progress of the religion to study Bahá'í history, Bahá'í administration in general and specifically electing local assemblies, and Bahá'í teachings.

Dissolution and reformation

The national and local assemblies were all dissolved between 1976 and 1981 due to legal restrictions. However Bahá'ís from Nepal were able to attend the October 1977 Asian Bahá'í Women's Conference with Hand of the Cause Rúhíyyih Khanum after which she toured in Nepal including addressing some 700 students at the Padma Kanya Women's College. In May 1981 45 Nepalese Bahá'ís from various localities attended a conference at the national center in Kathmandu. A highlight of the weekend conference was the first showing in Nepal of the film *The Green Light Expedition* about Rúhíyyih Khanum's trip up the Amazon River. The local and national assemblies were reelected in and since 1982 - this dissolution and reformation was during the reign of King Birendra. When the national convention gathered there were 25 delegates. In 1983 there is comment that a distinguishing effect of pioneers was that they "not only took an interest in our troubles, they also looked on conditions in

Nepal as their own and talked about our problems as their problems." Hand of the Cause Collis Featherstone attended the 1983 national convention. In 1984 the National Spiritual Assembly of the Bahá'ís of Nepal printed "Selected Writings on Baha'i Administration" in parallel English and Nepali scripts. Later in 1984 Nepalese Bahá'ís attended the conference at the almost completed Lotus Temple. By 1985 the Bahá'ís assembly of Malangwa has established a school that has about 30 students, several of whom receive scholarships. Low and high caste children eat and drink together, and the villagers have accepted that Bahá'í schools do not observe customs concerning caste. In 1988 the national assembly had expanded and improved its adult literacy program. In 1989 representatives of the national Assemblies of Nepal along with the Andaman and Nicobar Islands, Bangladesh, India, Sikkim and Sri Lanka along with Continental Counselors and members of sub-regional councils in India met in Pune, India to discuss creating a unified vision of the religion and its progress across the sub-continent.

On 29 September 1990 Hand of the Cause Collis Featherstone died and is buried in Kathmandu.

Modern community

Since its inception the religion has had involvement in socio-economic development beginning by giving greater freedom to women, promulgating the promotion of female education as a priority concern, and that involvement was given practical expression by creating schools, agricultural coops, and clinics. The religion entered a new phase of activity when a message of the Universal House of Justice dated 20 October 1983 was released. Bahá'ís were urged to seek out ways, compatible with the Bahá'í teachings, in which they could become involved in the social and economic development of the communities in which they lived. Worldwide in 1979 there were 129 officially recognized Bahá'í socio-economic development projects. By 1987, the number of officially recognized development projects had increased to 1482. Since the early 1990s the Bahá'ís of Nepal have involved themselves in diverse concerns in Nepal.

One group of Bahá'ís set up an organization "Education, Curriculum, and Training Associates", or "ECTA", which means "unity" in Nepali, in 1997 to promote rural development strategies and programs that can be done at low cost by village groups without extensive outside aid.

Nepalese Bahá'ís joined the Inter-religious Council of Nepal promoting peace in the country who have also met with CPN Maoist leadership and consulted on AIDS issues.

A "Sacred Gifts for a Living Planet" conference in Nepal in November 2000 was organized by the Alliance of Religions and Conservation and the World Wide Fund for Natureincluded Bahá'ís.

The Club of Budapest offered a "Change the World — Best Practice Award" given to four international educational projects that aim at empowering people through learning and enabling them to take full control of their economic development.

Marcia Odell was one of the awardees, representing the Women's Empowerment Program (WEP) in Nepal, which has developed an approach to microfinance and the empowerment of women.

The WEP program has reached more than 130,000 women in Nepal and has also received considerable support from the Bahá'í community of Nepal.

In December 2003 a conference entitled "Education: The Right of Every Girl and Boy," brought together representatives of five South Asian countries by government officials and members of the Bahá'í communities: Bangladesh, India, Nepal, Pakistan, and Sri Lanka and was co-sponsored and supported by: the Bahá'í International Community, UNESCO,World Vision India, National Foundation for India, Save the Children UK, Commonwealth Education Fund, and India Alliance for Child Rights.

In 2006 Bahá'ís participated in an international youth conference organized by Hindu Vidyapeeth Nepal. It was set as a peace conference with the theme of 'Deepening our Spirituality' in Kathmandu.

Demographics

Though it is illegal to convert others, occasional reports of police harassment, and reports of discrimination based on religious belief or practice by 2001 the national census reported 1211 Bahá'ís (but includes children down to 0–4 years old—indeed the largest segment of population was 10–14 years old.) There were more women than men, and of the 5 Divisions more Bahá'ís lived in the Eastern Division and the least in the Western one. The Association of Religion Data Archives (relying on World Christian Encyclopedia) estimated some 4350 Bahá'ís in 2005.

CHRISTIANITY IN NEPAL

The first record of a visit of a Christian missionary in Nepal dates back to 1628, when King Lakshminarasimha Malla received Portuguese Jesuit Father Juan Cabral graciously in the spring that year. He was awarded with a Tamra Patra, a copper plate, allowing him to preach Christianity. Protestant Christians initially came to Nepal primarily through the Nepalese who were living outside of Nepal during and prior to the Rana Regime. After the collapse of Ranas rule in Nepal in 1950, Nepali Christians living in India came in, along with some western missionaries. United Mission to Nepal, International Nepal Fellowship and others are a few earliest western mission agencies that came in and brought Christianity. According to the government data, Christian followers in Nepal accounts for about 1.4% of the population.

History

The first record of a visit of a Christian missionary in Nepal dates back to 1628, when King Lakshminarasimha Malla received Portuguese Jesuit Father Juan Cabral graciously in the spring that year. He was awarded with a Tamra Patra, a copper plate, allowing him to preach Christianity. In the year 1661, Albert d'Orville, a Belgian, and Johann Grueber, an Austrian visited Nepal as missionaries but did not stay long. On 14 March 1703, six Capuchin Fathers travelled from Rome to Nepal. Only two arrived in Kathmandu on 21 February 1707 and settled in Kathmandu in the middle of 1715's winter.

Over the next 54 years, they lived amongst the people of Bhaktapur and Patan in the Kathmandu valley. On 24 March 1760, Father Tranquillius made a small new church situated in Wotu Tole in Kathmandu under the title, The Assumption of Our Lady.

After Prithvi Narayan Shah's conquest in 1769, the Capuchin fathers and 57 newly converted Newar Christians were exiled to Bettiah, India. Then till 1950, missionaries were disallowed in Nepal.

Scottish missionaries in Serampore and Darjeeling worked on Bible translations into Nepali, which were completed by Ganga Prasad Pradhan in 1932.

Missionaries began to enter Nepal in the early 1950s, but engaged in development work, education and social service such as health care. Nepal was an officially Hindu state, and while conversion was never banned, proselytizing with the aim of converting was illegal and the Christian organizations who entered Nepal, including the Catholic church and the ecumenical United Mission to Nepal, followed a philosophy of witnessing by example rather than evangelizing.

Some of the schools and hospitals founded by these groups, such as St. Xavier's school, Patan Hospital and Tansen Hospital, became highly regarded for their quality.

Missionary activities with the intent to convert Nepalis to Christianity increased with the advent of democracy and, in particular, after Nepal was named a secular state in 2008. Christmas is now an official government holiday and the "door is widely open for evangelism."

By 2011, the small but growing community of Christians had emerged as a political pressure group, demanding that the government grant them land for cemeteries. After a decade of extensive missionary action, the 2011 census found Christians at 1.45 percent of Nepal's population, almost triple the number in 2001. The targeting of indigenous ethnic groups and low-income people with extensive proselytizing efforts, for instance as "unreached people," has been culturally controversial.

State of the Church in Nepal

Until 1990, most of the church groups in Nepal were united with few exceptions like Assembly of God and Church of Christ. But the democratic changes of 1990 brought relative freedom to practice one's faith. This freedom contributed towards a proliferation of various denominations and groups. Missionaries began to enter the open doors in the decades since 1990.

3

Important Festivals of Nepal

The Nepali calendar is clogged with festivals except during the rice-planting season, which coincides with the monsoon.

One of the most important festivals and celebrated by a majority of Nepalese people is Dashain but the more spectacular are the chariot festivals.

The other important festivals are Tihar, Gai Jatra (jatra=festival in the Newari language) Biska Jatra, Buddha Jayanti, Krishna Astami, Tihar, Lhosar, Seto Machhendranath Jatra, Rato Machhendranath Jatra, Indra Jatra and Mani Rimdu.

Some festivals are celebrated by the Newars (indigenous people of Kathmandu valley) alone; some by only Buddhists or only Hindus, yet others are generally celebrated by most Nepali people.

Bisket (Biska) Festival

This festival is unique to Bhaktapur and is celebrated during the Nepali New Year, which falls in mid-April. The two striking features are the chariot procession and the tall pole known as lingo that is erected. In fact there are two chariots, one for the God Bhairav and the other for his consort, Bhadrakali also known as Bhairavi. The festival lasts for nine days during which, different shrines of Goddess Durga is visited and offerings laid according to ritual. The 70 ft pole with two large banners of cloth hanging from the top crosspiece is erected near the open shrine of Bhadrakali. The two chariots are also brought here during the coarse of the festival. Huge crowds gather to watch the proceedings. An interesting feature of the celebrations is the tug of war that takes place between residents of the upper city and that of the lower half. This decides to whose half the chariot is pulled to first, and often leads to open hostilities, which can lead to brick throwing and brawls. The bringing down of the pole marks the beginning of the new Nepali year and the end of the festival. The chariots are then pulled back and dismantled.

Chhat

For people living in the terai belt (plains), Chhat is one of their important festivals. This is the worship of the Sun God. The first day is spent on preparations as various food stuffs must be prepared for offering the Sun God as well as to consume after a day long fast. The festival takes place by the banks of the rivers where devotees gather to pray to the Sun God. On the first day the gathering takes place in the late afternoon to wait for the sun to sink below the horizon at which time they lay offerings of fruits and other edibles along the banks. Lighted oil-wick lamps are floated on the river, suspended on paper boats. As the sun goes down, the worshippers wash in the river make offerings and pray. The following day the gathering takes place before sun up. There are many who observe penance by prostrating themselves along the way. As the sun comes up, many enter the water to bathe and pray turning several times around in the water. There are huge gatherings along the banks of the rivers during this festival. The offerings are taken home and distributed as prasad (blessed food).

Dasain

The Dasain festival takes place around Sept-Oct and is celebrated by most communities in Nepal. This, like Christmas is the time when family members come together regardless of where they are. The festival lasts for ten days and each day is marked with some ritual ceremony. During the course of Dasain many animals are sacrificed and unique to Nepal, there is even a military parade, which is attended by the King and Queen. Many people pass their time gambling, drinking, feasting and merry-making in general. The most important day is the tenth and last day when elders of the family bless their juniors by applying tika on their foreheads. All are dressed in new clothes for the occasion and feasting follows the tika ceremony. Tika however is not restricted to this day as it is not possible to visit all relatives on one day. The tika ceremony can be conducted until the full moon.

Lhosar

An important Buddhist festival is Lhosar, the Tibetan New Year. It usually falls around February and is celebrated by Tibetans, Sherpas, Manangays and some of the Tamangs and Gurungs who live in high altitudes. However, they do not all celebrate on the same day. Lhosar like Dasain also lasts for weeks as families travel to visit relatives over the week following Lhosar. The festival begins with the thorough cleaning of the house and everything in it. Each day is marked by a ritual like the throwing away of evil on the first day. There is much singing and dancing, feasting and there is even an opera like performance at Boudhanath. Drinking alcoholic beverages is a part of the Lhosar Festival, hence there is much merriment. It is also their tradition to sing and dance to entertain visiting relatives, who happily join in. The monks in the monasteries perform rituals for the good of all mankind and hold ceremonies to rid the earth of evil spirits.

Holi "The Festival of Colours"

This festival marks the beginning of spring and is celebrated by Hindus by dousing each other in coloured water. Many only play with coloured powder, which they rub on each other's forehead, cheeks and clothes. At Durbar Square in Kathmandu, a Pole bedecked with many multi-coloured cloth pieces is erected. Ethnic Indians living in Nepal pray and perform rituals at the pole lighting fires of cow dung and tying sacred thread around the pole. The playing of colour lasts only for a day and the festivities end when the pole at Durbar Square is brought down. It is then dragged to the open field at Tudikhel where it is ceremoniously burnt. The cinders and ash are then taken by devotees to use as protection as well as to bless their houses. The pieces of cloth from the pole are also worn as arm bands to ward off evil spirits. According to legend, the cloth pieces are said to represent the clothes of the Gopinis (Lord Krishna's female companions), which Krishna is supposed to have hung on a tree while they bathed in a nearby river.

Buddha Jayanti "Lord Buddha's Birthday"

This is one of the important Buddhist festivals when devotees gather around stupas like Swayambhunath and Boudhanath. The full moon day in late April or May is celebrated as Lord Buddha's birthday, which is also the day He achieved enlightenment and also the day he attained nirvana. Buddha was born in Lumbini in south Nepal more than 2500 years ago. During the full moon night of Buddha Jayanti, Swayambhunath is lighted up with butter lamps as well as electric lights. Devotees arrive from far and wide. Hundreds of prayer flags are strung up around the stupa strung from the spire. A large number of Buddha images along with a massive gilded image are displayed to the crowds. The devotees offer rice, flowers, coins and light oil wick lamps. Buddhist monks carry the image of Buddha down the steps to a place called Naghal. There the image is worshipped accompanied by elaborate rituals and is finally returned to Swayambhu. In all three cities; Kathmandu, Patan and Bhaktapur, images of Buddha, prayer flags and banners are carried through the streets in processions. At special functions to honour Buddha, the story of his life is told and reviewed. There is a special celebration at Bouddhanath where a large image of Buddha is placed on an elephant and paraded around the city.

Gai Jatra

The Gai Jatra festival (Gai=cow), which takes place in August is said to be the creation of a king named Pratap Malla who had lost a son. In the hope of consoling his Queen who was overcome with grief, he ordered all his subjects who had lost a member of their family during the past year to bring out a procession in their honour. In this way he hoped his queen would realize that she was not alone in her grief. Many people are seen leading a cow during the procession, hence the name Gai Jatra. Hindus believe that on this day Yamaraj, the God of death will open the gates to let the dead in. The cow being a sacred animal, leads the way.

It is common practice today to dress a young boy as a cow rather than find a real one. In these modern times most families do not own a cow. Other kids are dressed as holy men or a God such as Ram. The most interesting of the celebrations among the three cities takes place in Bhaktapur. Hundreds of drummers take to the streets playing traditional drums. These are followed by flautists and stick dancers neatly turned out in uniform. The carnival atmosphere lasts for several days. There is music and dancing everywhere and weirdly dressed people take to the streets. Some dress as gorillas; some as tourists with fake cameras; other men dressed as women. The funny dresses were originally meant to make the unhappy queen laugh. During Gai Jatra, the Government allows citizens to freely criticize political leaders without fear of a backlash and there are comic plays enacted on the brick platforms around street corners. The festival is celebrated in all three cities.

Krishna Astami

Krishna Astami (astami=eighth) falls on the seventh day of the dark lunar fortnight in August or September. It is the celebration of Lord Krishna's birthday. Krishna, one of the popular Hindu Gods is the eighth incarnation of Vishnu. Series of pictures depicting Krishna's life are displayed in street corners on this day. The day is marked by processions arriving from everywhere. There are hordes of people carrying idols of Krishna garlanded and decorated for the occasion taking to the streets. Then there are the processions on trucks with portraits of Krishna. To the accompaniment of musical instruments, devotional songs praising Krishna are sung the whole day right through the night.

The Krishna Mandir in Patan Durbar Square becomes the focus of celebrations. This beautifully carved stone temple itself is covered in images glorifying the life of Lord Krishna. Enormous crowds of devotees predominantly women gather here for the festivities and prayers. Krishna is known for his fondness for women and is often depicted surrounded by his gopinis (female cowherds). The temple is covered with oil wick lamps and incense kept alight through the night by vigilant devotees. The temple glows with a new aura from the thousands of lamps. All night one can hear female voices chanting Krishna's various names like Gopala and Narayan. Long queues of men and women struggle up the steps to receive tika from the temple priest. Arriving on the second floor where the idol is kept, they pay homage to Krishna offering him flowers, food and coins. Lord Krishna it is said was born at midnight and raised by a cowherd, which is why women shower his idol with butter, milk and sweets. The large crowd engulfing the Krishna temple lingers until the early morning. With the coming of dawn the festival is over and the crowd disperses.

Indra Jatra

The Indra Jatra festival lasts for eight days in the month of September. One of the most spectacular festivals, Indra Jatra has many legends intermingled with the acts of various deities and is also one of the rare occasions when Lord Indra is remembered. The festivities get under way with the erection of the ceremonial pole at Durbar Square. This takes place on the twelfth day of the waxing moon in September. The pole is believed to represent a similar flag- pole given to Lord Indra by the God, Vishnu. At Indra Chowk, the Akash Bhairav mask is brought out of the Bhairav temple and placed in front of the temple. It is then worshipped and covered in beautiful flowers, while sweets and other offerings are placed on it.

Legend has it that Lord Krishna decapitated a Kirati King when he showed an inclination to fight for the opposing side. The king's head is said to have flown all the way to the Kathmandu valley. His head has since been represented by the enormous blue mask kept in the temple. During the proceedings, masked dancers take to the streets and this dance is known as Lakhe nach. The elephant dance depicting Indra's steed in search of his lost master is also popular as they chase people around. The chariot procession of the Living Goddess is an integral part of the festival. There is great excitement when she is seen sitting on her chariot. At every stop she is worshipped and the attending priest anoints the devotees and gives them prasad. During this auspicious occasion the monarch of Nepal receives Tika on his forehead from the Kumari. This is said to symbolically give the king the right to rule over her people. The chariots of the Kumari and her two companions on their respective chariots are pulled by two rows of youths for whom it is a great honour.

On the last day of the festival the flag- pole is brought down amid sacrifices and gun salutes. It is then immersed in the Bagmati river before it is finally cut into small pieces and burned inside a shrine.

Mani Rimdu

Mani Rimdu is a festival that is celebrated only in the mountainous regions of Nepal. Celebrated by Sherpas living in high altitudes, the more famous one is held at the Tengboche monastery every year during the full moon period of the ninth month of the Tibetan calendar. According to the Gregorian calendar it falls between mid-October and mid-December. However at the Thame monastery it is held in June and at Chiwang, Solu district, it is held in the month of December. Mani=prayers to Chenrisig the God of Compassion of the Buddhists. Ril= the small red pellets that are distributed by lamas and Du= the blessing of the pellets. The Mani Rimdu festival attracts large crowds of both sherpas as well as tourists.

For ten days the lamas pray for the good of all mankind while public events last for only three days. The main events that take place are 1/ the Lama's blessings 2/ the masked dances and 3/the grand finale with a bonfire. Of greatest interest to tourists are the masked dances performed by the lamas, in which, the central characters are the Gods to whom the lamas have been praying. These dances are the main attraction of Mani Rimdu and the festival comes to a close when the lamas throw offerings into a huge bonfire.

Rato Machhendranath Festival

This is a long drawn out chariot festival held in Patan. The Rato Machhendranath (rato=red) is the God of rain as well as the God of mercy. The Buddhists refer to him as Lokeshwar. A large chariot is assembled in Patan and is moved in a procession from place to place often taking more than a month to reach its final destination. Legend has it that Lord Machhendranath once resided in Assam and in ancient times a pious King and two officials travelled all the way to fetch him. Using tantric mantras they changed Machhendranath into a bee and brought him to Nepal in a ceremonial vase. As Machhendranath is also known as Bungadeo, a town was built in his honour and named Bungamati. Many years after his arrival in the valley, a special temple was built for Machhendranath at Bungamati, Lalitpur district.

Two chariots are taken out in a procession, the second for Minnath, godson of Machhendranath. The procession of these two chariots gets under way on the fourth day of the bright fortnight of Baishak (April-May). A large enthusiastic crowd, including Newari musicians accompanies the chariots. There, the Living Goddess gives blessings to devotees until late evening. Where the chariot stops, devotees come out to make offerings, mostly of rice as the God ensures rain for its cultivation.

Feasting, animal sacrifices and loud music is part of the festival. On the final day of the festival the Bhoto (a bejeweled waistcoat) is displayed to the massive crowd that gathers at Jawalakhel. This sacred waistcoat is held up for all to see and the onlookers includes their majesties the King and Queen. This is popularly known as the “Bhoto Jatra” (jatra=festival) although it is part of the Chariot festival. Every twelve years the Rato Machhendranath festival is celebrated with greater fanfare and the next big one takes place in 2003.

Shivaratri

Shivaratri literally means "Night of Lord Shiva" and is celebrated around the temples of Shiva in late February or early March. The most important location is the Pashupatinath temple, which receives hundreds of thousands of Hindu pilgrims during this festival every year.

This is a one-day affair but sadhus (holy men) and other devotees start descending on Pashupati from months before the big day. On the day of Shivaratri there are massive crowds who come to pay homage and even the Royal family arrives to pay their respects.

Bathing in the holy Bagmati river and laying offerings at Shiva's shrine, the crowds mill around until evening when bonfires are lit that last until early morning. Pashupati witnesses the biggest crowds during Shivaratri and a large police force is required to maintain order.

Tihar

Dasain is soon followed by Tihar, which is popularly known as the Festival of Lights. The most striking feature of this festival is the lighting up of houses with hundreds of oil-wick lamps. Modernization has replaced the oil-wick lamps with electric bulbs.

But many follow tradition and light oil-wick lamps as they still do in the villages. This is a five-day festival with the most important being "Bhai Tika" when sisters put tika on their brothers' foreheads and give blessings. Each brother is expected to offer his sister a gift and the sister prays for the brother's protection and long life. The other important day is the day of "Laxmi Puja" when all pray to Laxmi, the Goddess of Wealth. It is believed that on this day, the Goddess visits all the houses that have been well lit; hence the tradition of lighting oil-wick lamps. Gambling, feasting and going from door to door singing Tihar songs make up the activities during this festival. While going from door to door singing traditional songs, they receive money and in return, they bless the household.

Seto Machhendranath

The Seto Machhendranath (Seto=white) chariot festival takes place in Kathmandu. This chariot with a long wooden steeple is constructed at Durbar Marg near the statue of King Mahendra. The image of Seto Machhendranath is brought to the chariot from Machhendranath temple at Jana Bahal near Indra Chowk in the heart of Kathmandu.

In the following four days the chariot is pulled in a procession from one stop to the next until it finally comes to rest in Lagankhel in the Lalitpur district (Lalitpur is the old name of Patan). At various locations where the chariot halts, people crowd around to pay homage to the deity. Oil wick lamps are lit, offerings are placed as the priests busily distribute prasad (blessed food) and tika to the gathering. At the end of the festival, the image is removed from the chariot and placed in a palanquin. From Lagankhel it is then carried in a procession back to the temple at Jana Bahal in Kathmandu. The chariot is dismantled and put aside for a year.

4

Nepali Nationalities and Peoples

Bankariyas

The Bankariya ethnic group is found in the villages of Handi Khola, Chourabesi, Sunkhola and the Chure Range of Makwanpur District. Like Chepanges, Bankariyas are also nomadic, and forage for tubers for their food. Believed to be only about 400 even in the best of times, there are now only about five families huddled in sheds in the deep of jungles. They are close to Chepangs in religious practices and languages. They gather wild asparagus and barter it for cereals in nearby villages. They like to fry and eat wild red ants.

Baramos

Baramos are from Gorkha while they are also found in Dhading, Makwanpur and Lalitpur and Tanahu districts. They claim to be close to the Sunuwars of east Nepal, and seem to have close affinity with the Jirels also. The Baramo language belongs to the Tibeto-Burman family. In religious practices, they are close to the Magars. Many Baramos trace their language and culture to Burma (Myanmar) and the Burmese. They are mostly engaged in farming.

Bahra Gaunle

The inhabitants of the Bahra Gauns (12 villages) above the Thak Khola (river) and to the south of Lho Manthang in Mustang

District are called the Bahara Gaunles. They resemble Lhopas in facial features, language and clothes. They also build their houses in the styles of the Lhopas of Lho Manthang. They practice both bon and Buddhism.

There are 18 settlements in Bahra Gaun. Though they also work as indentured laborers, their main professions are farming and trade. The indigenous people found in and around the sacred Buddhist temple of Muktinath (the temple is popularly known as Chhume Gyatsa in the Tibetan speaking world) are also included among the Bahara Gaunles.

Botes

Botes inhabit the banks of the Madi, Seti and Kali Gandaki Rivers of the districts of Tanahu and Kaski. The Bote religious practices, language and cultures are quite close to those of Danuwars, Darais and Majhis.

Their economic activities are similar to those of the Majhi community. Botes are of two kinds-Pani (water) Botes and Pakhe (land) Botes. While the former are engaged in boating and fishing, the land-based Botes are farmers and laborers. They have their own language. They are primarily animists and use alcohol in their religious rituals; hence their religion seems different from Hinduism.

Magars

Large numbers of Magars live in Palpa, Tanahu, Myagdi, Pyuthan and Rolpa. They are also found in Arghakhanchi, Syangja, Parbat, Baglung, Dolpa, Surkhet, Sindhuli and Udaypur. Research scholars opine that the Sen kings and Thakuris of the Magrant districts are also Magars. These facts make the Magars as one of the most pervasive ethnic groups of Nepal. Their language belongs to the Tibeto-Burman family, and they have their own unique dress codes and culture, which are doomed to extinction. They are Buddhist by religion. The Magar priest is called Bhusal. According to the census of 1991, the present Magar population stands at 7.2% of the national total.

Manangays

Manangays are those people residing in the upper regions of the Marsyangdi River in the Manang District. They are locally called Nesyangbas. Though resembling the Tibetans in language, culture as well as in physical features. they prefer to call themselves Gurungs. The occupations of the Nesyangbas of the Manang Valley are international trade in which they have earned much acclaim, cultivation of wheat, paddy, potato, and animal husbandry of sheep and goats. They practice Bon, Buddhism and shamanism. Lhosar is their major religious festival, and archery is their main cultural event of the year.

Majhis

Majhis are mostly found in the districts of Kavrepalanchok, Sindhupalchok, Ramechhap, Sindhuli, Dhankuta nad Okhaldhunga. They are also found living along large riverbanks. Like the Darai language, the Majhi language is a mixture of Tibeto-Burman strains as well as Bhojpuri and Maithili. They are engaged as boatmen. they also prospect for gold in the river sand. The river is their benevolent deity. The Majhis dance for three days in the memory of their recent dead. Many knowledgeable Majhi claim of Kipat ownership of riverbanks and the adjacent ghat-s.

Marphalis

Marphalis are the inhabitants of Marpha situated between Tukuche and Kagbeni in the district of Mustang. They are one of the Panch Gaunle confederations, and resemble the Thakalis in every conceivable way. In fact, they consider themselves Thakalis. Their clan names are Hirachan, Lalchan, Juharchan and Pannachan. Proffessing Buddhism, Marphalis are engaged in commerce, agriculture and horticulture.

Mugalis

The indigenous Mugalis are from the Mugu Karan area of the Mugu District of Karnali Zone. There are 12 Karan consisting of the 13 villages of Mugu, Dolphu, Maha, Chyute, Krimi, Mangri, Wongri, Katick and Daura and another village of Mugu where Mugalis live. They are Buddhist. They are similar in language, dress and culture to the Tibetans in the north. Lhosar is their principal festival. The Mugalis of 12 Karan are farmers whereas those Mugu are traders.

Meches

Being residents of the Mechi River banks and the neighborhoods in the district of Jhapa, they are aptly called the Meches. They are closer to the Botes in civilization. According to historians, Meches were nomadic until a few decades ago. They became settlers when the land range and forest frontiers of their free roaming became demarcated and restricted. Ai Bali Khungri and Batho Barau are their principal deities. They also worship the deities of the forest. Their language derives from the Tibeto-Burman family. Meches are also called Bodos. They are at present engaged in farming.

Rais

Rais belong to Kirant confederation. Since ancient times, Rais are living in the districts of Solukhumbu, Okhaldhunga, Khotang, Bhojpur and Udayapur. Rais speak many dialects of the Tibeto-Burman family. They have their own unique religion. Their principal scripture is Mundhum. Sitakhau Budo, Walmo Budi, Jalpa Devi and others are their local deities. Rich in culture, the Sakela (Chandi) Dance and the sharing of newly harvested foods in Nwagi are their principal festivals. Rais bury their dead. Pork is used for auspicious and holy occasions. They consider Sumnima and Paroohang as their primordial parents. There are many Rai clans. Their houses are scattered. Short in stature, round in face and stout in build, Rais are expert in farming and textile weaving. Following the unification of the Kingdom of Nepal Rais were given rights of kipat autonomy and ownership of land in the Majh (middle) Kirant. The Rai language, though it has no script, is rich in texture.

Rautes

The name Raute comes from the shed they fabricate. Such makeshift is called Rauti. Rautes are the most confirmed nomadic tribe of Nepal who forage for tubers and fruits and hunt animals for their living. They are indigenous of the dense forests in the districts of Dailekh, Jajarkot, Surkhet, Salyan, Achham, Jumla, Darchula and Baitadi. The national census figure show their number to be 2878, but most field researchers have estimated their number only about 900. They seldom live in one place for more than two months at the most. Therefore, they have not taken up farming yet. The speak Khamchi language of the Tibeto-Burman family, and worship nature. They intermarry within their close clans.

Rajbanshis

Rajbanshis live in the Nepal-India borderlands of the districts of Jhapa and Morang of east Nepal. Anthropologists opine that they are the kiths and kin of the peripheral Koch people of the adjacent states of West Bengal and Asom (Assam) in India. Though having Mongoloid features-they consider themselves as a branch of the Kirants-their language is akin to Bengali and Assamese. They wear clothes conforning to their climate and weather. They worship Thaku Brahmani and also practice shamanism. Consumption of alcohol is a must for worshiping the gods. They play with mud and water during their major festivals. The groom's side makes monetary payment to the bride's family during their marriage. This custom also prevails among some other ethnic groups of Nepal. Their principal occupation is agriculture. Rajbanshis were the indigenous people of Jhapa and Morang before the hill migrants of Nepal overwhelmed them. Most of the Rajbanshis bury their dead but now-a-days some of them have adopted cremation formalities.

Rajis

The districts of Dang and Surkhet are the native strongholds of the Rajis. Their numbers have dwindled. They speak a unique dialect of the Tibeto-Burman variant. They live in joint families. Farming is their newly embraced occupation, but have not given up their tradition of foraging for tuber and other forest products and fishing. They bury their dead. Marriages take place within their own clans. They practice shamanism, and worship such amorphous deities as Sunpal, Deopal and Rajuwali. Rajis use and consume alcohol and pork during their ceremonies and festivals.

Larkes (Nubribas)

Larkes live in Larke, which is in the north of Gorkha District and to the west of Siyar. Larkes are locally known as Nupribas. Their religion and culture are influenced by Tibet Autonomous Region of China in the north, and there is also much cultural commonality with the Sherpas of Solukhumbu. Traditionally traders with Tibet, they also occasionally do farming. Their language is Bhote. Some Larkes use Gurung as their clan surnames.

Lhomis (Shingsabas)

The Shingsa region is where the Arun River enters Nepal from Tibet, and is situated to the north of the district of Sankhuwasabha. The inhabitants of Shingsa are called Shingsabas or Karbhotes. They enjoy cultural and social affinity and geographical proximity with the Sherpas and other northerners. They adhere to Bon and Buddhism. The village headman is called Pombo. They migrate to the lower hills during winter. Most are engaged in farming and some are in trade. The Shingsaba society had already been formed in Darjeeling in India as far back as circa 1914. If a Shingsaba husband marries a second wife, he must leave the house.

Walungs

The Walung stronghold is the Olangchungola area at the top of the Tamor River in the district of Taplejung. Olangchungola is locally known as Walung, which is comprised of the five major settlements of Olangchungola, Yangma, Ghunsa, Lungthung, Lelep and other six or seven minor inhabitations. Trade is the major occupation of Walungs. Their religion, language, dres and social patterns are Tibetan in derivation. Walung has a great monastery. The Futuk festival relives the scenes of the battle between the Gyabo of Muksum and the Gyabo of Thudam. Walungs celebrate with great fervor the social and religious festivals of Lhosar, Neso, Futuk, Sakadawa, Dhukpachhesi and Ngyungnay.

Sherpas

According to linguists, the work sherpa means easterner, and this work comes from the Tibetan language. The ancestral place of these famous mountaineers is northern side of the Solukhumbu district. The traditional habitat of the Sherpas also lies in the valley between the Dudh Koshi and Sun Koshi rivers. The Sherpa language and script are derived from Tibetan. Sherpas are Buddhist. Lhosar is their major festival. They cremate their dead. They greet their guests with khada scarfs, Chhewa is performed for the dead. Tourism, trade and farming are the major occupation of the Sherpas.

Siyars (Chumbas)

Siyars live in the northeastern parts of Gorkha District. They are called Siyars because they live on the banks of the Siyar River. They are locally known as Chumbas. Their main occupations are farming and trade with Tibet. Some of their habits resemble those of the Gurungs in the south. They are Buddhist, and they maintain equal footing with the Tibet-influenced Nubriba community.

Sunuwars

Sunuwars live in the land between the Likhu and Khimti rivers and in the districts of Okhaldhunga, Ramechhap and Dolkha. They have their own unique language and culture. They had their kipat rights on their ancestral lands. Because of their adherence to the Kirant religion, they are considered closer to the Rais. However, sociologists opine that they are more akin to the language and culture of the Magars with whom they also share similar physical resemblance. Sunuwars, Surels and Jirels are socially close-knit communities. Sunwars are mostly engaged in farming.

Surels

The minority community of the Surels, numbering less than 200 at present, lives in the village of Bahuri situated on the banks of the Suri River in Dolkha District. Surels consider themselves Kirants, and their scriptures are also the Mundhum. Thei language is a variant of the Tibeto-Bueman family. Their shaman is called Moyambo. Surels are mainly engaged in farming and labour.

Syangtans

The Buddhist Syangtans belong to the Panch Gaunle confederation. They live in the village of Syang situated in the middle of Tukuche and Jomsom of Mustang District. They, like Thintans, are also similar to Thakalis. They are divided into the sub-clans of Sakar. Syangten, Pasing, San, Chi, Jhisin, Kya and Shren Phobe. Girls are eloped for marriage in this community. This arrangement is called Raholiboba. Mostly traders, Syangtans are also engaged in farming and horticulture.

Hayus

Hayus are another minuscule community of Nepal. They live along the neighborhoods of the Maryang River, and they are also found in the districts of Sindhuli and Ramechhap. However, the village of Ratanchura in Sindhuli is considered their ancestral home. Short in stature, flat-nosed and squinty-eyed, they have their own unique language and culture. In religious matters, Hayus are closer to Rais, but they do not perform Chandi Puja as Rais do. Hayus were nomadic until a few years ago; now they are mostly engaged in farming and labour.

Hyolmos

Hyolmos are from Helambu area which is situated in the North west of the Sindhupalchok District, and North East of Nuwakot district and they have much in common with Tamangs and Sherpas in linguistic, cultural and other ways of life. Hyolmos also have close cultural and linguistic affinities with the inhabitants of the Kerung and Rongsyar areas of Tibet Antonomous Region of China. Trade, tourism and farming are the major occupations of Hyolmos.

Kisans

The dwindling community of Kisans has only about 700 members left at present. They live in the villages of Dhulabari and Dhaijan of Jhapa District. Their language is Dravidian, and their script is Uraun. The traditional name of these people is Kuntam. At present, however, they are known by various other names, such as Kuda, Kora, Mirdha, Kola, Morbha, Birhor, and Nagesia. The men have the tradition of marrying their maternal cousins (maternal uncle's daughters). A widow may also be allowed to marry the younger brother (brother-in-law) of her deceased husband. The Kisans have their own king. Their ancestral deity is Samalai Mahaprobha. The Kisans both practice cremating or burying their dead. Animist and nature worshippers as they are, the Kisans had the infamous practice of killing their women accused of being witches. Though likely to be compared with the Uraun farmers of Orissa and Bihar in India, many characteristics of the Nepalese Kisans' ways of life, however, do not conform to them. The Kisans are farmers.

Kumals

Kumals are found in large numbers in the districts of Dolkha, Dhading, Sankhuwasabha, Palpa and Parbat. They are also found scattered in almost all the other districts of Nepal. They share physical characteristics and ways of life with the Tharus, Danuwars, Darais, Majhis and Botes. The main occupation of the Kumals is pottery. Their language is more accentuated to the Tibeto-Burman family. Their preferred inhabitation is on riverbanks, inner valleys and tropical areas. They relishpork and buffalo. The Kumals seek assistance from the Dhami and Jhankri shamans. They either bury their dead or consign them to the flow of the rivers.

Kushbadias (Kuhbadias)

Kushbadias are also known as Kuhbadias. They are found

in Banke and Bardia districts. Their facial features subscribe to some lesser Mongoloid strains. They ascertain their origin in east Bhairahawa. Carving stone grinding slates and wheels and weaving ropes and making brooms are their major professions. They worship Masounia as their principal deity. They strongly resemble the Tharus in their ways of life, language and dress patterns. Kushbadias bury their dead. After the burial, they sit around the cemetery and drink potent moonshine.

Chimtans

Chimtans are the inhabitants of one of the Panch (five) Gaun or villages between Kagbeni and Tukuche in the district of Mustang. Their village is known as Chimada or Chimang. They call themselves Thakalis, and have affinity of language and culture with the Thakalis. Though Buddhists, they also practice shmanism. There are two branches of Chimangs-1) Bhamphobe and 2) Dhyalkipal Phobe. Commerce is their main profession with farming, horticulture and animal husbandry as side businesses.

Chepangs

One of the most backward ethnic groups of Nepal, the Chepangs inhabit in the remote and sparse contours, outback and rolling precipices of the districts of Makwanpur, Chitwan, Gorkha and Dhading. They have their own distinct language, which belongs to one of the Tibeto-Burman strains. Like the Kusundas, the Chepangs also shun farming and prefer to forage for tubers for their food. However, they are born hunters. Their clan priests are called Pandes. It is felt that their religion and culture are influenced by the Tamangs.

Chhantyals

Scattered in the districts of Baglung and Myagdi, the Chhantyals have their own language quite akin to the Thakali. Their population is about 20,000. As inhabitants of the Magrant region, the Chhantyal culture and habits resemble those of the Magars. However, the Bhalanja section of Chhantyals considers the Kusundas as their ancestors. The Chhantyals are animists and profess shamanism. In religious practices, they are closer to the Magars. Previously believed to be employed in the Nepalese mines, Chhantyals are mostly concerntrated in farming at present.

Chhairottans

Chhairottans are considered the inhabitants of the Chhairo village, one of the Panch Gaun villages of the Mustang district. They resemble Marphalis and Thakalis in facial features, language and dress codes. Chhairottans are Buddhists though they also practice shamanism. Farming and animal husbandry are their major professions. The original Chhairottans have migrated from their stronghold of Chhairo village, which is now occupied by a few Thakali households and some ten Tibetan refugee families.

Jirels

Jirels are mostly concentrated in the villages of Jiri and Jugu of the Dolkha district. Many Jirels also live in the sindupalchok district. they speak a particular Tibeto-Burman dialect, which is akin to Sharpa. Other Sherpa influences are also evident in the Jirels' lifestyle.

Jirels call themselves Jiripas. They both profess Buddhism and shamanism. They address the Buddhist Lama as Pomba and the shaman as Phomba. Being farmers, they cultivate millet and live happily on the produce. Jirels either bury or cremate their dead on the recommendations of the Buddhist Lama.

Jhangads

Though they live in the wide expanse of Nausaya Bigha areas of the district of Dhanusha, Jhangads are also found spread from Sarlahi and Sunsari to Morang districts. The Dravidian Jhangads are a backward and minority group. They speak Kurukh Mundari. They are largly farmers and laborers. There are some differences between the Jhangads of Madhya Pradesh of India and those in Nepal. Jhangads of Nepal worship nature. They conclude their religious ceremonies by playing diga and feasting on pork and alcohol. Negroid or bury their dead. Pigs are their only domestic animals.

Thintans

Thintans are the inhabitants of Thini village situated between Tukuche and Kagbeni of the district of Mustang. Thintans are from among the larger Panch Gaunle or five-village confederation. though they resemble Thakalis in many ways, thintans have closer linguistic and cultural affinities with Chimtans and Shyangtans. Thintans have six branches-Omthin, Tapothin, Chhothin, Chakithin, Dhangyangthin, and Langlangthin. The latter seem to have vanished now. Though some thintans have adopted Buddhism, the old still adhere to Bon-po. Thintans are inherently traders, and practice farming and horticulture on the side.

Dolpos

The inhabitants of Dolpa are Dolpos (though they do not call themselves as such). Dolpa is located at the head of the Bheri river to the north of the Dhaulagiri Range and to the south of the Tibetan Plateau.

Dolpos live at the altitude of 13-14,000 feet, and they have 40 settlements in all. Their physical features and habits largely resemble those of the Lhopas, though the women have their own unique dress styles. They are farmers, but their chief occupation is also animal husbandry. They practice both Bon-po and Buddhism. They practice sky burial. Their dead are cut into pieces which are fed to the vultures. Dolpos practice polyandry, and their language and dress choices are similar to the Lhopas and Tibetans.

Tangbes

Tangbes, also called Tangbedanis, come from the village of Tangbe, which is a part of the Bahara Gaunle (12 villages) confederation in Mustang district. Like the Bahra Gaunle people, their ways of life are akin to the Lhopas. They are Buddhists.

Tangbes were traditionally salt traders. Since the decline in this trade many years ago, most Tangbes are engaged in farming and other vocations. Some Tangbe families are also found in Pokhara.

Tajpurias

Tajpurias are a minority group mainly found in the districts of Jhapa and Morang. Though their language and culture are almost akin to the Rajbanshis, Tajpuria women do not pierce their nose and use ornaments as Rajbanshi women do. No. Marrigae takes between these two communities.

Tajpurias have their own religion. Alcohol is a must in all religions rituals. They are engaged in artistic craftsmanship different from the Rajbanshis. Farming is the major occupation of Tajpurias. Though Rabanshis and Tajpurias dress similarly, the latter are expect at hand stitching. they bury their dead.

Tamangs

Tamangs are minly found in the districts of Rasuwa, Sundhupalchok, Kavrepalanchok, Makwanpur, Nuwakot, Dhading, Ramechhap, Dolkha and Sindhuli.

The census of 1991 places their population at 4.9% of the national total.

The Tamang language, culture and traditions are rich. They were already descried as a powerful nation in historic inscriptions going as far back as the 3rd century, attesting to their ancient civilization.

They are Buddhists, and their script originates from Tibetan. Their language belongs to the Tibeto-Burman family. The archives of Tamang religious scriptures are rich, varied and vast. Their intellectual hierarchy had categorizations of royal priests, raconteur of history and other scholastic divisions of labour. They celebrate with equal fervor such diverse religious occasions as Lhosar, Maghe Sankranti, Baisakh Purnima and Shravan Purnima. They are fond of buckwheat delicacies. Their dance culture is equally rich and varied. There are many Tamang sub clans.

Topkegolas

They live in Topkegola situated at the top of the Mewa River to the west of Walung. But they are different from the Walungs. Locally, Topkegolas are called Dhhokpyas. Their major occupation is trade. They ply their trade between Dhankuta, Dharan and Chinapur of Sankhuwasabha in Nepal and Sar in Tibet. Their language, religion, culture and dress styles are in essence similar to Tibet region of China as are those of the Shingsaba in the near west, Walungs in the east and the neighbouring Thudams.

Thakalis

The stronghld of the Thakalis is Thak Khola in Mustand District. They have their own language, which belongs to the Tibeto-Burman family, and is similar to Gurung (Tamu) and Tamang languages. Thakalis have four major clans-Chhyoki (Gauchan), Salki (Tulachan), Dhimchen (Sherchan), and Bhurki (Bhattachan), Lha Phewa is a major festival of the Thakalis, which is renowned as a 12-year cyclic fair. Thakalis adhere both to Bon and Buddhism. Their Toranlha festival coincides with the Fagu Purnima. The Thakalis' estimated number is only some 8,000. They are renowned as a mercantile community.

Thamis

Thamis are mainly found in Susma, Chhamawati, Khepachagu, Alamyu, Bigu, Kalinchok, Lapilang and Lakuri Danda villages of Dolkha District. Numbering about 30,000 in all, the Buddhist Thamis are considered the original people of these places. The Thami language is similar to the language of the Sunuwars, which again conforms ot the Rai language originating in the Tibeto-Burman family. Tamang influences are also quite prominent on the Thamis. Labour and farming are the Thamis' main occupations. In religious matters, Thamis are much closer to the Tamangs.

Tharus

Tharus pervade all along the east-west lowland Terai belt

as well as in the inner Terai valleys of Chitwan, Dang, Surkhet and Udaipur. They are considered the first native people of that part of Nepal. According to the regions of their inhabitation, each respective Tharu clan has its own ethnic identity, dialect and culture.

Tharus have their own languages but the respective Tharu languages are thus influenced by Awadhi, Bhojpuri and Maithili languages, depending on the regions of their inhabitation. Because of their facial and physical features, they are considered Mongoloid. They mainly practice Buddhism. The census of 1991 places the Tharus at 5.4% of the national total population of Nepal. their main occupation is farming, and Tharus enjoy many similarities with the agro-based Jyapus of the Kathamandu Valley.

Thudams

Thudam, formerly in the district of Talpejung, is now incorporated in the district of Sankhuwasabha. The unhabitants of Thudam are locally known as Thudambas. they are quite akin to the Topkegolas. In fact, Thudams make their living by tenant-farming the lands of Shingsabas and Walungs and also by looking after their livestock. Additionally, they are also traditionally known as exporters of agro-produces, timber and incense to Tibet, Autonomous region of China. The religion, language, culture and dress patterns of the Thudams conform more to the Walungs, rather than the Shingsabas.

Danuwars

Quite akin to the Tharus in numerous ways, the ancestral strongholds of the Danuwars are Banke and Bardia districts. They belong to four clans-loincloth wearer, janai thread wearer, Rai and Adhikari. The loincloth-wearing Danuwars live between the Chure and Mahabharat Ranges while the thread wearing ones live in the Terai plains. Rai and Adhikari Danuwars prefer the riverbanks. In religious matters, Danuwars are much colser to the Tharu and Dhimal ethnic groups. Farming is their major occupations.

Darais

Darais are mainly found in Damauli of Tanahu District and on the banks of Madi River. Flat-nosed, short in stature and stout in build, Darais are prominently boatmen and fishermen. The Darai language is imbued with Bhojpuri, Maithili, Magar and Gurung languages. Darai women have high place in their society. Darais marry after having children. They profess Buddhism, and alcohol accentuates their religious ceremonies.

Duras

Duras live on hills of Dura Danda, Turlungkot and Kunchha Am Danda of Lamjung District. TheirLanguage is also called Dura. they practice both Buddhism and Hinduism. Round-faced, flat-nosed and short in stature, Duras have their own unique traditions and though their religious and cultural formalities are quite akin to Gurungs. Their sons are fitted with bows and arrows on the very day of their naming ceremonies, a fact that reflects on their martial heritage. They have no definite history of their origin. Farming is the chief occupation of Duras.

Paharis

The minority group of Paharis is mainly found in the villages of Khopasi, Saldhara and Palanchok of Kavrepalanchok District. However, they consider Dailekh District as their ancestral place. They are also scattered in Lalitpur of Kathmandu Valley and elsewhere. Paharis have their own Pahari language, which is quite akin to the Tamang and Newar languages. Paharis consider ginger and soybeans as delicious and supreme. They practice Buddhism. Traditionally weavers of bamboo trays and baskets. Paharis are increasingly drawn to farming and labour these days.

Fris

The strongholds of Fris are the districts of Sindhupalchok, Kavrepalanchok, Makwanpur and Lalitpur. In Lalitpur, they are found in the settlements and villages of Bhadikhel, Sikarpa,

Fhade, Lele, Tomphel and Godawari. In Makwnapur, they live in Betani and Kulekhani. Their religious practices, language and culture are closer to the Newars and Paharis. According to their legends, the Fris were once chefs at the kitchen of the king of Bhaktapur. found filthy, they were exiled for 12 years during which they intermarried with Tamangs, and were thence called Fris. There is a strong fundation that because of similar legends and other factors, Fris are indeed Paharis.

INDIGENOUS PEOPLES OF NEPAL

Gurungs (TAMUs) - Middle in height and stout in build, the main habitats of the Gurungs are the districts of Kaski, Lamjung, Gorkha, Syangja, Manang and Tanahu in the Gandaki Zone while they are also scattered in Okhaldhunga, Sankhuwasabha and Taplejung in East Nepal. Animal husbandry is their main occupation. They speak languages related to the Mon-Khmer and Tibeto-Burma lineages. The Gurung history is ancient. Gurungs are predominantly Buddhist. Their institutions of Lhosar, They both practice cremation and burial of their dead. Gurungs call themselves Tamu.

Kusundas - Kusundas are probably the most endangered species of the aboriginal ethnic groups of Nepal They prefer to live separately and alienated from other people. They select secluded forest areas for their inhabitation. Sparsely found in the districts of Gorkha, Kaski, Salyan, Pyuthatn, Dang, Dailekh and Surkhet, the Kusundas resemble the Chepangs in their observances. Kusundas are also known as Ban Manchhe (wild people) and Ban Raja (kings of the forests). The have their own language. Some Kusundas call themselves Chhatyals. Others do not address themselves by their ethnic surnames. The Kusunda language and culture are on the brink of extinction. Instead of making their livelihood from agriculture, they prefer to forage for tubers for their food. They do not drink milk of bovines. Cow dung is almost taboo.

Gangais - Gangais are mostly concentrated in Jhapa and Morang districts of Nepal. They are also known as Ganesh or Mandal. Because of their flat nose, plain face, wheatish complexion and rough curly hair, anthropologists have compared them to the Lepchas. While the Gangais of Morang speak Maithili, the Gangais of Jhapa speak Rajbanshi. They also differ in their dress preferences. Mahabir and Thakur are their ancestral deities. They live in joint families. One group called Babu Gangais takes pork while the Besaram Gangais shun it. The Gangais are armers.

Dhanuks - Dhanuks live in the districts of Saptari and Dhanusha, and are spread along southern belt of the Chure Range. There are three clans of Dhanuks-Mandal Dhanuks, Sur Dhanuks, and Rajbanshi Dhanuks. Sur and Mandal Dhanuks, being Indo-Aryan Hindu untouchables, do not belong to the ethnic peoples of Nepal. Because of their facial and physical features, language and culture, the Rajbanshi Dhanuks are closer to the Tharus. Hence they are considered an ethnic group. However, scholars are presently challenging this claim, of Rajbanshi Dhanuks also of being an indigenous group. Farming and domestic labor are their chief occupations.

Dhimals - Dhimals live on the peripheries of the districts of Morang and Jhapa. Because of their facial features, language and religious practices, they are called the Limbus of the Nepalese plains. However, anthropologists place them next to the Meches. But, even if they are plainspeople, Dhimals have the characteristic habit of exhibiting the quick temper and unwarranted aggressiveness of the Limbus of the eastern hills. Dhimals have their own unique language, dress preferences and culture. They are fond of music, and in this there is a trace of the Rajbanshi ethnos. They bury their dead. Farming is their specialization.

Newars. - The name of the county Nepal itself derives from the Newars. Newars are the indigenous peoples of the Kathmandu Valley. They are also found in the neighboring hill settlements as well as in the towns and cities of the Terai plains. Originally Buddhists, Newars have increasingly become synceritc, and now a days some Newars practice both Buddhism as well as Hinduism. They are prominent in business, agriculture and craftsmanship. Their population exceeds 1.3 million. Newars have their own language, called Nepal Bhasha, which belongs to the Tibeto-Burman family. The Newar language has incorporated the rich corpus of Newa literature from historical times. Newars are considered a highlydeveloped nation state of many communities. They have a hierarchical clan system patterned after their respective occupations. The written history of the Newars is 2,5000 years old during which they developed their impeccable culture and arts into a great civilization. Newars maintained their unique kingdom even during the various reigns of the Gopala, Kirat, Licchavi and Malla dynasties. The Shahs finally amalgamated the Newar nation state in their unification drives.

Byasis - The villagers of Byas village to the north of Darchula and the foothills of the Byas Himal are called Byasis. Also called Souka, these Mongoloid animists call themselves Range. They have their own unique language and ways of life. Their 12th century scripts are found in the caves. Their dress is called chyungwala. The ancestral god of the Soukas of Rolpa is Namjung, who is a principal deity of Bon. Their major festival is called Dhhyoula. Byasis conduct the trade between Taklakot in Tibet and Darchula. They do not celebrate Hindu festivals. The Front of their houses are festooned with Buddhist prayer flags called dharchyo. According to linguists, the Souka language is somewhat close to the Magar language.

Bhujels/Ghartis - The Bhuji area in Baglung is considered as the ancestral place of the Bhujels. Nowadays they are scattered all over the Kingdom of Nepal. They are close to the Magars. The religion and culture of these backward people are close to extinction, and Hindu influences have been encroaching on their ways of life. In religious matters they have affinities with the Magars while in language they are closer to the Chepangs. They are known as either Bhujel or Gharti in one place or the other. They are engaged in farming and in domestic chores.

Bhutias - In Nepal, Bhutias are spread from Mahakali in the far west to the Kanchanjunga Range in the extreme east. They are found in Bajura and Darchula of the far western development region, and also in Humla, Dolpa, Surkhet and Mugu in the mid-Western region as well as in Mustang, Manag, Kaski and Tanahu of western region, and finally in the Himalayan heights of the middle regions and the east. They are also found in towns and large cities in the mid-ranges. In general, Bhutias are those people who do not belong to any of the particular or distinct stocks of indigenous people of the Nepal Himalaya. They resemble Tibetans in most of their ways of living. However, their statistics are not yet properly maintained. Trade and animal husbandry are the main occupations of the Bhutias.

Rajis - The districts of Dang and Surkhet are the native spanholds of the Rajis. Their numbers have dwindled. They speak a unique dialect of the Tibeto-Burman variant. They live in joint families. Farming is their newly embraced occupation, but have not given up their tradition of foraging for tuber and other forest products and fishing. They bury their dead. Marriages take place within their own clans. They practice shamanism, and worship such amorphous deities as Sunpal, Deopal and Rajuwali. Rajis use and consume alcohol and pork during their ceremonies and festivals.

Lepchas - The ancient Lepchas are believed to have originated from the foothills of Mount Kanchanjunga, which they revere as their deity. Lepchas presently live in the Ilam District of Nepal, and in Sikkim, Darjeeling and Kalimpong of India. They consider themselves of royal stock. Their language is a derivastion from the Tibeto-Bruman family. They have their own script, and their holy scripture is called Astachyo. Animist in origin, many Lepchas now adhere to Buddhism and Christianity. In Lepcha society, alcohol is considered “clean”. There is no animosity and caste system among the Lepchas. The dead are taken out through the broken wall of the house and are buried. The Lepchas social council is called Rong Senungthi. Their dance is called Loknen. Commerce and agriculture are their major occupations.

Lhopas - Lhopas are found in Lho Manthang of the upper Kali Gandaki region of Mustang District. They produce weat, paddy and potato, and raise sheep, yaks and horses, They carry out cross-border trade with Tibet Autonomous Region of China. Their language, dress codes and religion are all derived from Tibet with which they maintain social interactions. They are divided into three clans-Kutuk, Shelpa and Rigin. It is mandatory for the second son to be a monk. Polyandry is prevalent among Lhopas. The Mustang Raja Jigme Parbal belongs to the Lhopa people. A minor clan called Naka Dorje also has assimilated into the Lhopa ethnic community.

5

The Role of Civil Society in State Building in Nepal

Development is the process of economic and social transformation. It is a movement from traditional relations, traditional ways of thinking, traditional ways of dealing with health and education, traditional methods of production, to more 'modern' ways (Stiglitz, 1998). Modern means here scientific way of thinking that recognizes the individual, society and changes. Change is not an end in itself, but a means to other objectives. The changes that are associated with development enrich the lives of individuals by widening their horizons and reducing their sense of isolation. It improves the quality of life.

This is not straightforward to explain the development process of the country; however, the process follows well-ordered sequences and exhibits common characteristics across the society. The conventional economic theories that deal with scarcity problems or with the process of market clearance or equilibrium are not enough to understand development process. Economics does have something positive to offer the methods of analysis or way of thinking to analyze the political, sociological and non-economic factors to understand better process of development; however, economic issues fundamentally important to our well-being, individually and collectively. The roles of social relationships in development were frequently ignored in previous economic theories of development. In contrasts, some of the theories, such as dependency theory, capital accumulation theory, and institutionalism focused on social relations as obstacles of development. Most of the development theories concentrated on the production-function approach to the measurement of sources of growth (Thirlwall, 1989).

The creation of new social capital and new capacities need to change the society. Process of changes is the movement to 'scientific' ways of thinking, identifying critical variables that affect macroeconomic outcomes. Materials and other resources can be brought or borrowed from outside the country but the creative and productive society, democratic culture and social trust are true assets of the community or the nation. Other resources and constraints are important, but the social trust, social networks, social cohesion, democratic norms are more crucial resources to improve the process of economic and social transformation, if they are developed and encouraged and utilized properly. These resources work together as an active factor of production and reduce the high concentration of economic, social and political power at all levels. Working together creates positive externalities for the society; consequently, there will be economies of scale in the production process. Progress adjusts need of people and social transformation will be in continuous process.

The study of the interaction between the economy and other aspects of society (such as cultural values and distributions of power) and the interaction of social contexts (such as ideology, or beliefs) and economic outcomes is important to understand the development process (Cohn, 2007); however, orthodox economics frequently ignores these important issues. Recently, development economists are working with holist ideas of how societies work and what works in the society with the analysis of the full impact of economic phenomena on social structures.

It is necessary to forge a more coherent and constructive way of analysis of development process of Nepal in line with the holist approach. The paper lays particular emphasis on the social capital and its contribution on economic development process. The paper explores the ideas how economic, social and political sectors interact in order to improve the culture of democracy, social capital, and socioeconomic standard of the people. In addition to this, how the civil society can play the roles to maintenance of democracy and the nurturing of community as macroeconomic outcomes is the major contribution of this paper. The paper seeks to provide an overview of the role of civil society in state building and a scholarly contribution to it further development. It has been written in the conviction that interactions among the economic, social and political sectors are fundamentally important for the development process. The paper has adopted the exploratory method to look at the interaction among the sectors, rather than econometrics tools; however, it illuminates the measurement issues.

A SKETCH OF DEVELOPMENT PROCESS IN NEPAL

Similar to other developing countries, international debates and trends of economics affect largely in the development process of Nepal. Major debates were on the roles of state in the development process. In the early 1950s, Nepal attempted with first five year plan with recognizing the role of state for her economic development. Later, in the 1970s and 1980s, the failures of the central planning system were widely recognized in the international level. Social sector was treated as unproductive sector. Nepal had aggressively followed the international concept in the development process. Consequently, social sector was largely ignored until late 1990s. Anecdotal evidences suggested that there were some levels of interactions among economic, social and political sectors in the early 1950s. Due to change in political regime, the possibilities of interactions between and among the sectors were very limited. There was a big departure from the interaction process among the sectors in 1970s to early 1990s. Consequently, the process widened the socio-economic inequality among the groups and geographical areas. Wrongly adopted development process supported to concentrate political, social and economic power to the certain groups.

The following figure sketches the development thinking in Nepal. It should be a balance between the state and market, productive and the social sector. Politics plays the central role to mobilize all the sectors to make the balance. It doesn't mean that this relationship will be static; but it means that it mobilizes all sectors in such a balanced way that it contributes to social transformation. The state has a greater role because without creating the space in the public sector, market cannot function. For example, resources from the public sector were skewed directly and indirectly to central and eastern regions of Nepal before 2000s, now private sectors are enjoying more in central and eastern regions than mid- or far western regions. Similarly, private sectors are involved in health and education sectors because the huge amount of resources has been spent by the state in these sectors. International evidences suggested that the state has been integral part of the capitalist development (Stilwell, 2005). At first, state has created the market by using its mechanism, then private sector enjoys in that market.

Therefore, state and market are complementary, not competitive in many underdeveloped areas or initial situation of the development process; after having some degree of development of this area, the roles of state will be different; it will be more regulatory, encouraging to competiveness and improving quality of goods and services. The figure depicts that in 1950, development policy made almost balance among the sectors in line with the political process. There was balance between the productive sector and social sector with the lead by the Government during 1960s to 1970s. Due to change in political regime, the development process was also shifted. The interaction with political process was very weak and role of private sector in economic development was minimal. Consequently, the economic system could not function with its full capacity. After 1970s, the development policy focused on the productive sector and market. The role of government in the economic system was limited and investment in social sector was significantly reduced. In the decade of 1990s, the political process for the development was improved, but the economic policy was more market oriented. Privatization and liberalization policy was aggressively introduced. Social sector remained relatively ignored. After 2000s, the situation was shifted one point to another. The Millennium development goals (MDGs) were established by the United Nations in 2000. Most of these goals are related to social sectors. Nepal has also showed commitments to meet MDGs in 2015 and social sector became a priority sector. At the same time, participation, civil society engagement, social network are improving and political regime has been shifted. After 2000s, the interactions between and among the sectors has improved; however, it remains fluid. It is not sure whether it is towards the centre or not.

Inadequacy of information, inadequacy of infrastructure, weak government regulation, limited resources and inadequate decentralization among others are the common characteristics of underdevelopment. Consequently, inefficiency occurs in the economic system, in terms of price distortion in the market, corruption in the public sectors, low quality of services in both private and government sectors among others. It leads to outputs that are markedly below the economy's potential output. Therefore, interactions between and among the economic, political and social sectors are required for better outcomes. The interactions can take place through participation, broadly active civic engagement, internalization of social as well as development process, democratic political process.

The interaction process or the relationship between political democratic process and economic development process has long been debated. The involvement of democratic process, participation and active civic engagement in the economic development process may be a "luxury good"; the cost of economic development will significantly be high (Stiglitz, 2002). In contrast, other view is that "development" is not the different product that is imported from abroad people. To understand "development for whom and what development is" is important. Definitely, development is for the people and development is "development of people". Development is not an end in itself, but a means to other objectives. Development can be defined in a wider way, with distinguishing three core values: life-sustenance, self-esteem and freedom (Goulet, 1971). Life-sustenance is concerned with the provision of basic need; self-esteem is concerned with the feeling of self- respect and independence; and the freedom reflects achieving freedom from poverty, diseases and ignorance. The societies and individuals ought to investigate these aspects within a value based context of the "good life".

Given this discussion, it is clear that interactions among the sectors are important for the development process. Consensus-building, participation and the promotion of an active civil society are key ingredients to long term sustainable development. It may not be a single way to develop the nation if there is lack of creative and productive society; however, it will be one of the best options to move the social transformation ahead.

After 1990s, similar to other developing countries, civic engagement has increased in the development process in Nepal. Civil society became a "Mantra" for everyone from political leaders to social scientists. Civil society is treated as a means of social renewal. However, definition and use of civil society is being made differently by the philosophers in different situation; for example, market philosophers defined the civil society as a tool of market facilitating; however, Marxist philosophers portrayed the civil society as a special nucleus of independent political activity. It is perhaps the right time for discussion of the role of civil society in development process of Nepal and its limitations. It will be fruitful for the policy makers.

CIVIL SOCIETIES IN NEPAL

Defining Civil Societies in Nepal

In society, there are three sectors, which include government, business, and civil societies. A civil society organization (or CSOs) "is a fascination with nongovernmental organizations (NGOs), especially advocacy groups devoted to public interest such as human rights, women's issues, anticorruption, public hearing among others. Such groups have been multiplying exponentially after 1990s in the country. Nevertheless, it is a mistake to equate civil society with NGOs or similar organization or groups. In fact, civil society is a broader concept, encompassing all organizations and associations that exist outside the state; labour unions, professional associations, chamber of commerce, ethnic association, religious organizations, student groups, and informal community groups among others. An active, diverse civil society often does play a valuable role in helping advance democracy." (Adhikari). Nepalese civil societies can be constructive to develop communities through volunteerism, though there are debates on whether this engagement is progressive due to corruption in leadership. These community groups can be categorized into Mother groups, Women/Single Mother groups, Forest User groups, Youth groups, Child Groups, and Community Development groups. For the purposes of this study, the significance and importance of CSOs will be explored and discussed.

A Brief History of the Development of Local Level CSOs in Nepal

Prior to 1990, the Nepalese government existed as an autocratic political regime that discouraged the registration of civil society organizations and did not protect freedoms of speech and association. Due to this strict governance, NGOs/CSOs could not function efficiently and were few in numbers. In 1960, Nepal declared the Society Registration Act, which legitimized the civic sector through legal registration of groups. This law was amended and renamed the Association Registration Act in 1977 so that the registration included clubs, public libraries, literary societies, self-help groups, NGOs, and cultural groupings. However, due to the Social Service National Coordination Council Act of 1977, most NGOs and other civil society organizations were politically driven (this act was later repealed and replaced by the Social Welfare Act of 1992).

In 1990, the democratic movement of Nepal overthrew the autocratic regime and established the Constitution of the Kingdom of Nepal, which guaranteed freedom of speech, assembly, respect for the International Declaration of Human Rights and other International Covenants that were important for the growth of civil societies in Nepal. Civil societies experienced a sudden emergence and development. However, simultaneously, these groups were in dire need of structural organization. The Local Self-Governance Act encouraged the local government to play a role toward promoting CSOs through the District Development Committee and the Village Development Committee (VDC). These committees were in charge of organizing and registering the civil society groups in the communal level. As of now, there is little known about how civil society organizations are functioning in the local level. Since the current trend of the non-profit world is to work from the grassroots upward and there are large democratic movements in the formation of the constitution, this report will focus on the study of functioning civil society organizations and how they are currently transforming village societies.

CONCEPTUALIZATION OF CIVIL SOCIETY

The term 'civil society' entered the development lexicon in the1980s. Over the past two decades, an impressive body of literature on 'civil society and development' has been produced, and efforts to strengthen civil society have become a common feature of the agendas and programmes of many development organizations (Dahal, 2006). Civil society is a fascination with nongovernmental organizations (NGOs), especially advocacy groups devoted to public interest such as human rights, women's issues, anticorruption, public hearing among others. Such groups have been multiplying exponentially after 1990s in the country. Nevertheless, it is a mistake to equate civil society with NGOs or similar organization or groups.

In fact, civil society is a broader concept, encompassing all organizations and associations that exist outside the state; labour unions, professional associations, chamber of commerce, ethnic association, religious organizations, student groups, and informal community groups among others. An active, diverse civil society often does play a valuable role in helping advance democracy. It can discipline the state, ensure that citizens' interests are taken seriously, and foster greater civic and political participation. On the other hand, a weak civil society leads to a lack of "civic engagement" and "social trust".

In recent years, there has been renewed interest in the concept of civil society in development and governance circles. Broadly understood as the space in society where collective citizen action takes place, civil society has, in fact, proved an extremely difficult concept to define and operationalize (Foley and Edwards, 1996).

In general, the word "civil" means polite, lawful, non-military and civil society relates to the notion of a well-governed social system. However, civil society is used with broader perspective. It can be defined as individual and collective action towards the common public good (Hyden, 1997). The unit of analysis of civil society is 'individual and collective action'. Such individual and collective action may include actions by government officials and business entrepreneurs as citizens, acting for the common public good in their communities and neighborhoods.

Some other definitions contradict with this definition, for example, civil society is defined as the arena, outside the family, the government, and the market, where people associate to advance their interests (Foley and Edwards, 1996). Based on this definition, we wish to emphasize the importance of its role in providing a public space where diverse societal values and interests interact, i.e. where people come together to discuss, associate, and seek to influence broader society. Conceptualizing civil society as an arena enables us to examine not only actors and activities within civil society (Sobel, 2002). Conceptualizing civil society as a public arena allows us to take a holistic view of it.

Even today it continues to be described by scholars as an 'elusive' and 'vague' concept. The elusive concept of 'civil society' has become a major 'buzz word' within development literature and practice. Despite its varied interpretations, civil society can be broadly understood as the societal perspective. Interpersonal trust and civic participation are fundamental to strengthening the state. The citizens who participate in the civil society lean to work together, and eventually learn to trust each other. It is important because it increases tolerance for others by fostering interaction between people who may not think alike, but are willing to work together. Working together creates positive externalities for the society. Many studies confirmed a correlation between high levels of civic culture, comfortable lifestyles and positive economic outcomes (Putnam 1993). We recognize our communalities in the diversity of humanity. Membership of multiple communities breeds civic confidence and civic virtue and provides a basis for trust of strangers, enabling us to work together to create social capital. Multiple links create, at best, robust societies where people can see themselves through the eyes of many others.

In real civil societies, the scope of interests advanced collectively in the public sphere, and the methods used by those actors, is broad. It includes democratic, progressive, and civil interests and methods, as well as undemocratic, fundamentalist, and uncivil ones, such as violent demonstrations, hate speeches, or deal-striking behind closed doors. Certain groups may be actively harmful to other parts of society-criminal organizations. It can produce a negative externality or negative social capital which we can think of as the radius of distrust. Therefore, the civil society should be defined broadly that encourage to building a good society, at the same time, discouraging to create negative social capital (Larry, 1994).

More rightly, civil society can be defined as the collection of somewhat forgotten values - such as trust, co-operation and goodwill - that hold society together *(Cox, 1995)*. Civil society builds the social bridge and breaks the barriers. It is an important social adhesive. This is related to holist theory. Individuals are social beings. Civil society looks at the aggregate maximizing choices rather than individual maximizing choices. Holism begins with a focus on the structure (or structures) of society.

This definition is against with the neoclassical theory of economics. Neo- classical economists tend to think of individuals as the bearers of a human nature that leads them to try to maximize their isolated self-interest in a rational way. The basic idea of holist theory is that social wholes need to be studied as structured entities, rather than society as the sum of individuals.

Whole is greater than sum of its parts. There is a cluster of social roles, institutions, and beliefs that evolve collectively over time. This cluster creates the context within which individuals experience the world. It also creates the incentive structures, organizational vehicles, opportunities for group action, and distributions of power among others that bring about change in the world. The concept of individual choice maximization destroys society. The logic of a social system helps to understand civil society from a holist perspective (Cohn, 2007).

Civil societies are also civic societies. Trust, mutuality and reciprocity are nuts and bolts of the civil society. The civil society can be recognized the supreme importance of social connections which include plenty of robust goodwill to sustain difference and debate. It can contribute to an optimum society that will allow us to move co-operatively and not only competitively towards a more civilized future. The concept of civil society offers an opportunity to understand and influence the process of development. We need to encourage new ideas, dissident views, debates and critics to make more productive and creative society. What we have had is a 'convergence' of views and a desire for the false certainty of consensus. Some of the studies suggested that civil society is primarily a theoretical, normative, and abstract idea. It can be considered such conceptions useful in defining civil society as an 'ideal', but less useful in seeking to understand and assess the reality of civil society around the globe. But several other studies confirmed that civil society and civic participations are key ingredients to long term sustainable development, sustainable democracy and sustainable government performance.

Trust, reciprocity and mutuality are powerful forces that connect us as social beings; however, these are not reflected in public policy and therefore are losing ground. Ideologies that are systems of beliefs determine the creative and productive society (Stilwell, 2005). The ideologies prove support for an existing social, economic and political order. All of us are influenced by the ideologies, knowingly or unknowingly; most of the time unknowingly. Beliefs can be defined as subjective judgments about the issues and their relationships. Beliefs are based on existing stock of knowledge. What we have learned about the society and its importance determines what we believe about the society. More evidences, logics and information lead to change the way of thinking and beliefs.

SOCIAL CAPITAL

A central feature of civil society is the concept of social capital. Social capital is the sum of our social connections, the levels of trust and tolerance. We need to draw on social capital for co-operative and mutually satisfying interactions (Persell et al, 2001). Social capital refers to the processes between people which establish networks, norms, social trust and facilitate co-ordination and co-operation for mutual benefits.

An accumulation of social capital enhances our quality to life and provides the base for the development of other forms of capital such as financial, physical and human capital. With an adequate level of social capital we can enjoy the benefits of a truly civil society. Trust leads to co-operation. We know that working together is preferable to working alone. We need to build a store of trust and goodwill as part of our social capital - a collective term for the ties that bind us. Accumulated social trust allows groups and organizations to develop the tolerance sometimes needed to deal with conflicts and differing interests. Social interactions and the development of trust relationships, technology enhances social capital. Social capital can be measured and quantified so we can distribute its benefits and avoid its losses. There is a strong correlation between high levels of civic culture, comfortable lifestyles and positive economic outcomes (Putnam, 1993). If the social system isolates people, it discourages informal and formal contact, or just fails to offer the time and space needed for social contact, then, social capital will be reduced. The decline of social capital threatened the quality of life (Putnam, 1993). The social capital concept includes the household and informal sectors which can also create social trust relationships and forms of civic wellbeing.

Accumulation Social Capital and Economic development

Formation of social capital is mainly based on interactions. Interactions involve space, time, opportunities, precedence and the valuing of process. We need the opportunities to interact with a reasonably broad spectrum of people, and to build up a level of trust through positive rather than negative experiences. We need the time to engage in satisfactory processes of discussion, to acknowledge the input of others, and to develop outcomes which reflect their inputs. An accumulation of social capital enhances our quality of life and provides the base for the development of other forms of capital. With an adequate level of social capital we can enjoy the benefits of a truly civil society. The concept of social capital (or civil society, interchangeably used in this paper) is used as a contributing factor to economic development, transition economies, common-resource property use, health and education.

Accumulation of social capital refers to the breadth and density of representative societal organizations. Putnam's definition of social capital as the "stock" of "norms of reciprocity and networks of civic engagement" helps explain how citizens overcome the obstacles through collective action (Putnam 1993). As mentioned earlier, ideology, leadership and social structure determine the size of social capital. Cycle of interaction and creation of "spillover effects" represent the quality of capital accumulation.

There are four distinct dimensions of social capital - integration and linkage at the micro level, integrity and synergy at the macro level (Woolcock, 1998). At the micro level, intra community and inter communities relations are most important. The fostering of "synergy" between the state and the societies is important at the macro level. Both the micro and macro levels interact with one another. The different combinations of these four dimensions of social capital can account for a range of development outcomes. The same dimension of social capital can serve very different developmental purposes when combined with other forms.

While individual groups form the building blocks of civil society, the value of the concept lies in the extent and density of relations among groups as well as the synergy between civil society, state and market. Therefore, social capital is an integral part of civil society at the micro and macro levels. Civil society is not a constant, rather it is continuously evolving and its roles vary in different contexts and at different levels of economic development.

The structure and composition of social capital is well established in literatures. This dimension explores the overall size, importance, level of organization, and resources of the civil-society arena in a given country. It also seeks to assess the main characteristics of civil-society actors, and the relationships among them. The structure and composition of social capital can be discussed in terms of breath, depth and diversity of participation of citizens.

Breadth of Citizen Participation reflects civil society's overall size and strength. It can be measured in term of the proportion of citizens involved in the formation of social capital this or that way. Depth of citizen participation shows the strength of social capital. It is important to know how frequently and extensively people engage in civil-society activities. Diversity within the process of capital formation is important. Since social capital is understood as an arena where conflicting interests and power relations are played out, the equitable representation of different social groups within civil society, especially traditionally marginalized groups, is considered an important feature.

Ethnic relations come up frequently in discussions of social capital. Whether it is immigration, micro-enterprise development, tribal nepotism or racial conflict, ethnic ties are a clear example of how actors who share common values and culture can band together for mutual benefit. Key concepts in ethnicity and social capital are: reciprocity, bounded solidarity, and enforceable trust. They serve simultaneously as a way to bind some people together while keeping others apart. By bringing similar people together, ethnicity, race and religion can mobilize human and physical resources towards some common goal.

Recent researches on social capital have confirmed a very strong effect on economic outcomes (Durlauf, 2002). Socialcapital has become central to explaining a multitude of developmental processes ranging from participation in local development schemes to the successful implementation of national policies. The concept of social capital reflects the realization among the policy makers that certain social facts – such as trust, norms, values, hierarchies and solidarity – may be part of the process of wealth accumulation at the individual, community and national levels (Portes, 1998).

Social ties provide access to information, influence, social credentials, and reinforcement. These features of social capital reduce the need for formal marketing, staffing, contract negotiation and enforcement – all costs incurred in the process of economic transactions (Lin, 2001). The primary function of social capital in development processes is to reduce the costs of economic and other transactions. According to social capital theory, the bonds of collective identity as well as the formal structures and procedures provided by civic associations generate a collaborative spirit among members. The different arguments about the problems with cooperation, collective action, and public goods remain vague in explaining the linkage between the level of social capital and the other attribute of government performance or administrative efficiency. Recent studies of social capital have drawn a potentially powerful explanatory variable accounting for government performance. These studies argue that social capital is equally positively related to both government policy activism and administrative efficiency (Tavits, 2006). A number of research studies on social capital constitute one of the most influential sources of inspiration for the literature on social and cultural factors of economic growth (World bank, 1998).

Both heterogeneous and homogeneous civil society can contribute to economic development. The homogenous civil society with common norms and values and trust between the citizens has a positive impact on regional development (Putnam, 1993). However, Florida (1995) suggested that a heterogeneous civil society with diverse values combined with tolerance influences regional growth in a positive way. The study of heterogeneous society is more realistic than homogeneous society to accumulate the social capital.

The social capital offers the opportunities for trust and cooperation. Trust must be the basis of healthy debate in a civil society. There is nothing wrong with dissent, debate or conflict when they are based on mutual respect and trust. We need to value and validate the thoughtful critics of the system and debate them, as we value and debate those who maintain social cohesion. We need to continue to debate, discuss, and disagree on where we are going. The processes of participation and debate underpin a truly civil society. This process ensures the creative and productive society. Trust, reciprocity, mutuality, tolerance, collective decisions are the most important functions to create the productive society. Social tolerance has usually been measured by variables indicating attitudes toward members of different social groups. A schematic picture of the model of economic and social development. The concept of this figure was drawn from Florida et al, 2007; however, content and components are different. The arrows show the relationship and contribution of the concerned factors. The general pathway of the model shows that there is a joint contribution of tolerance, trust, reciprocity, mutuality and collective decisions to construct the creative and productive society. The creative and productive society contributes to economic and social development with support of existing technology. The model allows us to test the direct relationship between creative and productive society and economic and social development. Creative and productive society is also the social capital; but it is self-motivated society. Community forest user groups, mothers' clubs (Aama samuh), public facility users groups, youth or student clubs etc. are some of the examples of creative and productive civil societies at the local level in Nepal. Mass Medias can be used as an example of national level civil society; however, some of them are frequently involved to create the negative social capital knowingly or unknowingly. Therefore, it should be careful to interpret the role of mass media to accumulate the social capital in Nepal.

Similarly, the model allows to examining interpersonal trust and levels of citizen participation in solving community problems. Both interpersonal trust and civic participation that are fundamental to strengthening democracy can be used as indicators of politics of redistribution. Interpersonal trust enables people who do not necessarily think alike to willingly work together, fostering the consolidation of democratic political culture among citizens. As discussed earlier, debates with healthy trust, active participation, cooperation, reciprocity, and mutuality are forces of and regular phenomenon of active social life. Higher degree of participation, debates with healthy trust, reciprocity, cooperation and mutuality ensures the higher degree of creative and productive society.

The interactions with economic, social and political sectors

Civil society is simultaneously a goal to aim for, a means to achieve it, and a framework for engaging with each-other about ends and means. Therefore, it allows to interacting with economic, social and political sectors. Civil society (or social capital) plays the central role to make functional (in the positive way) of these sectors. A strong social capital ensures the creative and productive society which has power to positively influence to these sectors. A schematic representation of these three influences and civil society. The civil society is central of this analysis. How the three dimensions interact with civil society is the primary question; at the same time, if there is no civil society what will be the situation- is the next question.

As discussed earlier, a strong civil society can reduce the high concentration of economic, political and social power at all levels. The interactions between the civil society and economic sector ensure the economic development of the regions or the country. The interaction between civil society and political sector shows the democratic progress in the country. The interaction between civil society and social sector shows the interpersonal trust and minimizing possible discrimination. Area (1) represents the civil society. The interactions of the civil society with all sectors should be improved equally to maximize the welfare of the society or state. The area (2) represents the interaction between political and social; but there is no civil society. In this situation, the economic sector is isolated. Political sector adopts the social issues; but without participation of the citizens, it will be just a political slogan. It creates the conflicts among the social groups; but social issues are not addressed. Area (3) shows the interaction between economic sector and social sector. In this case, there is a overlapping of social and economic inequalities. Socio-economic issues are not the political agenda. There is no possibility of civic participation and democracy is not functioning. Area (4) shows the interaction between political and economic sectors. In this situation, political and economic power is skewed to the one sector. Corruption, rent seeking behaviour, smugglings are the common characteristics of this area. Political parties will have economic agenda, but not for the people, to get the political power. The areas (5), (6) and (7) represent the extreme power of political, social and economic respectively. This situation is an acute situation and it cannot be functioned in the long run. The situations of areas (2), (3) and (4) are frequently observed in the country; therefore the scope of civil society should continuously be expanded. It does not mean that all three sectors should be coincided in one circle. The certain portions of these sectors can be overlapping; but they cannot be coincided. The civil society can cover all sectors and can provide the support to improve the economic, social and political situation. The role of civil society is more effective in the local society. They assess their needs and priorities on the basis of their perceptions. The complex relationships among the issues, nature, intensity and their process of interactions may not be easily understood from outside of the society or top-down approach. Local people can use their stock of indigenous knowledge, experiences to identify actual the problems and their deepness and to find their solutions. Therefore, role of civil society in the local level is pertinent.

SECURITY SECTOR REFORM IN NEPAL: THE ROLE OF CIVIL SOCIETY

What is the role of civil society in Nepal? In the wake of ongoing peace negotiations that resulted in the signing of a peace agreement, USIP sponsored a two day program in Nepal to discuss the concepts of Security Sector Reform, Disarmament, Demobilization, and Reintegration, and how they fit within the context of Nepal.

On August 31 and September 1, 2006, the United States Institute of Peace sponsored a two-day program in Kathmandu, Nepal. This two-day program brought together a broad spectrum of Nepali civil society, including representatives of human rights organizations, dalit and janjayti rights groups, development agencies, and student, media, and academic communities, to discuss the issue of security sector reform in Nepal and civil society's role in the wake of ongoing peace negotiations that subsequently resulted in a peace agreement signed by the government of Nepal and the Communist Party of Nepal-Maoists (CPN-M) in November 2006.

The program was organized by Karon Cochran-Budhathoki of Defend Human Rights Movement-Nepal andColette Rausch, deputy director of USIP's Rule of Law program. It was facilitated by Ann Fitz-Gerald and Gordon Hughes of the Centre for Security Sector Management at Cranfield University, who presented participants with a broad range of case studies on security sector reform from other countries in transition.

This USIPeace Briefing provides an overview of the in-depth discussions that took place during the course of this program. It reviews the concepts of Security Sector Reform (SSR) and Disarmament, Demobilization, and Reintegration (DDR), and how they fit within the context of Nepal, as well as the ongoing challenges and needs for SSR, and the potential role for civil society. The areas of SSR that are highlighted in the report were identified as priority areas by members of civil society who participated in the USIP program. These priority areas include defense reform, the rule of law, democratic oversight, and DDR. The annex to the reportcontains the recommendations and action plan for civil society that directly resulted from USIP's program.

Context

On April 24, 2006, under pressure from daily public demonstrations that began April 6, Nepal's King Gyanendra reversed his February 1, 2005, declaration of direct palace rule and reinstated the House of Representatives (HoR). The seven political party alliance (SPA), which had opposed the King's absolute rule, came together to form a partial cabinet and select a prime minister. The government agreed to hold a constituent assembly election that would lead to a new constitution.

Following these events, the government and Communist Party of Nepal-Maoists (Maoists) continued to build on the dialogue that had begun between the Maoists and the SPA in November 2005, which had led to a 12-point understanding. The first "official" round of talks took place on May 26, 2006, and resulted in a 25-point ceasefire code of conduct. The second "official" round of talks finished on June 15, 2006, resulted in a four-point agreement to hold summit talks between the prime minister and Maoist Chairman Prachanda; to form a truce monitoring team (Ceasefire Code of Conduct National Monitoring Committee); to request the UN to assist the truce monitoring team and to monitor human rights; and finally, to hold further talks under observers.

Subsequently, summit talks were held on June 16 and resulted in an eight-point agreement to, among other things, dissolve the HoR, set up an interim government that would include the Maoists, enforce an interim constitution, and dissolve the Maoist de facto parallel government and judicial system that had been established in as much as 70% of the countryside. While some steps were taken for implementation, such as establishing a six-member interim constitution drafting committee, the peace process stalled over the sticking points of arms management and the future role of the king.

On November 21, 2006, Nepal's government and the Maoists signed a comprehensive peace agreement to formally end the ten-year conflict in Nepal that had resulted in an estimated 13,000 deaths. The peace agreement reaffirmed calls for UN involvement in arms management and elections monitoring, pledged to abide by international human rights and humanitarian laws, and called for the establishment of committees to undertake aspects of implementation. Under the agreement, and the November 28, 2006, Agreement of Monitoring the Management of Arms and Armies, the Maoists will sequester their armed fighters in cantonment sites, and the Nepalese Army will return to its barracks. The peace agreement has been widely hailed as historic within the country and many feel cautiously optimistic given the hurdles that lie ahead. Security sector issues remain in the forefront of challenges facing Nepal and implementation of the peace and arms management agreements.

Security Sector Reform and Disarmament, Demobilization, and Reintegration

Security Sector Reform (SSR) is "another term used to describe the transformation of the 'security system'—which includes all the actors, their roles, responsibilities and actions—working together to manage and operate the system in a manner that is more consistent with democratic norms and sound principles of good governance, and thus contributes to a well-functioning security framework." The security system mentioned in this definition encompasses, among other agencies, core security actors like armed forces, police, paramilitary forces, intelligence and security services (both military and civilian), the judiciary, penal systems, human rights commissions, and customary and traditional justice systems. It includes security and management oversight bodies such as the executive, the legislature, ministries of defense and internal affairs, and civil society. Furthermore, the concept of "security sector" also encompasses non-statutory security forces such as liberation armies and private security companies. The protection of human security is a key goal of development with each affecting and informing the other at the strategic, operational, and programmatic levels. Likewise, SSR is part of a democratization agenda and post-conflict reconstruction strategy.

At a programmatic level, SSR includes initiatives such as defense reform, police reform, judicial reform, parliamentary oversight, democratic accountability and transparency, and strengthening civil society.

Defense reform includes the reform of uniformed forces, the ministry of defense, and the home ministry, and consists of restructuring or strengthening these institutions and their interaction both strategically and operationally.

Training is often prioritized in countries in transition; however defense reform is a much broader initiative that may include capacity-building programs to increase the ministries' ability for oversight or the redesign or development of oversight mechanisms. Beyond defense reform, police, judicial, and penal system reform may also be high on the SSR agenda. In a country transitioning out of conflict there is often a breakdown of law and order, and the police, as internal security actors, may not be fully operationally effective. Efforts may be made to provide training, equipment and other institutional or legal reforms to improve upon its operational effectiveness and ensure that it operates under democratic principles. The judiciary, the penal system, and the intelligence services may undergo similar reforms. Strengthening civil society is also a core component of SSR. A robust civil society acts as an effective oversight mechanism. In addition, civil society may stimulate dialogue on SSR reforms, often working with policymakers by providing much-needed data and research to inform their decisions.

SSR requires strategic planning and developing programs based on a holistic approach that looks at the various security actors as an integrated and comprehensive unit. SSR also requires a strong partnership between domestic actors (both policymakers and civil society) and development donors. But there is general agreement in the development community that SSR should be locally owned, led, and driven. As part of this reform process, widespread consultation is fundamental as the community as a whole seeks to define and respond to threats. Sufficient political will and strong leadership are vital to ensure effective long-term SSR strategies and their effective implementation. Also vital is the role of civil society as a key driver of change.

Disarmament, Demobilization, and Reintegration (DDR) is a core component of SSR and is usually conducted at the front-end of SSR reforms, close to the cessation of a conflict or the signing of a peace agreement. Disarmament involves the collection and disposal of weapons and/or their surveying, storage, registration, and/or destruction. Demobilization involves the disbandment of armed groups for administrative processing and discharge orientation. It may include, among other things, the establishment and management of temporary camps in which ex-combatants receive training for returning to civilian life or for integration into the national security forces. Finally, Reintegration programs seek to reintegrate former combatants into society through compensation, training programs, and employment opportunities. As part of reintegration programs, ex-combatants might receive social counseling and incentives for returning to their communities and re-establishing civilian life. DDR will be most successful if it supports a national agenda and development strategy. For example, if former combatants are being provided with new professional skills, it is crucial that there be a demand for these skills in the country. Reconstruction and development programs are often included as part of DDR, and depending upon the national needs and agenda, disarmament, demobilization, and reintegration may not be sequential. No matter the sequence or process for DDR, it is a program that should be designed and implemented as part of the broader SSR agenda.

Security Sector Reform Priorities in Nepal: Identifying Needs & Challenges

Nepal is a country attempting to transition into a sustainable democratic system and out of a ten-year violent conflict. The country must have a long-term development strategy to address issues such as its high unemployment rate, high illiteracy rate, lack of access to health facilities, and socio-economic trends that are steeped in caste, gender, and ethnic discrimination. While the peace process continues, splinter groups and criminal gangs are operating freely, causing increasing insecurity. This insecurity, the challenges to transition, and the need for a development agenda all indicate the necessity of having an SSR in Nepal. A strong and effective SSR strategy and programs, which would include DDR as well as development and democratization agendas, will greatly reduce the risk of failure of the comprehensive peace agreement. Under the USIP-run civil society program in Nepal, four areas were identified by civil society as SSR priorities: Defense Reform; Rule of Law; Good Governance and Democratic Oversight; and DDR. Challenges within each of these priority areas highlight the need for SSR in Nepal.

Defense Reform

For more than 200 years the Nepal Army (formerly the Royal Nepal Army) has been under the control of the monarchy of Nepal. Consequently, many at USIP's civil society program viewed the army as protecting the interests of the king rather than the security and interests of the Nepali people or a democratic government. Furthermore, they raised concerns about the army's human rights record, its involvement in internal security matters, and allegations of discriminatory practices within the ranks. In light of these concerns, many argued for reform of the army.

Rule of Law

Under the broad heading of the "Rule of Law" as a priority area for SSR in Nepal, civil society identified police reform, justice reform, and intelligence reform as key areas to address. The need to undertake police, justice, and intelligence reform has been increasingly emphasized due to the increase in domestic and cross-border crime since the restoration of the HoR and the start of the formal dialogue between the government and the Maoists. Organized criminal gangs, splinter groups of the Maoists, and vigilante and other armed groups are operating freely in Nepal. The Nepali police, and the entire criminal justice system, are struggling to adequately address serious crimes. In the absence of state action in criminal matters, many are taking the law into their own hands. Coupled with this, a parallel system of justice, run in Maoist-held territory, has continued to operate. The significant crime problems Nepal faces, in addition to the problem of illegitimate actors filling the "rule of law vacuum," needs to be urgently addressed. The police force as a whole needs to be strengthened, trained, and provided adequate resources in order to confront this phenomenon. Beyond the police force, the entire criminal justice system may need to be strengthened in order for Nepal to move toward a society based on the rule of law and justice. Issues of corruption and nepotism also need to be urgently addressed.

Another major rule of law challenge is the issue of accountability of Maoists and the security sector, including the army and the police, for violations of domestic law and international human rights and humanitarian law. In many cases, the Maoists and the army have operated with impunity and the Maoists have continued to violate signed understandings by continuing to extort, abduct, and recruit minors. Victims of the conflict must be granted access to justice to seek recourse for such violations of their fundamental rights. Currently, access to justice, both for violations during the conflict and more broadly for criminal offenses committed, has been limited due to lack of political will, a weak justice sector, and a lack of lawyers, judges, and courts outside of district headquarters.

Good Governance and Democratic Oversight

This priority addresses the interface between the security forces and the democratic government, as well as the politics of transformation. The concept of democratic oversight has never been implemented in Nepal. Furthermore, insufficient financial oversight of the security sector has been a long-standing issue. In Nepal, where the government is bound to democratize and oversee the operation of the army, a lack of coordination and information-sharing between civilian and military authorities has created many logistical and operational walls to the government effectively implementing its oversight function.

Lack of political will, hesitancy in overseeing the security forces, and lack of division of labor within the government ministries has further hampered the police force's ability to effectively fight crime within the country.

DDR

DDR was a major sticking point for the peace process, and is still not viewed through the wider lens of SSR.

Civil society members in Nepal strongly believe that a DDR program for the Maoists' Peoples Liberation Army (PLA) will not be sufficient unless there are concurrent programs for changing state security institutions.

The international community has also created challenges through demands for complete disarmament. The timeframes discussed for a DDR program, whether by the government, civil society, or the international community, have been unrealistic. Because so many of the root causes of the conflict revolve around socio-economic discrimination and other development challenges, DDR should be part of a national recovery agenda.

While the November 28, 2006, Agreement of Monitoring the Management of Arms and Armies addresses issues of cantonment and the possible integration of the PLA into the Nepal army, reintegration modalities have not been determined, concerns regarding the interests of women and child combatants were not addressed, and reform of the security sector was neglected. Furthermore, civil society has been largely excluded from the process, but is expected to assist in the implementation of the peace and arms management agreements. Reconstruction, rehabilitation, and restorative justice have not been considered while planning for DDR. The agreements continue to see DDR as alien to a larger development and democratization agenda, or as part of a larger SSR strategy.

LOCAL BODIES AND CIVIL SOCIETY

Anecdotal literature suggested that social capital, community participation in civic organizations, and other forms of political participation are positively correlated with participation in activities of local government. The interactions of civil society and local bodies are most important to improve the society. Social capital proponents claim communities with larger stocks of horizontal social capital exhibit better development outcomes (Putnam, 1993). To effectively build social capital, local government must share autonomy with citizens, shifting its emphasis from controller to regulator and provider to new roles as catalyst, convener and facilitator (Crocker et al, 1998). These partnership approaches to local government will improve service delivery but they require a level of public capital or civic infrastructure with which to partner. In areas where such social capital infrastructure is weak, government can help build it by decentralizing programs to the neighborhood level. In the local level, politics are undemocratically dominated; generally local bodies are not included as an agenda for reform. For example, during the last almost one and half decades Nepal had no local election; local bodies were not a major agenda in discuss about the federalism in the country; however, local governance is the major issue in the countries where federal governments exist, such as India and Pakistan

The section discusses the political and social transformation while introducing the role of civil society. Social capital formation can be fostered by public sector institutions, but those institutions are themselves a product of social relations. This circularity requires development interventions give attention to both underlying social relations and bureaucratic organizational design. In places with horizontal social capital and robust, democratic governance structures, we can expect governmental interventions to promote horizontal community social capital development which will in turn impact program and organizational design as well as further reinforce social capital and democratic political structures. Autonomy and linkage are both strong, synergy between state and society is effective. However, there are certain factors that ensure the greater involvement of civic society and sustainable democratic practices in the root of national politics.

Breath, depth and range of participation of society are important factors to build the foundation of the democracy (Cohen, 1971). Breadth means the coverage of the fraction of the citizenry participating in making and carrying out decisions. Participation nourishes the democratic spirit of individuals. It is also determined by the proportion of the community members who participate directly or indirectly in all decision making activities.

The interactions, opportunities, and networks among others determine the coverage of social capital. The breadth of social capital supports to expand the participation of democratic process. An active, diverse civil society often does play a valuable role in helping advance democracy. It can discipline the state, ensure that citizens' interests are taken seriously, and foster greater civic and political participation. The essence of the breadth in a democracy is the proportion of the community that participates in determining its policies. Participation may be the choice of the people; but it is crucial that whether there are any barriers created by law, rules, regulations or social norms or not. The system remains essentially democratic. A number of underlining factors that determine the number of participation, or change in number of participation in the decision making process should be identified. The involvement of voting activities may not be sufficient to know the breadth of the democracy; however, relative changes in participation of voting right can be used one of the indicators. The breadth of democracy is determined by the measuring the ratio of participants to total membership in the community.

The depth of the democracy is determined by the characteristics of the participants in the decision making process. Depth is related to quality of democracy that determines effectiveness and continuation of participation in the democratic process. Depth of the democracy refers to the potential for efficacy and autonomy of popular participation. Use of voting right in the election is breadth of democracy; however, involvements in process of candidate selection, process of preparation of election manifesto are related to depth of the democracy. The participation of women, disadvantaged and marginalized groups is related to depth of democracy. Interpersonal trust, tolerance, mutuality, reciprocity are the quality indicators. Quality indicators matter in the construction of creative and productive society. The quality of democracy that is the independent of power supports to improve socioeconomic equality in the society. The depth or quality of democracy is the indicator of maturity of democracy. There is a causality and positive relationship between depth of the democracy and civil society.

Range of the democracy is related to sovereignty power of the participants. Breadth and depth of the democracy ensure the large number of participations with various levels, groups, and classes of the community in the decision making process; however, the ultimate authority of the participants to make decision on the discussion issues is important. The authority over power of the local bodies on various issues is related to rage of the democracy. The effective use of delegated power is also important. How effectively the members of the community may influence or alter decisions is also related to range of democracy. The members of the community can influence the decisions through direct or indirect methods. The civil society is the part of the member of the society. Civil society supports to increase the participants, to improve the representation of the various groups of the participants and to make effective decisions. The community will enjoy in the more democratic process if it has greater breadth, depth and range of the democracy.

Nepal is in the political transition; however, there remains a practice of majority based democracy. Majority rule, majority based decision making process may limit the breadth, depth and range of the democracy. Participatory based rule or decision making increases the dimensions of the democracy.

6

Languages of Nepal

The 2011 National census lists 123 language spoken as a mother tongue (first language) in Nepal. Most belong to the Indo-Aryanand Sino-Tibetan language families. An overview of Nepali languages is found in the work of Toba, Toba, and Rai.

The official language of Nepal is Nepali, formerly called Khaskura then Gorkhali. According to the 2011 national census, the percentage of people with Nepali as the mother tongue is 44.6%.

Classification

Three quarters of the hundred or so languages native to Nepal belong to the Tibeto-Burman language family; this includes Nepal Bhasa (Newar) (the original language of Kathmandu), the Tamang, Magar and various Rai and Limbu languages.

However, the official and numerically most important language, Nepali, belongs to the Indo-Aryan (Indic) branch of the Indo-European family, so that Indic languages constitute 79% of the population to Tibeto-Burman's 18%, even though most languages of both families are spoken by small numbers of people.

The Dravidian languages are represented by Kurux, and the Munda languages of the Austroasiatic family by Santali and Mundari. The indigenous languages of Nepal that predated the influx of Indic, Tibeto-Burman, and other families barely survive in the Kusunda language, which is nearly extinct today. Nepal also has at several indigenous village sign languages, Jhankot Sign Language, Jumla Sign Language, and Ghandruk Sign Language, in addition to the Nepali Sign Language designed for national use.

Constitution

Interim Constitution of Nepal 2063 (2007):

1. All the languages spoken as the mother tongue in Nepal are the national languages of Nepal.
2. The Nepali Language in Devanagari script shall be the official language.
3. Notwithstanding anything contained in clause (2), it shall not be deemed to have hindered to use the mother language in local bodies and offices. State shall translate the languages so used to an official working language and maintain record thereon.

Major languages

The following languages are some of the major languages spoken as mother tongue:

- Nepali (44.6%, 2011 census)
- Maithili (11.7%)
- Bhojpuri (8.0%)
- Tharu (5.8%)
- Tamang (5.1%)
- Kirati (3.3%)
- Nepal Bhasa (3.2%)
- Magar (3.0%)
- Bajjika (3.0%)
- Doteli (3.0%)
- Urdu (2.6%)
- Awadhi (2.0%)
- Baitadeli (1.02%)

Nepali is spoken as a lingua franca.

English is taking over as the lingua franca of the educated population as English is sole language of higher education in all the technical, medical, scientific studies and some of the economics and trade. There is a significant rise in the number of English-medium schools throughout the nation and a decline in Nepali-medium schools. Except for the government-funded schools, there are very few Nepali-medium schools.

NEPALI LANGUAGE

Nepali or Nepalese is an Indo-Aryan language. It is the official language and *de facto* lingua franca of Nepal and is also spoken in India, Bhutan and Burma. Nepali has official status in the Indian state of Sikkim and in West Bengal's Darjeeling district. Nepali developed in proximity to a number of Indo-Aryan languages, most notably the Pahari languagesand Magahi, and shows Sanskrit influences. However, owing to Nepal's geographical area, it has also been influenced byTibeto-Burman. Nepali is mainly differentiated from Central Pahari, both in grammar and vocabulary, by Tibeto-Burman idioms owing to close contact with the respective language group. Nepali language shares 40% lexical similarity with Bengali language. British Resident at Kathmandu Brian Houghton Hodgson has observed that it is, in eight-tenths of its vocables, substantially Hindi.

Historically, the language was first called the Khas language (*Khas kurâ*), then Gorkhali or Gurkhali (language of the Gorkha Kingdom) before the term *Nepali* was coined. Other names include *Parbatiya* ("mountain language", identified with the Parbatiya people of Nepal) and Dzongkha *Lhotshammikha* ("Southern Language", spoken by the Lhotshampa people ofBhutan).

Literature

Nepali developed a significant literature within a short period of a hundred years in the 19th century. This literary explosion was fueled by Adhyatma Ramayana; Sundarananda Bara (1833); Birsikka, an anonymous collection of folk tales;

and a version of the South Asian epic *Ramayana* by Bhanubhakta Acharya (d. 1868). The contribution of trio-laureates Lekhnath Poudyal, Laxmi Prasad Devkota, and Balkrishna Sama took Nepali to the level of other world languages. The contribution of expatriate writers outside Nepal, especially in Darjeeling and Varanasi in India, is also notable.

In the past decade, there have been many contributions to Nepali literature from the Nepali diaspora in Asia, Europe, and America.

Number of Speakers

According to the 2011 national census, 44.6 percent of the population of Nepal speaks Nepali as a first language. The Ethnologue website counts more than 17 million (2007) and 42 million (2012) speakers worldwide, 17 million within Nepal (from the 2001 census).

Nepali is traditionally spoken in the Hill Region of Nepal, especially in the western part of the country. Although the Newar language dominanted the Kathmandu valley, Nepali is currently the most dominant. Nepali is used in government and as the everyday language of a growing portion of the local population. Nevertheless, the exclusive use of Nepali in the courts and government of Nepal is being challenged. Recognition of other ethnic languages in Nepal was one of the objectives of the Communist Party of Nepal's long war.

In Bhutan, those who speak Nepali, known as *Lhotshampa*, are estimated at about 35 percent of the population. This number includes displaced Bhutanese refugees, with unofficial estimates of the ethnic Nepali population as high as 30 to 40 percent, constituting a majority in the south (about 242,000 people).) Since the late 1980s, over 100,000 Lhotshampas have been forced out of Bhutan, accused by the government of being illegal aliens. A large portion of them were expelled in an "ethnic cleansing" campaign, and presently live in refugee camps in eastern Nepal.

In India, there is a large number of Nepali-speaking people. In Northeast India there are several million Nepali speakers.

A considerable number of Nepali-speaking people are also present in many Indian cities such as Kolkata, Delhi, Bangalore, Visakhapatnam, Goa, Bihar, Darjeeling, Sikkim, Chennai, Mumbai, and Hyderabad.

Combining the Ethnologue figures with strong population growth in Nepal and India, the assumption of 20 million people with Nepali as their native language is a reasonable estimate for 2006.

History of the Language

Around 500 years ago, Khas people from the Karnali-Bheri-Seti basin migrated eastward, bypassing inhospitable Kham highlands to settle in lower valleys of the Gandaki Basin that were well-suited to rice cultivation. One notable extended family settled in the Gorkha Kingdom, a small principality about halfway between Pokhara and Kathmandu. In 1559 AD a Lamjunge prince, Dravya Shah established him in the throne of Gorkha with the help of local Khas and Magars. He raised an army of khas with the commandership of Bhagirath Panta. Later, in the late 18th century his heir Prithvi Narayan Shah raised and improvised an army of Chhetri, Thakur, Magars and Gurung people and possibly other hill tribesmen and set out to conquer and consolidate dozens of small principalities in the Himalayan foothills. Since Gorkha had replaced the original Khas homeland, Khaskura was redubbed *Gorkhali* "language of the Gorkhas".

The most notable military achievement of Prithvi Narayan was conquest of the urbanized Kathmandu Valley, on the eastern rim of the Gandaki basin. This region was also called *Nepal* at the time. Kathmandu became Prithvi Narayan's new capital, from which he and his heirs extended their domain east across the Koshi River basin, north to the Tibetan Plateau, south into the plains of North India, and west across the Karnali/Bheri basin and beyond.

Expansion – particularly to the north, west, and south – brought the growing state into conflict with the British and Chinese. This led to wars that trimmed back the territory to an area roughly corresponding to Nepal's present borders. Both China and Britain understood the value of a buffer state and did not attempt to further reduce the territory of the new country. Since the Kathmandu Valley or *Nepal* had become the new center of political initiative, this word gradually came to refer to the entire realm and not just the Kathmandu Valley. So *Gorkhali* came to be known as *Nepali.* In all these years, Nepali has had influences from many languages. While Nepali is technically from the same family as languages like Hindi and Bengali, it has taken many loan words. Words like *dhoka* "door", *jhyaal* "window", *pasal* "shop", *kukhura* "rooster" and *raango* "water buffalo' have Tibeto-Burmese roots. Words like *saheed* "martyr" and *kaanun* "law" come from the Arabic language through Persian roots. Many English words are in use nowadays due to the rising popularity of America in the region and the previous British aid in schools and other fields.

Nepali is spoken indigenously over most of Nepal west of the Gandaki River, then progressively less further to the east. This is shown graphically in detailed language maps of western and eastern Nepal as language number 73.

7

Culture of Nepal

The culture of Nepal is rich and unique. The cultural heritage of Nepal has evolved over the centuries. This multi-dimensional heritage encompasses the diversities of Nepal's ethnic, tribal, and social groups, and it manifests in music and dance; art and craft; folklore andfolktales; languages and literature; philosophy and religion; festivals and celebration; foods and drinks.

DANCE AND MUSIC

Legends state that dances in the Indian subcontinent originated in the abode of Lord Shiva — the Himalayas and the Himalayan Kingdom of Nepal — where he performed the tandava dance. This indicates that dance traditions of Nepal are very ancient. With altitudes and ethnicity, the dances of Nepal slightly change in style as well as in the costumes. The Dishka, a dance performed at weddings, includes intricate footwork and arm movements. Accompanying music and musical instruments change in tune with the themes, which revolve around topics like harvesting of crops, marriage rites, war stories, a lonely girl's yearning for her love, and several other themes and stories from everyday life in the villages.

MUSIC OF NEPAL

Music of Nepal refers to the various musical genres of Nepal. With more than fifty ethnicity, the music of this country is a highly dispersed phenomenon. Although genres like pop, rock, Nep-hop ko bato, folk, and Classical music exist, a huge number of such genres are yet to be cataloged.

Many musical bands exist in Nepal, with a huge number in Kathmandu – most of the recent ones focused in pop and rock. Rap has been known to emerge on the charts from time to time.

Nepali Music Genres

Dohori

Dohori music is Nepali folk songs. It is a unique style of music. Dohori means from two side or a debate. This debate is in rhythm, and involves quick and witty poetry.The two teams in Dohori usually involves boys in one group girls in the other.The song is started with a question usually from the boys side. The girl follows the question with a quick response and continues the musical conversation.

Dohori songs can last for a long periods of time, even up to a week long. The length of the Dohori depends on the quick thinking ability of the players.

Aadhunik geet

Aadhunik geet or modern songs are popular songs in Nepal. It is also known as sugam sangeet. These type of songs are soft and melodious.

Nepalese hip hop (Nep-hop)

Mostly preferred by people in this generation,Nep-hop is a modern genre of Nepal which represents Nepali hiphop music.

Ethnic Music in Nepal

Newar music

Newa Music or Newar Music, is traditional music developed in Nepal by the Newars. The musical instruments mainly consist of percussion and wind instruments.

Gurung Music

Gurungs have a very rich tradition of music and culture. Gurungs have an ancient tradition of Rodhi where young people meet, sing and dance to folk songs, and share their views. Young men and women at Rodhi often sing call-and-response songs called dohori, which are largely improvised. Some musical dances like Ghantu and Chudka are still in existence, and are still performed in many Gurung villages. These dances are many hundreds of years old, and are performed either solo or in a group. Music also plays a big role in the Gurung ritual of Argum, which is performed when someone in the community dies.

These traditions are still very much alive in rural Gurung villages. Gurung films are also popularizing some of these songs and dances. Jyoti Gurung is considered as the finest Gurung singer from this community. She has contributed the most number of Gurung film songs than any other artist.

Kirat music

The Yakthungs (Limbu) have various forms of dance, songs and musical instruments. Of them, Dhaan Nach (paddy dance) and Chya:brung (Dhol Nach "drum dance") are popular symbolics. Khambu celebrate Sakela, a dance performed during the occasion of "Udauli" and "Ubhuali" which is the greatest festival of khumbu (Rai,kirat). Sakela which are sometime wrongly referred as Chandi Naach. Chandi is Hindu goddess and is not related in any way with Kirat culture. Many forms of their dance involve rituals or religious offerings towards Mundhum (native Kiranti religion). Traditional dance and songs are also practiced for weddings, festivals or gatherings.

Tamang Music

Tamang community is well known for Damphu, a traditional instrument. Tamang Selo music is based on the usage of Damphu and Tungna. It is said that British people got an idea of making Drum Sets from Damphu during their stay at India. Western and Indian instruments are also found in some modern Tamang

Selo music. Recently due to the re-mixing trend of classic Nepali songs, Tamang Selo tuned songs like changba hoi changba, Man chadey Maichyang lai have been a hit in Nepali radio stations. Also, Modern artists like Sindhu Malla, Raju Lama Avinash Ghising, Roj Moktan, Bijay Lama, etc. have used Tamang Selo tunes in their songs and those songs have also been a hit.

Magar Music

Salaijo, Kauda and Sorathi are the three unique and exclusive musical genre of Magar music.

Sherpa Music

Sherpa Music is based on Tibetan Buddhism. This is identical to Music of Tibet around the trans-Himalayan region. First and foremost Tibetan music is religious music, reflecting the profound influence of Tibetan Buddhism on the culture.

Maithili Music

Maithali music is one of the ancient music existing in south Asia and even in Nepal. It has a very great histoy and has many aspects. No one knows from when the maithali music came into existence since it has a very long history.

Mithila was an independent nation ruled by the king Janak and it was used then also so it might have become one of the boon for other music developed and flourished here in Nepal. Malla kings in Kathmandu were very fund of music and since maithali songs were very popular at its time they also used to enjoy it. maithali musing includes different instruments specially classical. Now the maithali songs has been modernized and has been using different modern instruments. so in short maithali song has its own identity and has been flourished on its own basis. Some of the great contributor to it are Maha kabi vidhyapati jha, Udit Narayan Jha, Binit Thakur, Rama Mandal.

Imported Music

The musical genres which was introduced to Nepal from

outside and thrived here can be considered as imported music. This contains:-

Bhajan

A Bhajan is any type of devotional song. It has no fixed form: it may be as simple as a mantra or kirtan. It is normally lyrical, expressing love and pray for the Divine. Shiva, Krishna, Vishnu, Sai Baba bhajan are popular in Nepal.

Filmi music

Filmi music is popular music as written and performed for cinema. Since history of cinema of Nepal is not so long the filmi music is developing. As Bollywood movies are also popular in Nepali urban areas Nepali filmi music heavily inspired by Indian filmi music. Music directors make up the main body of composers; and the songs are performed by playback singers.

Ghazal

The ghazal is a poetic form consisting of rhyming couplets and a refrain, with each line sharing the same meter. A ghazal may be understood as a poetic expression of both the pain of loss or separation and the beauty of love in spite of that pain. The form is ancient, originating in 6th-century Arabic verse. The ghazal spread into South Asia in the 12th century due to the influence of Sufi mystics and the courts of the new Islamic Sultanate. Although the ghazal is most prominently a form of Dari poetry and Urdu poetry, today it is found in the poetry of many languages of the Indian sub-continent. Motiram Bhatta introduced the written form of Ghazal in Nepali language in 1890. Seturam Shrestha (1891-1941) has been credited with pioneering ghazal music in Nepal. The tradition of singing ghazals has been gaining popularity in the last few years.

Western Music

- Rock & Roll (Introduced by the Hippies)
- Blues
- Rock

- Electronic Music
- Metal
- Pop
- Rap/Soul

Awards

With the growth and development of Nepali music industry, different award ceremonies began being held in different parts of the country, some of them being focused on local talents. The awards of National standard are held each year by media houses, mainly Hits FM and Image FM.

Annual Hits FM Music Awards

Hits FM (Nepal) was established in April 1996 with the intention to help the music industry grow beyond what it was. Since then, Hits Nepal Pvt. Ltd., the parent organization and the event organizer of Hits Awards has been greatly involving in encouraging and promoting Nepali artists and music. Then came the concept of further involvement throughAnnual Hits FM Music Awards, which was held for the first time in 2054 BS (1998 AD) with seven categories to award, and it became the first ever musical award to be organized by a private company in national level. The award ceremony celebrated its 14th birthday recently, with artists awarded in 19 categories, including the prestigious Life Time Achievement Award (awarded to a senior member of music industry for their contribution for the development of Nepali music), and performances by top Nepali artists. The songs and albums nominated in each category are based on the votes of the public and the winner is then evaluated by an independent panel of judges.

LANGUAGES AND LITERATURE

As per the 2011 census, 123 languages are spoken in Nepal. Nepal's linguistic heritage has evolved from three major language groups:Indo-Aryan, Tibeto-Burman, and indigenous. The major languages of Nepal (percent spoken as mother tongue) are Nepali (44.6%),Maithili (11.7%), Bhojpuri (6%), Tharu (5.8%), Tamang (5.1%), Nepal Bhasa (3.2%), Magar (3%) and Bajjika (3%).

Nepali, written in Devanagari script, is the official national language and serves as *lingua franca* among Nepalese ethno-linguistic groups.Maithili language that was originated in Mithila region of Nepal is the de-facto official language of Nepal and Madhesh as a whole. Maithili is spoken in Nepal as a second language. Extinct languages of Nepal include Kusunda, Madhesiya and Waling.

Religions and philosophy

The 2001 census identified 80.6% of the population being Hindu. Buddhism was practiced by about 11% of the population (although many people labelled Hindu or Buddhist often practice a syncretic blend of Hinduism, Buddhism, and/or animist traditions). About 3.2% practice Islamand 3.6% of the population follows the indigenous Kirant religion. Christianity is practiced officially by less than 0.5%.

Hindu and Buddhist traditions in Nepal go back more than two millennia. In Lumbini, Buddha was born, and Pashupatinath temple, Kathamandu, is an old and famous Shiva temple of Hindus. Nepal has several other temples and Buddhist monasteries, as well as places of worship of other religious groups. Traditionally, Nepalese philosophical thoughts are ingrained with the Hindu and Buddhist philosophical ethos and traditions, which include elements of Kashmir Shaivism, Nyingma school of Tibetan Buddhism, works of Karmacharyas of Bhaktapur, and tantric traditions.Tantric traditions are deep rooted in Nepal, including the practice of animal sacrifices. Five types of animals, always male, are considered acceptable for sacrifice: water buffalo, goats, sheep, chickens, and ducks. Cows are very sacred animals and are never considered acceptable for sacrifice.

Festivals and celebrations

Several of the festivals of Nepal last from one to several days. Dashain is the longest and the most important festival of Nepal. Generally Dashain falls in late September to mid-October, right after the end of the monsoon season. It is "a day of Victory over Demons". The Newarscelebrate the festival as Mohani. Tihar or Swanti and Chhath are another important festivals of Nepal. New Year's Day of the lunar calendar Nepal Sambat occurs at this time.

Other important festivals include Buddha Jayanti (the celebration of the birth of Buddha), Maha Shivaratri (a festival of Lord Shiva), and during Maha Shivaratri festivities, some people consume excessive drinks and smoke charas. Sherpas, mostly located at higher altitudes and in the Mount Everest region, celebrate *Mani Rimdu*, for *the good of the world.*

Most festivals include dancing and music, as well as all kinds of local delicacies. A variety of foods are consumed during festivals and on special occasions. If one has to taste Nepali food, Newa cuisine and Maithil Cuisine are must have; a festive meal, like one served during a marriage, is a real treat, and include vegetarian and non-vegetarian dishes.

The Sagan ceremony is the ritualized presentation of five food items (boiled egg, smoked fish, meat, lentil cake and rice wine) to a person which is done to bring good fortune as per Tantric tradition..

Architecture and archeology

Nepal Sumpada Sangha (Nepal Heritage Society) has compiled an inventory of 1,262 significant architectural and archeological sites in Nepal outside Kathmandu Valley.

CULTURAL AREA

The extent of Nepal Mandala has been traditionally defined by the locations of 64 Hindu and 24Buddhist pilgrimage sites. The Hindu shrines consist of 64 Shiva lingas scattered from Brahmeswar inNuwakot district in the west to Bhimeswar in Dolakha District in the east.

The 24 Buddhist pilgrimage sites are spread from the Trishuli River in the west to Dolalghat in the east. When seen as an ordered pattern, they form the picture of the mandala of Chakrasamvara, the principal deity of Vajrayana Buddhism. Nepal Mandala was conceived on the basis of the Chakrasamvara Mandala.

Francis Buchanan-Hamilton has written in *An Account of the Kingdom Of Nepal* published in 1819 that four pilgrimage spots marked the boundaries of Nepal Proper: Nilkantha (an eight-day journey north from Kathmandu), Nateswar (three days to the south), Kaleswar (two days to the west) and Bhimeswar (four days to the east).

Political area

The term mandala also means a country, and it has been used to represent traditional political formations such as federation of kingdoms. The area comprising Kathmandu, Lalitpur, Bhaktapur and Dolakha during the Malla period is generally known as Nepal Mandala.

According to the Outline History of Nepal, Nepal Mandala was situated between the Khas and Simraungarh kingdoms. The Khas kingdom extended from Garhwal in the west to the Trishuli River in the east, and from Lake Mansarovar in the north to the Terai in the south. Karnatak, also called Simraungarh, was situated in the Terai.

Western travelers in the late 18th century have written that Nepal's borders extended to Tibet in the north, the nation of the Kirata in the east, the kingdom of Makwanpur in the south and the Trishuli River in the west which separated it from the kingdom of Gorkha.

In 1661, Jesuit Fathers Johann Grueber and Albert d'Orville travelled from Tibet to India through Nepal. They mentioned in their report that they passed through "Cuthi", the first town in the kingdom of "Necbal" (Nepal), and arrived in "Cadmendu" (Kathmandu), the capital of "Necbal". From "Cadmendu", a journey of five days brings one to "Hedouda", a market town in the kingdom of "Maranga". The town of Hedouda is known as Hetauda today.

The inhabitants

The oldest inhabitants of Nepal Mandala are the Newars who are of multiple racial strains that combined over millennia. Newar civilization is a blend of different cultures that came together in Nepal Mandala. According to sociologists, the people of Nepal gradually became known as Newar.

History

The Buddhist text *Manjushrimula Kalpa* has mentioned Manadeva (reigned 464-506 AD) as being the king of Nepal Mandala.

The term Nepal Mandala also appears in the popular Buddhist text *Swayambhu Purana*. It occurs in a stone inscription at Gyaneswar, Kathmandu dating from the eighth century during the reign of Licchavi king Jayadeva II.

The term Nepal Mandala has been used through the centuries in stone and copper inscriptions and the colophons of manuscripts when mentioning the dedicator's address. It is also referred to during important Buddhist ceremonies.

LUMBINI

Lumbini is a Buddhist pilgrimage site in the Rupandehi District of Nepal. It is the place where, according to Buddhist tradition, Queen Mayadevi gave birth to Siddhartha Gautama in 623 BCE. Gautama, who achieved nirvana some time around 543 BCE, became the Gautama Buddha and founded Buddhism after achieving Enlightenment. Lumbini is one of many magnets for pilgrimage that sprang up in places pivotal to the life of Gautama Buddha; other notable pilgrimage sites include Kushinagar, Bodh Gaya and Sarnath.

Lumbini has a number of temples, including the Mayadevi Temple and several others which are still under construction. Many monuments, monasteries and a museum — the Lumbini International Research Institute — are also located within the holy site. Also located there is the Puskarini or Holy Pond where the Buddha's mother took the ritual dip prior to his birth and where he, too, had his first bath. At other sites near Lumbini, earlier Buddhas were, according to tradition, born, achieved ultimate Enlightenment and finally relinquished their earthly forms.

Lumbini was granted World Heritage status by UNESCO in 1997.

In Pratham's time

In the Buddha's time, Lumbini was situated between Kapilavastu and Devadaha (both in Nepal). It was there, that the Buddha was born. A pillar now marks the spot ofAshoka's visit to Lumbiní. According to an inscription on the pillar, it was placed there by the people then in charge of the park to commemorate Ashoka's visit and gifts. The park was previously known as Rummindei, two miles (3.2 km) north of Bhagavanpura.

In the Sutta Nipáta (vs. 683) it is stated that the Buddha was born in a village of the Sákyans in the Lumbineyya Janapada. The Buddha stayed in Lumbinívana during his visit to Devadaha and there preached the Devadaha Sutta.

Rediscovery

In 1896, Nepalese archaeologists (led by Khadga Samsher Rana and assisted by Alois Anton Führer) discovered a great stone pillar at Lumbini. Führer postulated that the pillar was placed at the site by Ashoka (emperor of the Maurya Empire) circa 245 BCE. Records made by the Chinese pilgrim Faxian in the early fifth century CE were also used in the process of identifying this religiously acclaimed site.

Recent excavations beneath existing brick structures at the Mayadevi Temple at Lumbini have uncovered evidence for an older timber structure beneath the walls of the newer brick Buddhist shrine, which was constructed during the Ashokan era. The layout of the Ashokan shrine closely follows that of the earlier timber structure, which suggests a continuity of worship at the site. The pre-Mauryan timber structure appears to be an ancient bodhigara (tree shrine), consisting of postholes and a wooden railing surrounding a clay floor containing mineralized tree roots that appears to have been worn smooth by visitors. Radiocarbon dating of charcoal from the wooden postholes and optically stimulated luminescence dating of elements in the soil suggests human activity (possibly pre-Buddhist tree worship) began at the site around 1000 BCE, followed by the development of a Buddhist monastery-like community by approximately 550 BCE.

Present-day

The present-day Lumbini historic site is 4.8 km (3 mi) in length and 1.6 km (1.0 mi) in width. The holy site of Lumbini is bordered by a large monastic zone in which only monasteries can be built, no shops, hotels or restaurants. It is separated into an eastern and western monastic zone, the eastern having the Theravadin monasteries, the western having Mahayana and Vajrayana monasteries.

The holy site of Lumbini has ruins of ancient monasteries, a sacred Bodhi tree, an ancient bathing pond, the Ashokan pillar and the Mayadevi Temple, where the supposed place of birth of Buddha is located. From early morning to early evening, pilgrims from various countries perform chanting and meditation at the site.

A non-governmental organization named Samriddhi Foundation started in 2013 working extensively in the field of education and health specially in government schools of the area where underprivileged children study. A non-governmental organisation called "Asia Pacific Exchange and Cooperation Foundation" (APECF) backed by chairman of the Unified Communist Party of Nepal (Maoist)and then Prime Minister Prachanda, the Chinese government and a UN group called "United Nations Industrial Development Organization" (UNIDO) signed a deal to develop Lumbini into a "special development zone" with funds worth $3 billion. The venture was a China-UN joint project. A broader 'Lumbini Development National Director Committee' under the leadership of Pushpa Kamal Dahal was formed on 17 October 2011. The six-member committee included Communist Party of Nepal (Unified Marxist-Leninist) leader Mangal Siddhi Manandhar, Nepali Congress leader Minendra Rijal, Forest Minister Mohammad Wakil Musalman, among other leaders. The committee was given the authority to "draft a master plan to develop Lumbini as a peaceful and tourism area and table the proposal" and the responsibility to gather international support for the same.

Nipponzan Myohoji decided to build a Peace Pagoda in the park in 2001, which is visited by many different cultures and religions every day.

Hindus regard the Buddha as an incarnation of Vishnu and thousands of Hindu pilgrims come there on the full moon of the Nepali month of Baisakh (April–May) to worship Queen Mayadevi as Rupa Devi, the mother goddess of Lumbini. There are controversy about the birthplace of Gautam Buddha, however on the basis of enough evidence from the Lumbini it is found that Buddha was born in Madesh. Actually Buddha was from Madeshi descent. Lumbini was granted World Heritage status by UNESCO in 1997.

On the Nepali rupee

Nepal's central bank has introduced a 100-rupee Nepali note featuring Lumbini, the birthplace of Buddha. The Nepal Rastra Bank said the new note would be accessible only during the Dashain, Nepal's major fiesta in October 2013. It displays the portrait of Mayadevi, Gautam Buddha's mother in silver metallic on the front. The note also has a black dot which would help the blind recognise the note. The name of the central bank in Latin script would be printed on the note along with the date of printing in both the Christian Era and the Bikram Era. The new note is being issued following a cabinet decision 27 August.

CULTURE AND TRADITION

Religous Traditions and Festivals

Nepal is a multicultural,multilingual and multiethinic country.Similarly, Nepal has the people of different religious tolerance among the people.However,the people who follow Hindu religion are in great number.Besides this,Buddhism is another popular religion of Nepal.The founder of Buddhism is Gautam Buddha.Who was born in Lumbini,Nepal.He is famous as the Light of Asia.There are many followers of Islam, Christianity, Shikhism, Jainism and Kirat religion.Every religion has its own values and norms.People of every religion can celebrate their festivals according to their culture and traditions.Some important festivals are as follow.

Some festival which is celebrated by different religious communities of Nepal.And This festival is also known as national festivals

Dashain

The Hindus all over the world celebrate Dashain.It is also known as Bada Dashain,Durga Puja,Dusshera and Kalipuja.It falls in autumn in the months of either September or October every year.It is celebrated for fifteen days from the day of Ashwin Shukla Pratipada i.e., Ghatasthapana till Purnima,Goddess Durga is worshipped on the occasion.She is regarded as the Goddess of Power.

The elder members in the family put Tika and Jamara and bestow blessings to the younger members on the tenth day to mark this occasion.The tenth day is remembered as the Day of Victory i.e,Vijaya Dashami.The other major days of Dashain are Phulpati of Saptami,kalaratri or Mahasthami and Mahanawami, which fall on the seventh,eighth and the ninth day respectively.

It is a festival of union in the family,of great joy and extreme delight.People put on new clothes and eat delicious food.They go to Dashain fair and exchange greetings and good wishes.People,rich or poor,enjoy alike.

It is believed that this festival is celebrated to mark the victory of Goddess Durga over Maisasur,a demon,and Lord Rama over Ravana,the demon King of Lanka.This festival,therefor,symbolises the victory of good over evil and truth over falsehood.

Tihar

It is another great festival of the Hindus.People celebrate it with great pomp and show.It comes about fifteen days after Dashain.This festival is also called Diwali or Deepawali i.e.,the festival of lights.It is observed for five days from Kartik Krishna Dwadashi up to Kartik Pratipada.The first two days of this festival are dedicated to Kag i.e.,the crow,and Kukur,i.e.,the dog.The third day is called Gai Tihar or Laxmi Puja.Cows are worshipped on this day in the morning and Goddess Laxmi in the evening.She is regarded as the Goddess of Wealth.People clean their houses,decorate and illumine them all night by putting candles,small oil lamps or colourful electric bulbs.And they pray that Goddess Laxmi dwell in their house.People,particularly girls and women play Bhailo in groups on the night of Laxmi Puja.The Gobardhan Puja is observed on the fouth fay and oxen are worshipped.People play Dheusi during the night and the next day.

The final day is called the Bhaitika.On this day,sisters worship their brothers and wish for their long and healthy life.They put tika and garland them.They serve different varieties of sweets,fruits and delicacies to their brothers.The brothers,in turn, give them cash and gifts.

It is believed that this festival is celebrated to mark the return of Lord Rama to his Kingdom in Ayodhya after fourteen years in exile.

Chhat

Chhat is a great festival of the Hindus of central Terai.especially the Maithili people.It is a festival of the Sun-God.It is celebrated on the fifth day of Kartik Shukla,six days after the Laxmi Puja.Both men and women celebrate this festival.However,only women observe fast during the day for three days,worship the setting sun in the evening and then only eat.On the sixth day,they all gather around richly decorated platforms near a local pond or a nearby river early in the morning.They take bath and workship the rising sun with flowers and lamps for the long life and good health of their husbands.After finishing the worship,all the family members sit together and eat variety of sweet.It brings happiness and joy in the family and community.

Lhosar

Lhosar is a Buddhist festival.Lho means year and Sar means new.Lhosar thus basically is a New Year festival.It is celebrated mainly in the Himalayan region by the Gurungs,Tamangs and the Sherpas.They celebrate Lhosar according their own community and customs.Some celebrate it on 15th of Poush,some on Magh Shukla Pratipada and others on Falgun Shukla Pratipada.The Gurungs have Tamu Lhosar,the Tamangs celebrate Sonam Lhosar and the Sherpas observe Gyalpo Lhosar.

Lhosar is a festival of feast,joy and dance.people draw swastiks,symbol of peace and good fortune,in their homes.They also decorate their homes with paintings of natural elements like the Himalayas,the sun,and the Moon.

They wear new clothes and eat sumptuous meals.They generally gather at public places and play games,engage in fun,sing and dance.They alos visit their elders and seek their blessings for a healthy and prosperous New year. They exchange greetings and gifts with each other.

Christmas

The most important festival for the Christians is Christmas.It is also known as X-Mas.The letter X represents the holy sign Cross for the Christians.It falls on 25 December every year.It marks the birth anniversity of Jesus Christ,the founder of Christianity.It is generally celebrated for three days from 24 to 26 December.

Christmas eve is celebrated on 24 December.On Christmas eve,they decorate a pine tree called Christmas Tree with candles,colourful papers,balloons and flowers.They keep the presents and cards given by their friends and relatives under this tree.They open them later to know who owns the most and best of them.They have great fun.

The Christmas father is Santa Claus.It is believed that he comes during the night and leave presents for the children in their socks.During the day,they go to church and pray together.They put on special caps and new clothes.

26 December is known as Boxing Day.Rich people give boxes full of gifts or money or food and clothes ot the poor people.They visit their friends and relatives on the occasion and have a lot of fun,is celebrated as the New Year Day.The christian era started from this date from the time of jesus Christ.They exchange New Year greetings and wish each other good health and prosperity in life.

Eid

Eid is a New Year festival of the Muslim community according to the Hijri or Hijaratera.The Hijriera began from the time of Prophet Mohammad who is the messanger of their Allah.All the Muslims follow the Hijri calender.It is believed that some people threatened to kill Prophet Mohammad while he was preaching his ideas.

He along with his followers,therefore,left Mecca for Medina.This journey is called Hijara which means migration.Mecca and Medina are thus the two most holy places of the Muslims.

The Muslims observe a month long fast called Roza during the month of Ramjan.They do not eat anything,not even drink water during daytime.All the family members sit together and eat after sun set.They believe that this will purge and discipline them.They celebrate the last day of Ramjan as Eid-ul-Fitr.They congratulate,embrace and greet each other Eid Mubark which means Happy New Year.They put on new clothes,eat variety of sweets and visit their friends and relatives.They go to the mosques and read Namaz.They also give alms called Zakat to the poor,disabled and needy people.

All these religious festivals carry the message of love and peace.They help to foster friendship,brotherhood and peace in society.Hence,they promote national unity and integration.

Maghe Sangkranti

Maghe Sangkranti has a great importance in the Nepalese society.Most of the Nepalese festivals are based on lunar calender.Yet there are some festivals which are based on solar calender.Nawabarsha(New Year),15th Asar,Saune Sangkranti along with the Maghe Sagrakanti are the festivals based on solar calender.

Sangkranti means the first day of the month. Therefore, Maghe Sangkranti is observed on the first day of the month –Magh. This festival is observed to mark the end of winter season.During December 22nd the sun comes gradually to norhern hemisphere,and the palces at the nothern hemisphere start to get warmer.

Maghe Sangkranti is a social festival.It is celebrated in different ways in different parts of the country.In hilly regions people gather at the riverside and take bath early in the morning and eat Til ko Laddu(a kind of sweet made of sesame),boiled roots(yam,sweet potato,potato,etc.)and Khichadi (dish made with rice and lentil together).It is believed that all the food that we eat on this day shall have been cooked at the previous day(end of the Poush month)except Khichadi.In terai,especially in Tharu community,this day is celebrated as 'Maghi'.This day marks the New year in their community.Many of the fairs are organized at different parts of the country.The fun and excitement of these fairs are remembered throughout the year.

This is the one of the days of celebration of social value.such celebrations construct our culture and traditions.It is our duty to conserve these festivals which are celebrated by different communities of the country.

Ram Nawami

Ram Nawami is one of the important festivals of all the Hindu people of Nepal.It falls on the 9th day of the full moon fortnight of Chaitra.It is believed that the Lord Ram was born on this day.Lord Ram was one of the most influential incarnations of Lord Vishnu who is one of the Trinity.Lord vishnu is the God who takes care of all the living beings after being created by Brahma.It is believed Lord Mahesh (Shiva)takes the life later on.

Ram was an ideal person.He was obedient to his parents and the caretaker of responsibilities.We gain Knowledge of obedience,brotherhood,peace,endurance,tolerance,apology,justice and above all the truthfulness by studying his life.

Many people observe this day with fasting.Early in the morning people visit the temples of Lord Ram.A grand fair takes places at Ram Janaki Temple in Janakpur.

Religous Traditions and Festivals

Nepal is a multicultural,multilingual and multiethinic country.Similarly Nepal has the people of different religious tolerance among the people.However,the people who follow Hindu religion are in great number.Besides this,Buddhism is another popular religion of Nepal.The founder of Buddhism is Gautam Buddha.Who was born in Lumbini,Nepal.He is famous as the Light of Asia.There are many followers of Islam, Christianity, Shikhism, Jainism and Kirat religion.Every religion has its own values and norms.People of every religion can celebrate their festivals according to their culture and traditions.Some important festivals are as follow.

Janai Purnima

Janai Purnima is the common name of the festival Rishi Tarpani or Raksha Bandhan.This festival falls on Shrawan Shukla Purnima (The full moon day of Shrawan).This day is one of the most important days for the Hindu community because it has highly religious value.People take bath early in the morning and the male members of Brahman and Chetri change Janai for the year.Janai is the sacred thread,which they start to wear after the Bratabandha or Upanayan ceremony.On the same day all the people receive another sacred thread yagyopavit(Raksha Bandan).It is believed that this tread prevents them from on every kind of misfortunes.In the terai sisters tie Rakhi on the brothers' wrists,secure their brothers making from any kind of mishaps.On this day all the people of Newar community prepare a special Kind of soup,Kwanti which is made by mixing nine different kinds of seeds.

Teej

This festival is celebrated by the women of Hindu society.This festival falls on Bhadra Shukla Tritiya (the third day of the full moon of Bhadra).

This festival is also known as Haritalika.On this day all the women observe fasting for the whole day.It is believed that in the Vedic period,Parvati observed fasting on this day hoping to marry with Lord Shiva.And just after that she got married with him.So,the married women celebrate this festival for better status and long lives of their husbands,and the unmarried girls wish for good husbands.On the eve of Teej(The evening before the fasting day)all the women eat 'Dar' with the family members.Dar is a special meal,prepared for that special day of Teej.

Shree Panchami

The festival which is celebrated on the fifth day of Magh Shukla Panchami (the fifth day of the full moon day of Magh)is famous as Shree Pancchami.This is also called as Basanta Panchanmi as spring season begins from this day.Saraswati is worshipped on this occasion Saraswati is the goddess of learning and wisdom.Most of the people of Hindu community go to the near by Saraswati temple and worship her.This is the special day for the students.People believe that this students.People believe that day is the best day for their children to start formal learning because they believe that goddess Saraswati gives them a divine blessing on this day. In Buddhist community,this day is called as Manju Panchami.Manjushree is the god of learning for the Buddhists.

Udhauli/Ubhauli

This is the main festival of the Rai c ommunity.This festival is celebrated on two days of the year.The first is the Udhauli and other is the Ubhauli.Udhauli falls at Kartik/Mangsir and Ubhauli in Baishakh/Jestha.This festival is celebrated differently at different places.

Some people celebrate it with chandi Nach,some with Sakela or Sakewa or some with Sakela or Sakewa or some other with Baishake or Badanmet.It is because Rai community has different cultures at different places.At this festival Nakchhong(the priest)recites Mundhum at different religious places like Chandithan,Margathan or Mangkhim.At every household people celebrate this festival worshipping ancestors and dance playing with Dholjhyamta.They eat different delicious foods and enjoy together.

8

Land of the Landless of Nepal

In Hebrew, Nepal is still referred to as a "poor country," but in English development practitioners have long ago adopted the much nicer sounding term "impoverished." Progress seems to have come to the very discourse of progress itself. But in my bilingual program Tevel Be'Tzedek (The Earth in Justice), the interchangeability of "poor" and "impoverished" raises a question about the substance of this switch. "Impoverishment" is a word that promises a lot in terms of political consciousness. Not only does "impoverished" disrupt any assumed relationship between a person or community's moral character and their economic capabilities, it also implies an agent of impoverishment, a responsibility that goes beyond present circumstances and into history.

For example, when Nepal is introduced as a "poor" country, what is being referred to is the present. On the one hand, they are talking about the government's tiny budget, endlessly supplemented by program-specific grants from non-governmental organizations, foreign governments and different branches of the international government like the World Bank. More than 80% of the health, education and probably other budgets comes from these non-governmental governments, systems that are largely dysfunctional and unaccountable (while the Nepali Royal Army is an image of efficiency and uncommon job security). The idea is that the government is weak and poor, so the nongovernments have to help the government. The assumption is that if the government "worked," then everything in Nepal would be fixed, that essentially the problem with Nepal is poor governance.

On the other hand, they are talking about the poverty of the people. Although the vast majority of people in Nepal live in rural villages, when foreigners talk about poverty they are mostly talking about what they see in Kathmandu, the extremes symbolic of the rule. People collecting garbage to recycle, fishing through trash to find fruits to sell. Child porters carrying 170kg at a time, many under 12 years old (10% of the GDP or more is from child labour). Slum dwellers living on the banks of the garbage-choked Bagmati river, where no one else wants to live because of the monsoon floods. And of course, the infamous street children, who live their lives in the streets getting high on glue. Yesterday, one of the kids pointed to a stray dog and said cheerfully in Nepali "Just like me."

Probably like many third-world cities, Kathmandu assaults the average middle-class first worlder with both presence and absence. The presence of piles of burning garbage and throngs of people. The absence of recognizable signs of authority, from street signs and street lights to animal control, from paved roads to city planning. On the other hand, the absence of central authority only makes it all the more amazing at how good people can be at managing with each other. Although most of Kathmandu's residents have no access to any discussion on governance, Kathmandu (miraculously) works, day after day, probably with less theft and violent crimes than most of America's heavily-policed cities. Despite the poverty and inequality, Kathmandu's residents offer each other admirable amounts of their already limited space. One of the TBT workers said that his greatest culture shock upon returning to Israel is all about buses. In Nepal 30 people or more cram into a microbus and still manage patient smiles, even when sitting on top of each other. On the other hand in Israel, despite the large, roomy, air-conditioned bus traveling on the fully paved road, the people are far more impatient to say the least.

The poverty in Kathmandu is undeniable, sometimes described as "crushing." But when we say these people are 'impoverished,' that implies causes, agents, reasons. If they are impoverished, who or what is doing the impoverishing? And if they are crushed, who is doing the crushing? (And no, it can't just be a 'lack of awareness'). Unfortunately, the questions implied by the word 'impoverishment' remain largely inert in the absence of history.

My first exposure to history in Nepal is Forget Kathmandu: An Elegy for Democracy by Manjushree Thapa, a problematic and conflicted book by one of Nepal's elite liberal humanists trying to understand her country. The book and from the smattering of historical content in the program is that Nepal's "history" is actually two histories. First there is the widely known 'political history' of Nepal, frustrating as it is irrelevant. Beginning with the 'unification' of the country by a particular royal dynasty 250 years ago, this history is an endless series of soap-opera successions, betrayals, and power struggles with local and international powers backing opponents and making deals to top the intrigue. Most of Nepal's people are not mentioned, the assumption being that they are somehow implied in the endless royal drama. In 1950 the royal dictatorship was briefly replaced by their elite challengers/inheritors, political parties, who rode on popular desire for some alternative. They behaved in much the same way as different lineages of royal inheritors had, except with more instability, with ten governments taking power in as many years. The second half of the 20th century is a struggle for power between different segments of the royal family and the political parties, culminating in a second 1950's style popular movement followed by the reinstitution of parliamentary democracy in 1990. Then, out of nowhere, the People's War from 1996 to 2006, a ten year insurgency led by the Maoist communists of Nepal. Violence, refugees, natural disasters, broken treaties, a strange massacre in the royal family, and the negotiated settlement with the Maoists come in a rapid and incoherent succession, a feeling of watching a massive spectacle that one has no active part or understanding in. Thapa communicates this brilliantly in her book.

On the other hand, very much in the background and totally separate from this traditional telling of Nepali history, is the (depoliticized) economic history. Development projects exploding with the reinstitution of the royal dictatorship in 1960, and roughly since then a growing corpus of increasing statistics in a myriad of areas such as literacy, poverty, nutrition rates, number of schools, number of people. The arc of progress made of tiny numbers stretching out like rainbow while the politicians bicker.

If accepted, this history would lead one to forsake politics for the sake of the pure, light-bringing progress of economic development. While the politicians quibble, the apolitical non-governments have been the only ones to do Nepal any good. Give us economics, save us from politics. Although this history is unintelligible and explains nothing, it is its very unintelligibility that achieves its political ends: to make people stay as far away from politics, to make it reasonable to think that economic development can be apolitical, to dismiss history as hornet's nest of cynical power-politics that no person should even try to know or understand.

But under scrutiny, this history raises questions. For example, the People's War turns out not to have been launched by the Maoists. It began with government attacks on villages where the movement later to be known as the Maoists was operating. Apparently, they were trying to organize people separately from the political system, something that threatened the sovereignty of the government was considered a threat existential enough to warrant massacring some unarmed civilians (this pattern would be repeated). The resulting insurgency fought the government to a standstill and even today controls large swaths of Nepal's countryside.

Now, I'm not saying that the Maoists were perfect or selfless or even good, but rather that no insurgency can survive for one year, much less ten, much less*fight the government to a standstill* without massive popular support whose origins cannot be dismissed. Apparently they redistributed land in some places, forced banks to return confiscated land deeds, made landlords forgive massive debts, etc. On the other hand, Manjushree Thapa, the author of "Forget Kathmandu," probably echoes widespread assumptions among Kathmandu's urban intelligentsia about the Maoists: that the Maoist insurgency is a mindless pastime of impressionable villagers trying to vent their frustration at their own backwardness, or that most of their rural supporters are being coerced or threatened. These liberal elites explain that the insurgency is just an extreme symptom of a lack of development and/or "true" democracy. The march of development must be restored. The cynical, political past must be left behind in favour of it.

But there are more troubling facts. Leaders from a new 'Janjati' (ethnic/indigenous) party came to visit TBT, and they talked about all kinds of crazy things like the imposition of the caste system through a 'Hindu state,' how this imposition was used to dispossess people of their lands, how as recently as sixty years ago many people lost their land because elites had registered it in their own names. And of course, the sharecropper system that is one of the universal constants in Nepali rural life: most villagers must work the lands of rich, upper-caste, absentee landlords and pay half of their harvest as rent. Many if not most have lived on land that is not legally theirs for hundreds of years. Although the leaders who told us this were themselves elites with long histories in politics, quite possibly instrumentalizing their ethnic background for political support (but why is that only a problem when members of indigenous or marginalized ethnic groups do it?), this history was something different than the banal power contests that passed for history until then.

Yes, it turns out that not all is quiet and pastoral in the average Nepali village.TBT workers explained that most farmers did not own enough land to feed themselves, with the best land usually owned by a minority of wealthy (sometimes absentee) landlords. The unequal land situation forces poor/impoverished farmers to relentlessly plow both their lands and the lands they sharecrop, leading to soil degradation and decreasing yields. The choice between rural hunger and backbreaking labour on the one hand, and urban poverty on the other is steadily sharpening. Like so many third world cities, Kathmandu actually a refugee camp for the rural poor, whose minimal services are mostly funded and partially administered by nongovernmental organizations and foreign grants to prevent the situation from becoming too bad to be suffered quietly. Through first-hand experience, Tevel Be'Tzedek workers have learned that virtually all of Kathmandu's poverty is village poverty transported, that the urban poor are largely first generation rural refugees exchanging rural debt slavery for urban wage slavery.

Virtually everyone with a grassroots experience of social problems in Nepal knows that the problem is in the villages, that the problem disproportionately affects lower-caste/ethnic groups, and that the problem is land. Much fewer people have an idea of *how* this situation came about, how 80% of rural people came to own only 20% of the arable land.

But precisely at this point, the conversation ends. This is the end of the road for NGOs, because the history of land ownership is Nepal is a *political* history, and the question of land distribution is a political question. The separation of Nepal's political history and its economic future must remain sacred and respected. After all, politics/history is impossible to understand and frustrating, it is best avoided. For all intents and purposes, then, the question of the historical origins of the very crushing poverty that NGOs seek to address is avoided.

This is a testament to how coincidental history is to the work of most development NGOs, a testament also to the limits of what "impoverishment" can mean in these circles. Obviously, the answer to the question of "how things came to be this way" would force nongovernmental organizations to deal with what is *politically* wrong in Nepal, to trace economics and politics back to the point where they become inseparable, then to trace it back to the present and stitch economics and politics back up again. It would force NGOs to grapple not only with the "impoverished," but also with the political, economic and social actors, processes and systems that *have and continue to impoverish them.*

Perhaps the negative practical consequences of such a move are so great that they make it impossible to think it about openly. Wealthy land owners are after all actively running both Nepal's government and many of its non-governments. But there is also a sense that TBT as a foreign organization has no legitimacy to look at the issue historically and politically. In Tevel B'Tzedek a series of largely informal understandings have arisen out of the direct experience of two years of trial and error. One is the sense that the mission is to learn about and empower the people we work with to think about the problems themselves, because they have legitimacy we do not to resist their enslavement. Although TBT volunteer activities have been formally confined to educational work related to health, nutrition, and agricultural improvement, there is a sense that there is a broader direction to the work that will somehow lead to greater autonomy and independent action, mainly exemplified by women's groups and theater groups that aim to develop autonomous thought and expression in groups.

9

Buddhism in Nepal

About 11% of Nepal's population practices Buddhism, consisting mainly of groups of Tibeto-Burman origin.

OVERVIEW

Buddhist influences are evident in the culture of Nepal, including that of many Hindu and Animist castes. Due to Nepal's close proximity to Tibet, Tibetan Buddhism is the most widely practised form.

The Newar practice Vajrayana Buddhism, which is another name for Tibetan Buddhism. Many Buddhist groups are also influenced by Hinduism. Buddhism is the dominant religion of the thinly-populated northern areas, which are inhabited by Tibetan-related peoples, namely the Sherpa, Lopa, Manangi, Thakali, Lhomi, Dolpa and Nyimba. They constitute a small minority of the country's population.

Ethnic groups that live in central Nepal, such as Gurung, Lepcha, Tamang, Magar, Newar, Yakkha, Thami and Chepang, are also followers of Buddhism. These ethnic groups have larger populations compared to their northern neighbours. They came under the influence of Hinduism due to their close contacts with the Hindu castes. In turn, many of them eventually adopted Hinduism and have been largely integrated into the caste system.

The Kirant tribes, especially the Limbu and the Rai, have also adopted Tibetan Buddhist practises from their Buddhist neighbours. The Jirel, which is considered a Kirata tribe, have also adopted Tibetan Buddhism.

BUDDHIST TEMPLES IN NEPAL

Bodnath: Bodnath is one of the holiest Buddhist sites in the area of Kathmandu, Nepal. The Buddhist stupa of Bodnath dominates the skyline. The influx of large populations of Tibetan refugees from China has seen the construction of Tibetan Gompas around the Bodnath.

Swayambhunath: Swayambhunath is one of the holiest Buddhist sites in the area of Kathmandu. It sits on a hill overlooking the city.

Mythology: According to Swayambhu Puran, the entire valley was once filled with an enormous lake, out of which grew a lotus. The valley came to be known as Swayambhu, meaning "Self-Created." The Bodhisatva Manjushri had a vision of the lotus at Swayambhu and traveled there to worship it. In order to make the site more accessible to human pilgrims, Manjushri cut a gorge through the mountains surrounding the valley. The water drained out of the lake, leaving the valley in which Kathmandu now lies. The lotus was transformed into a hill and the flower become the Swayambhunath stupa.

History: Swayambhunath is among the oldest religious sites in Nepal. By the 5th century, it had already become an important destination for Buddist pilgrims. The history of the site itself dates back to long before the arrival of Buddhism in the Kathmandu valley. Although the site is considered Buddhist, the place is revered by both Buddhists and Hindus. Numerous Hindu kings are known to have paid their homage to the temple including the most powerful king of Kantipur-Pratap Malla.

Architecture: The stupa consists of a dome at the base. Above the dome, there is a cubical structure present with eyes of Buddha looking in all four directions. There are pentagonal Toran present above each of the four sides with statues engraved in them. Behind and above the torana there are thirteen tiers.

Above all the tiers, there is a small space above which the Gajur is present.

Symbology: The dome at the base represents the entire world. When a person awakes (represented by eyes of mercy and self knowledge) from the bonds of the world, the person reaches the state a bit higher. After that, the person has to cross thirteen stages represented by the tiers before attaining Nirvana.

DEPARTURE AND ASCETIC LIFE

At the age of 29, Siddhartha left his palace in order to meet his subjects. Despite his father's effort to remove the sick, aged and suffering from the public view, Siddhartha was said to have seen an old man. Disturbed by this, when told that all people would eventually grow old by his charioteer Channa, the prince went on further trips where he encountered, variously, a diseased man, a decaying corpse, and an ascetic. Deeply depressed by these sights, he sought to overcome old age, illness, and death by living the life of an ascetic. Siddhartha escaped his palace, accompanied by Channa aboard his horse Kanthaka, leaving behind this royal life to become a mendicant. It is said that, "the horse's hooves were muffled by the gods" to prevent guards from knowing the Bodhisatta's departure. This event is traditionally called "The Great Departure". Siddhartha initially went to Rajagaha and began his ascetic life by begging for alms in the street. Having been recognised by the men of King Bimbisara, Bimbisara offered him the throne after hearing of Siddhartha's quest. Siddhartha rejected the offer, but promised to visit his kingdom of Magadha first, upon attaining enlightenment.

Siddhartha left Rajagaha and practised under two hermit teachers. After mastering the teachings of Alara Kalama (Skr. Ara a Kalama), Siddhartha was asked by Kalama to succeed him, but moved on after being unsatisfied with his practices. He then became a student of Udaka Ramaputta (Skr. Udraka Ramaputtra), but although he achieved high levels of meditative consciousness and was asked to succeed Ramaputtra, he was still not satisfied with his path, and moved on.

Ṡiddhartha and a group of five companions led by Kaundinya then set out to take their austerities even further. They tried to find enlightenment through near total deprivation of worldly goods, including food, practising self-mortification. After nearly starving himself to death by restricting his food intake to around a leaf or nut per day, he collapsed in a river while bathing and almost drowned. Siddhartha began to reconsider his path. Then, he remembered a moment in childhood in which he had been watching his father start the season's slowing, and he had fallen into a naturally concentrated and focused state that was blissful and refreshing, the jhana.

Enlightenment

After asceticism and concentrating on meditation and Anapana-sati (awareness of breathing in and out), Siddhartha is said to have discovered what Buddhists call the Middle Way—a path of moderation away from the extremes of self-indulgence and self-mortification. He accepted a little milk and rice pudding from a village girl named Sujata, who wrongly believed him to be the spirit that had granted her a wish, such was his emaciated appearance.

Then, sitting under a pipal tree, now known as the Bodhi tree in Bodh Gaya, India, he vowed never to arise until he had found the Truth. Kaundinya and the other four companions, believing that he had abandoned his search and become undisciplined, left. After 49 days meditating, at the age of 35, he attained Enlightenment; according to some traditions, this occurred approximately in the fifth lunar month, and according to others in the twelfth. Gautama, from then on, was known as the *Buddha* or "Awakened One." Buddha is also sometimes translated as "The Enlightened One." Often, he is referred to in Buddhism as Shakyamuni Buddha or "The Awakened One of the Shakya Clan."

At this point, he is believed to have realized complete awakening and insight into the nature and cause of human suffering which was ignorance, along with steps necessary to eliminate it. This was then categorized into 'Four Noble Truths'; the state of supreme liberation—possible for any being—was called Nirvana. He then allegedly came to possess the Nine Characteristics, which are said to belong to every Buddha.

According to one of the stories in the *Ayacana Sutta* (Samyutta Nikaya VI.1), a scripture found in the Pail and other canons, immediately after his Enlightenment, the Buddha was wondering whether or not he should teach the *Dharma* to human beings.

He was concerned that, as human beings were overpowered by greed, hatred and delusion, they would not be able to see the true *dharma*, which was subtle, deep and hard to understand.

However, Brahma Sahampati, interceded and asked that he teach the *dharma* to the world, as "there will be those who will understand the *Dharma*". With his great compassion to all beings in the universe, the Buddha agreed to become a teacher.

Formation of the Sangha

After becoming enlightened, two merchants whom the Buddha met, named Tapussa and Bhallika became the first lay disciples. They are given some hairs from the Buddha's head, which are believed to now be enshrined in the Shwe Dagon Temple in Rangoon, Burma. The Buddha intended to visit Asita, and his former teachers, Alara Kalama and Uddaka Ramaputta to explain his findings, but they had already died.

The Buddha thus journeyed to Deer Park near Varanasi (Benares) in northern India, he set in motion the Wheel of Dharma by delivering his first sermon to the group of five companions with whom he had previously sought enlightenment.

They, together with the Buddha, formed the first sough, the company of Buddhist monks, and hence, the first formation of Triple Gem (Buddha, Dharma and Sangha) was completed, with Kaundinya becoming the first stream-enterer. All five soon become arahants, and with the conversion of Yasa and fifty four of his friends, the number of arahants swelled to 60 within the first two months. The conversion of the three Kassapa brothers and their 200, 300 and 500 disciples swelled the sangha over 1000, and they were dispatched to explain the dharma to the populace.

It is unknown what the Buddha's mother tongue was, and no conclusive documentation has been made at this point. It is likely that he preached and his teachings were originally preserved in a variety of closely related Middle Indo-Aryan dialects, of which Pail may be a standardization.

Travels and Teaching

For the remaining 45 years of his life, the Buddha is said to have travelled in the Gangetic Plain, in what is now Uttar Pradesh, Bihar and southern Nepal, teaching his doctrine and discipline to an extremely diverse range of people— from nobles to outcaste street sweepers, mass murderers such as Angulimala and cannibals such as Alavaka. This extended to many adherents of rival philosophies and religions. The Buddha founded the community of Buddhist monks and nuns (the *Sangha*) to continue the dispensation after his *Parinirvana* (Pail: Parinibbana) or "complete Nirvana", and made thousands of converts. His religion was open to all races and classes and had no caste structure. He was also subject to attack from opposition religious groups, including attempted murders and framings.

The sangha travelled from place to place in India, expounding the dharma. This occurred throughout the year, except during the four months of the vassana rainy season. Due to the heavy amount of flooding, travelling was difficult, and ascetics of all religions in that time did not travel, since it was more difficult to do so without stepping on submerged animal life, unwittingly killing them. During this period, the sangha would retreat to a monastery, public park or a forest and people would come to them.

The first vassana was spent at Varanasi when the sangha was first formed. After this, he travelled to Rajagaha, the capital of Magadha to visit King Bimbisara, in accordance with his promise after enlightenment. It was during this visit that Sariputta and Mahamoggallana were converted by Assaji, one of the first five disciples; they were to become the Buddha's two foremost disciples. The Buddha then spent the next three seasons at Veluvana Bamboo Grove monastery in Rajagaha, the capital of Magadha. The monastery, which was of a moderate distance from the city centre was donated by Bimbisara.

Upon hearing of the enlightenment, Suddhodana dispatched royal delegations to ask the Buddha to return to Kapilavastu. Nine delegations were sent in all, but the delegates joined the sangha and became arahants. Neglecting worldly matters, they did not convey their message. The tenth delegation, led by Kaludayi, a childhood friend, resulted in the message being successfully conveyed as well as becoming an arahant.

Since it was not the vassana, the Buddha agreed, and two years after his enlightenment, took a two month journey to Kapilavastu by foot, preaching the dharma along the way. Upon his return, the royal palace had prepared the midday meal, but since no specific invitation had come, the sangha went for an alms round in Kapilavastu. Hearing this, Suddhodana hastened to approach the Buddha, stating "Ours is the warrior lineage of Mahamassata, and not a single warrior has gone seeking alms", to which the Buddha replied. That is not the custom of your royal lineage.

But it is the custom of my Buddha lineage. Several thousands of Buddhas have gone by seeking alms Suddhodana invited the sangha back to the royal palace for the meal, followed by a dharma talk, after which he became a sotapanna. During the visit, many members of the royal family joined the sangha. His cousins Ananda and Anuruddha were to become two of his five chief disciples. His son Rahula also joined the sangha at the age of seven, and was one of the ten chief disciples. His half-brother Nanda also joined the sangha and became an arahant. Another cousin Devadatta also became a monk although he later became an enemy and tried to kill the Buddha on multiple occasions.

Of his disciples, Sariputta, Mahamoggallana, Mahakasyapa, Ananda and Anuruddha comprised the five chief disciples. His ten foremost disciples were completed by the quintet of Upali, Subhoti, Rahula, Mahakaccana and Punna.

In the fifth vassana, the Buddha was staying at Mahavana near Vesali. Hearing of the impending death of Suddhodana, the Buddha went to his father and preached the dharma, and Suddhodana became an arahant prior to death. The death and cremation led to the creation of the order of nuns. Buddhist texts record that he was reluctant to ordain women as nuns. His foster mother Maha Pajapati approached him asking to join the sangha, but the Buddha refused, and began the journey from Kapilavastu back to Rajagaha.

Maha Pajapati was so intent on renouncing the world that she led a group of royal Sakyan and Koliyan ladies, following the sangha to Rajagaha. The Buddha eventually accepted them five years after the formation of the Sangha on the grounds that their capacity for enlightenment was equal to that of men, but he gave them certain additional rules (Vinaya) to follow. This occurred after Ananda interceded on their behalf. Yasodhara also became a nun, with both becoming arahants.

During his ministry, Devadatta (who was not an arahant) frequently tried to undermine the Buddha. At one point Devadatta asked the Buddha to stand aside to let him lead the sangha. The Buddha declined, and stated that Devadatta's actions did not reflect on the Triple Gem, but on him alone. Devadatta conspired with Prince Ajatasattu, son of Bimbisara, so that they would kill and usurp the Buddha and Bimbisara respectively. Devadatta attempted three times to kill the Buddha. The first attempt involved the hiring of a group of archers, whom upon meeting the Buddha became disciples. A second attempt followed when Devadatta attempted to roll a large boulder down a hill. It hit another rock and splintered, only grazing the Buddha in the foot. A final attempt by plying an elephant with alcohol and setting it loose again failed. Failing this, Devadatta attempted to cause a schism in the sangha, by proposing extra restrictions on the vinaya. When the Buddha declined, Devadatta started a breakaway order, criticising the Buddha's laxity. At first, he managed to convert some of the bhikkhus, but Sariputta and Mahamoggallana expounded the dharma to them and succeeded in winning them back.

When the Buddha reached the age of 55, he made Ananda his chief attendant.

Death/Mahaparinirvana

According to the Mahaparinibbana Sutta of the Pail canon, at the age of 80, the Buddha announced that he would soon reach Parinirvana or the final deathless state abandoning the earthly body.

After this, the Buddha ate his last meal, which he had received as an offering from a blacksmith named Cunda. Falling violently ill, Buddha instructed his attendant Ananda to convince Cunda that the meal eaten at his place had nothing to do with his passing and that his meal would be a source of the greatest merit as it provided the last meal for a Buddha. Mettanando and von Hinuber argue that the Buddha died of mesenteric infarction, a symptom of old age, rather than food poisoning. The precise contents of the Buddha's final meal are not clear, due to variant scriptural traditions and ambiguity over the translation of certain significant terms; the Theravada tradition generally believes that the Buddha was offered some kind of pork, while the Mahayana tradition believes that the Buddha consumed some sort of truffle or other mushroom.

The Mahayana Vimalakirti Sutra claims, that the Buddha doesn't really become ill or old but purposely presents such an appearance only to teach those born into samsara about the impermanence and pain of defiled worlds and to encourage them to strive for Nirvana.

"Reverend Ananda, the Tathagatas have the body of the Dharma—not a body that is sustained by material food. The Tathagatas have a transcendental body that has transcended all mundane qualities. There is no injury to the body of a Tathgata, as it is rid of all defilements. The body of a Tathagata is un-compounded and free of all formative activity. Reverend Ananda, to believe there can be illness in such a body is irrational and unseemly!' Nevertheless, since the Buddha has appeared during the time of the five corruptions, he disciplines living beings by acting lowly and humble."

Ananda protested Buddha's decision to enter Parinirvana in the abandoned jungles of Culinary (present-day Kushinagar, India) of the Malla kingdom. Buddha, however, reminded Ananda how Kushinara was a land once ruled by a righteous wheel-turning king that resounded with joy:

Kusavati, Ananda, resounded unceasingly day and night with ten sounds—the trumpeting of elephants, the neighing of horses, the rattling of chariots, the beating of drums and tabours, music and song, cheers, the clapping of hands, and cries of "Eat, drink, and be merry!"

Buddha then asked all the attendant Bhikshus to clarify any doubts or questions they had. They had none. He then finally entered Parinirvana. The Buddha's final words were, "All composite things pass away. Strive for your own liberation with diligence." The Buddha's body was cremated and the relics were placed in monuments or stupas, some of which are believed to have survived until the present. For example, The Temple of the Tooth or "Dalada Maligawa" in Sri Lanka is the place where the relic of the right tooth of Buddha is kept at present.

According to the Pail historical chronicles of Sri Lanka, the Dpavasa and Mahvacsa, the coronation of Ashoka (Pail: Ashoka) is 218 years after the death of Buddha. According to one Mahayana record in Chinese, the coronation of Hooka is 116 years after the death of Buddha. Therefore, the time of Buddha's passing is either 486 BCE according to The ravada record or 383 BCE according to Mahayana record. However, the actual date traditionally accepted as the date of the Buddha's death in The ravada countries is 544 or 543 BCE, because the reign of Hooka was traditionally reckoned to be about 60 years earlier than current estimates.

At his death, the Buddha told his disciples to follow no leader, but to follow his teachings (dharma). However, at the First Buddhist Council, Mahakasyapa was held by the sangha as their leader, with the two chief disciples Mahamoggallana and Sariputta having died before the Buddha.

Physical Characteristics

Buddha is perhaps one of the few sages for whom we have mention of his rather impressive physical characteristics. A kshatriya by birth, he had military training in his upbringing, and by Shakyan tradition was required to pass tests to demonstrate his worthiness as a warrior in order to marry. He had a strong enough body to be noticed by one of the kings and was asked to join his army as a general. He is also believed by Buddhists to have "the 32 Signs of the Great Man".

The Brahmin Sonadanda described him as "handsome, good-looking, and pleasing to the eye, with a most beautiful complexion. He has a godlike form and countenance, he is by no means unattractive."

"It is wonderful, truly marvellous, how serene is the good Gotama's appearance, how clear and radiant his complexion, just as the golden jujube in autumn is clear and radiant, just as a palm-tree fruit just loosened from the stalk is clear and radiant, just as an adornment of red gold wrought in a crucible by a skilled goldsmith, deftly beaten and laid on a yellow-cloth shines, blazes and glitters, even so, the good Gotama's senses are calmed, his complexion is clear and radiant."

A disciple named Vakkali, who later became an Arahant, was so obsessed by Buddha's physical presence that Buddha had to tell him to stop and reminded Vakkali to know Buddha through the Dhamma and not physical appearances.

Although the Buddha was not represented in human form until around the 1st century CE, the physical characteristics of fully-enlightened Buddhas are described by the Buddha in the Digha Nikaya's *LakkhaGa Sutta.* In addition, the Buddha's physical appearance is described by Yasodhara to their son Rahula upon the Buddha's first post-Enlightenment return to his former princely palace in the non-canonical Pail devotional hymn, *Narasiha Geisha* ("The Lion of Men").

Many Westerners associate the name "Buddha" with figurine depictions of a certain fat, bald, smiling person. This is inaccurate, as the person in these figurines is not Buddha at all, but Budai, a Chinese Buddhist monk who lived in the 10th century CE.

Teachings

Some scholars believe that some portions of the Pail Canon and the Agamas could contain the actual substance of the historical teachings (and possibly even the words) of the Buddha. This is not the case for the later Mahayana Sutras. The scriptural works of Early Buddhism precede the Mahayana works chronologically, and are treated by many Western scholars as the main credible source for information regarding the actual historical teachings of Gautama Buddha. Some of the fundamentals of the teachings of Gautama Buddha are:

- The Four Noble Truths: that suffering is an inherent part of existence; that the origin of suffering is ignorance and the main symptoms of that ignorance are attachment and craving; that attachment and craving can be ceased; and that following the Noble Eightfold Path will lead to the cessation of attachment and craving and therefore suffering.

- The Noble Eightfold Path: right understanding, right thought, right speech, right action, right livelihood, right effort, right mindfulness, and right concentration.
- Dependent origination: that any phenomenon 'exists' only because of the 'existence' of other phenomena in a complex web of cause and effect covering time past, present and future. Because all things are thus conditioned and transient (anicca), they have no real independent identity (anatta).
- Rejection of the infallibility of accepted scripture: Teachings should not be accepted unless they are borne out by our experience and are praised by the wise.
- *Anicca* (Sanskrit: *anitya*): That all things are impermanent.
- *Dukkha* (Sanskrit: *dukha*): That all beings suffer from all situations due to unclear mind.
- *Anatta* (Sanskrit: *anatman*): That the perception of a constant "self" is an illusion.

However, in some Mahayana schools, these points have come to be regarded as more or less subsidiary. There is some disagreement amongst various schools of Buddhism over more esoteric aspects of Buddha's teachings, and also over some of the disciplinary rules for monks. According to tradition, the Buddha emphasized ethics and correct understanding. He questioned the average person's notions of divinity and salvation. He stated that there is no intermediary between mankind and the divine; distant gods are subjected to karma themselves in decaying heavens; and the Buddha is solely a guide and teacher for the sentient beings who must tread the path of Nirvga (Pail: Nibbana) themselves to attain the spiritual awakening called *bodhi* and see truth and reality as it is. The Buddhist system of insight and meditation practice is not believed to have been revealed divinely, but by the understanding of the true nature of the mind, which must be discovered by personally treading a spiritual path guided by the Buddha's teachings.

THE MATERIALISM OF BUDDHA

Let us assume that, far from denying the Ego, Buddha believed in it, in his heart of hearts,—believed in it with the depth and subtlety of belief which are characteristic of Indian idealism,—believed in it as the "unbeholden essence" of all things, as the all-generating, all-sustaining life which individualizes itself in every human breast, yet is what it really is at the heart of the Universe, and nowhere else. What would be the attitude of one who so conceived of the Ego towards the popular belief—popular, one may safely conjecture, in Buddha's day as in ours—in the intrinsic reality of the individualized Ego, or individual soul? That the Ego is not real, in the fullest sense of the word, till it has become one with the Universal Soul, is the postulate on which all his philosophy, both as a whole and under each of its aspects, would be hinged. On its way to the goal of union with the Divine, the individual soul must needs pass through many stages of unreality. So long as it retains its sense of isolation, its mistaken sense of I-ness, it is, comparatively speaking, unreal. What is real in it is its potential universality. What is unreal is what it regards as of its very essence,—its individuality, its sense of separateness from all other things. Had Buddha looked at the problem of selfhood from the standpoint of Indian idealism, he would have seen that the popular belief in the intrinsic value of the individual Soul is fundamentally false, not on the plane of metaphysical speculation only, but on every plane of human life; and he would have set himself to combat it in each of its many forms.

Of the many forms that it takes I need not speak at length. The materialism of him who identifies his soul (his "self") with his body, or who conceives of it as the "totality" of his own sensations, perceptions, or other states of consciousness; the semi-materialism of him who (like the pious Christian) regards the soul as "something which flies out away from the body at death," or as one of many parts or organs of a complex being; the sentimental clinging to individuality; the metaphysical clinging to individuality;—these may be mentioned as typical forms of that reluctance to regard the Universal Soul as the only true self, which is so characteristic of popular thought in all the stages of its development, and against which Buddha, if I have not misread his philosophy, must have waged a relentless war.

If I am asked why Buddha, who eschewed metaphysical controversy, should have thought it necessary to combat a belief which seems to be primarily metaphysical, my answer is that the belief is not primarily metaphysical, that on the contrary it is the reflection in consciousness of a deep-seated instinct which has vital ethical consequences—the instinct to affirm the ordinary self, to accept it, minister to it, magnify it, rest in it—in a word, the egoistic instinct, the hidden root of every form of spiritual evil, and the first and last of moral defects. As the suppression of egoism was the very end and aim of Buddha's scheme of life, and as in this matter the distinction between theory on the one hand and sentiment, desire, and impulse on the other, is hard to draw and easy to efface, it was but natural that Buddha should wage war against the egoistic instinct even when it disguised itself as a semi-philosophical theory.

But he waged that war, as he did everything else that he took in hand, within the limits prescribed by his own "sweet reasonableness" and exalted common-sense. Leaving it to the metaphysical experts to wrangle over the more abstract aspects of the problem of selfhood, he contented himself with combating on quasi-popular grounds the popular delusion that the individual Ego is real, permanent, self-contained.

Let us assume this much; and we shall see a new meaning in each of the many passages on which Western criticism has based its theory that denial of the Ego was the cardinal article of Buddha's creed. We shall see that, whenever he seems to be denying existence to the Ego as such, what he is really doing is to deny reality to the individual Ego, to the ordinary surface self.

Let us first consider a dialogue in which the principal speaker is the venerable Sariputta, but in which the arguments advanced may well have been devised by Buddha himself, coinciding as they do with arguments which he is reported to have used in one of his early discourses.

A monk, named Yamaka, had convinced himself, as many modern interpreters of Buddhism have done, that the "doctrine taught by the Blessed One "amounted to this, "that on the dissolution of the body the monk who has lost all depravity is annihilated, perishes, and does not exist after death." His fellow-monks urged him to abandon what they regarded as a "wicked heresy," but to no purpose. At last they besought the venerable Sariputta to "draw near" to Yamaka and try to convert him to a truer view of the Blessed One's teaching.

"And the venerable Sariputta consented by his silence. Then the venerable Sariputta in the evening of the day arose from meditation, and drew near to where the venerable Yamaka was; and having drawn near he greeted the venerable Yamaka, and having passed the compliments of friendship and civility, he sat down respectfully on one side. And seated respectfully at one side, the venerable Sariputta spoke to the venerable Yamaka as follows: 'Is the report true, brother Yamaka, that the following wicked heresy has sprung up in your mind: Thus do I understand the doctrine taught by the Blessed One, that on the dissolution of the body the monk who has lost all depravity is annihilated, perishes, and does not exist after death?'

"'Even so, brother, do I understand the doctrine taught by the Blessed One, that on the dissolution of the body the monk who has lost all depravity is annihilated, perishes, and does not exist after death.'

"'What think you, brother Yamaka? Is form permanent, or transitory?"

"'It is transitory, brother.'

"'And that which is transitory—is it evil, or is it good?'

"'It is evil, brother.'

"'And that which is transitory, evil, and liable to change—is it possible to say of it: This is mine—this am I—this is my Ego?'

"'Nay, verily, brother.'

"'Is sensation... perception... the predispositions... consciousness, permanent, or transitory?'

"'It is transitory, brother.'

"'And that which is transitory—is it evil, or is it good?'

"'It is evil, brother.'

"'And that which is transitory, evil, and liable to change—is it possible to say of it: This is mine; this am I; this is my Ego?'

"'Nay, verily, brother Yamaka.'

"'Accordingly, brother Yamaka, as respects all form whatsoever—as respects all sensation whatsoever—as respects all perception whatsoever—as respects all predispositions whatsoever—as respects all consciousness whatsoever, past, future or present, be it subjective or existing outside, gross or subtle, mean or exalted, far or near, the correct view in the light of the highest knowledge is as follows: This is not mine; this am I not; this is not my Ego.

"'Perceiving this, brother Yamaka, the learned and noble disciple conceives an aversion for form, conceives an aversion for sensation, conceives an aversion for perception, conceives an aversion for the predispositions, conceives an aversion for consciousness. And in conceiving this aversion he becomes divested of passion, and by the absence of passion he becomes free, and when he is free he becomes aware that he is free; and he knows that rebirth is exhausted, that he has lived the holy life, that he has done what it behaved him to do, and that he is no more for the world.

"'What think you, brother Yamaka? Do you consider form as the Saint?'

"'Nay, verily, brother.'

"'Do you consider sensation... perception... the predispositions... consciousness as the Saint?'

"'Nay, verily, brother.'

"'What think you, brother Yamaka? Do you consider the Saint as comprised in form?'

"'Nay, verily, brother.'

"'Do you consider the Saint as distinct from form?'

"'Nay, verily, brother.'

"'Do you consider the Saint as comprised in sensation?... as distinct from sensation?... as comprised in perception?... as distinct from perception?... as comprised in the predispositions?... as distinct from the predispositions?... as comprised in consciousness?... as distinct from consciousness?'

"'Nay, verily, brother.'

"'What think you, brother Yamaka? Are form, sensation, perception, the predispositions and consciousness united the Saint?'

"'Nay, verily, brother.'

"'What think you, brother Yamaka? Do you consider the Saint as a something having no form, sensation, perception, predispositions or consciousness?'

"'Nay, verily, brother.'

"'Considering now, brother Yamaka, that you fail to make out and establish the existence of the Saint in the present life, is it reasonable for you to say: Thus do I understand the doctrine taught by the Blessed One, that on the dissolution of the body the monk who has lost all depravity is annihilated, perishes, and does not exist after death?"

"'Brother Sariputta, it was because of my ignorance that I held this wicked heresy; but now that I have listened to the doctrinal instruction of the venerable Sariputta, I have abandoned that wicked heresy and acquired the true doctrine.'"

Mr H. C. Warren, from whose translation of the dialogue in his learned work, "Buddhism in Translation," I have made this extract, heads each page in the dialogue with the significant words, "There is no Ego." That is how he interprets the teaching of Sariputta. But surely what Sariputta intended to teach was the exact opposite of this. The monk Yamaka believed that at the death of the "Saint"—at the moment when his cycle of earth-lives had come to an end—he ceased to be. This belief, we are expressly told, was regarded as a "wicked heresy"; and Sariputta disabused Yamaka's mind of it by showing him that it was as difficult for him to "make out and establish" the existence of the "Saint" in the present life as in the life beyond death (and beyond rebirth). He reminds him, in words which, according to tradition, had been used by Buddha himself, that the Ego is not to be identified with form, with sensation, with perception, with the "predispositions," with consciousness, since each of these is transitory and therefore evil, and "of that which is transitory, evil and liable to change it is not possible to say 'This is mine; this am I; this is my Ego.'"

"The ignorant unconverted man... considers form in the light of an Ego, considers sensation... perception... the predispositions... consciousness in the light of an Ego," and therefore clings to those apparent "selves" though they are all transitory and evil. "The learned and noble disciple does not consider form, sensation, etc., in the light of an Ego," and he therefore detaches himself from each of those delusive "selves." Not a word is said, in any part of the discourse, in disproof of the existence of the Ego. The point of the argument is that each of the apparent Egos—the Ego of form, the Ego of sensation, and the rest—is unreal; and that the man who regards the Ego of the "Saint" as non-existent after death, because it will then be finally detached from form, sensation, etc., is bound by the logic of his own delusion to regard the Ego of the "Saint" as non-existent while on earth, since, if the "Saint" has indeed won deliverance, he will have finally detached himself, even while on earth, from each of those phantom Egos, and in doing so will have found his true self.

From this point it is possible to advance to two conclusions. As disbelief in the after-death existence of the "Saint" is a "wicked heresy," it stands to reason that it is also a "wicked heresy" to regard the "Saint"—the true Ego—as non-existent now. This is the first conclusion, which the Western critic who seeks to father upon Buddha his own denial of the Ego will do well to bear in mind. The second seems to have been tacitly drawn by both Sariputta and Yamaka, and to have carried conviction to the latter's mind. As it is obviously absurd to say that the "Saint" is non-existent now, it stands to reason that it is also absurd to say—as Yamaka had said—that the "Saint" will cease to be after death. The whole discourse is directed nominally against Yamaka's "wicked heresy," but really against the erroneous belief that the individual Ego, the Ego which is associated with form, with sensation, and the rest, is the true Ego,—a belief which had generated in Yamaka's mind the "wicked heresy" that "on the dissolution of the body" the Saint "is annihilated, perishes, and does not exist." Indeed it is no exaggeration to say that in this discourse disbelief in the reality of the Ego—the true Ego which transcends the limits of the transitory, and therefore passes beyond the reach of thought and language—is authoritatively condemned.

Dr. Rhys Davids lays great stress on a discourse in which various attempts to conceive of the existence of the Ego after death are condemned as heresies. Here, as in the dialogue which has just been considered, the Ego is that of the man who has won deliverance while still living on earth, and whose cycle of earth-lives is therefore coming to an end.

The prying attempt to follow the liberated Ego into the life beyond death, into the unimaginable bliss of Nirvana, is repelled as impertinent and delusive, and every form that it takes is condemned as a "heresy." The discourse ends with these words: "Mendicants [Monks], that which binds the Teacher [the Saint, the Perfect One] to existence is cut off; but his body still remains. While his body shall remain he will be seen by gods and men, but after the dissolution of the body, neither gods nor men will see him." "Would it be possible," asks Dr. Rhys Davids, "in a more complete and categorical manner to deny that there is any soul—anything of any kind, which continues to exist, in any manner, after death?"

This criticism (so characteristically Western) is as wide of the mark as is Mr Warren's headline comment on the dialogue between Sariputta and Yamaka. What the preacher is trying to enforce is what Sariputta had impressed upon Yamaka, that the Ego of the "Saint"—the true Ego, for the "Saint" is one who has found his true self does not exist after death in any form or mode which is comprehensible by human thought. Far from denying the existence of the Ego, the preacher is insisting on its transcendent reality. "Neither gods nor men" will see the "Saint" after death, not because he will then be non-existent, but because his being will have out-soared all the categories of human thought.

In these and other such discourses Buddha falls into line with the thinkers of the Upanishads, who described by a series of negations what they regarded as the true Ego,—the Divine in man. The coincidences between his teaching and theirs are so significant that the only way to account for them is to assume that his faith—the deepest faith of his heart—was in its essence identical with theirs.

If the account that he gave of the Ego was purely negative, if he abstained from positive statements (even in that paradoxical form which was dear to the thinkers of the Upanishads), the reason was that he wished men to find out for themselves, by following the Path of soul-expansion, what the Ego really is. He said to them, in thought if not in words: "The Ego is not this thing or that; it is not any of the things with which you are used to identify it. If you wish to know what it is, enter the Path and follow it to the end. Your question will then be answered, for it will have transformed itself into a burning thirst for the ideal and the divine; and in the bliss of Nirvana that thirst will be eternally slaked and eternally renewed."

Dr. Rhys Davids is confirmed in his belief that Buddha denied the Ego, by the fact that the "heresy of individuality" is one of the three "Fetters" which have to be broken on the very threshold of the new life. But here, as elsewhere, Buddha is denying the reality, not of the Ego as such, but of the individual Ego; in other words, he is condemning by implication the blindness of him who regards the limitations which his individuality imposes upon him as the essential conditions of his existence. So, too, when he names among the fetters which have to be broken in the later stages of the Eightfold Path, the desire for life in the worlds of form, and the desire for life in the formless worlds, he is thinking, not of the desire for life as such but of the desire for separate life, for the continuance of individuality,—the hydra-headed desire which is ever tending to counteract the centripetal energy of love.

There is one set of discourses on which those who regard Buddha as a negative dogmatist lay great stress,—the so-called Milinda dialogues, or conversations between the Greek King, Menanda, of Baktria, and Nagasena, the Buddhist teacher. Nagasena seems to have been an acute controversialist who loved argument for its own sake almost as much as Buddha disliked it, and who, had he lived in Europe in the Middle Ages, would probably have nailed theological or metaphysical theses to church-doors. That he had caught the deeper spirit of the Master's teaching is, to say the least, improbable; but that his discourses present to us an interpretation of that teaching, which had gained currency in his day, can scarcely be doubted.

I have elsewhere allowed, for argument's sake, that he may have had an academic antipathy to the Ego. If he had, his discourses do less than justice to their theme. The arguments by which a merely academic belief (or disbelief) is sustained are in the nature of things ineffective. The spiritual atmosphere of his age, the words that he finds himself compelled to use, even his own subconscious convictions—are all against the thinker. In the well known Chariot dialogue, Nagasena is supposed to have proved conclusively that "there is no Ego." I cannot see that he has done this, and I am by no means sure that he has attempted to do it. What he has proved is that, just as the name chariot belongs to the vehicle as a whole and not to any of its parts, so the name Nagasena belongs to the living being as a whole and not to any of his organs or faculties.

If the dialogue is directed against anything, it is directed against the vulgar belief that the Soul is a quasi-material something (like the babe of vapour in mediaeval art) which can be separated from the rest of the man, just as a wheel can be separated from the rest of the chariot; or again that the soul is one among many faculties which go to make up the whole man. The flame simile, which is also supposed to be directed against the soul-theory of the Brahmanic philosophy, is one which that theory, far from rejecting, would accept as singularly apt. For just as fire uses up fuel, and in doing so manifests itself as flame (that is, as burning fuel), so the Soul, in its journey through the earth-life, continually uses up physical matter, and in doing so manifests itself as a living body (that is, as physical matter fused and vitalized by the Soul-fire). When the Soul retires from the physical plane, the body, deprived of its vitalizing influence, disintegrates into dust, just as fuel, when its fire is extinct, turns to ashes; but the Soul itself (if we may follow its progress through the intervening stages of existence) continues to use up matter, though, as the matter used is now impalpable, the Soul-flame becomes invisible till the time comes for it to feed again on the fuel of physical nature,—in other words, to appear again on earth.

Even when Nagasena's hostility to the Ego is unmistakable, his belief in re-incarnation causes his arguments to miscarry. He may flatter himself that he has disproved the identity between A (who is living now) and B (the future inheritor of his Karma); but, as a believer in re-incarnation, he must needs take pains to prove that B will justly be held responsible for what A has done or left undone; and in his attempt to make good this point he has to admit (or rather insist) that the relation between A and B is exactly analogous to that between a "young girl" and the same girl "when grownup and marriageable."

Dr. Rhys Davids has truly said that Buddha's "whole training was Brahmanism; and that he probably deemed himself to be the most correct exponent of the spirit as distinct from the letter of the ancient faith." If this is a true statement of Buddha's attitude towards Brahmanism, it surely behoves the student of Buddhism to seek initiation into the deeper mysteries of the "ancient faith," before he attempts to interpret the creed of one who, while breaking with the letter of that faith, "deemed himself to be the most correct exponent of its spirit." This, however, is what the Western critic, with his instinctive contempt for alien modes of thought, is extremely reluctant to do. What he does, in nine cases out of ten, is to carry with him to the study of Buddhism the prejudices and prepossessions of Western thought—foremost among which is the assumption that nothing exists, in the order of nature, except what is perceptible by man's bodily senses—and to insist that the teaching of Buddha shall conform to these, and be measured by their standards. Hence arise misconceptions and misunderstandings which might have been avoided.

If Buddhism seems to our Western minds to abound in errors and anomalies, the reason is that we insist on looking at it through a distorting medium. One who had steeped himself in the spirit of the Brahmanic philosophy before he began his study of Buddhism, would see that wherever Buddha seems to be denying existence to the Ego, what he is really doing is to deny reality to the apparent Ego or superficial Self, so that he may thereby clear the way for the exposition, not in words but in the unwritten language of conduct, character, and life, of the profound conception which is the very quintessence of the "ancient faith,"—the conception "that Brahma and the Self—the true Self—are one."

THE SILENCE OF BUDDHA

IT is the silence of Buddha which has misled so many of his commentators. The teacher who, while pointing out to us the ultimate issues of life, keeps silence as to its ultimate realities and ultimate principles, must be prepared for his philosophy—the philosophy that is at the heart of his silence—to be misunderstood. It is not merely that he gives us no clue to the labyrinth of his deeper thoughts, and so leaves each of us free to explore that labyrinth for himself. There is another and a graver danger to which he exposes the faith of his heart. Of those who take a speculative interest in his ideas, few will be content to regard his silence as purely agnostic. The majority will see in it either the negation or the confirmation of their own philosophical prejudices. The positive dogmatist, who has made up his mind that the ultimate realities of existence are such and such, will regard it as a challenge and a defiance, and will apply to it the epithets which he reserves for denial of his own creed. The negative dogmatist will insist that it is a polite concession to the weakness of the "orthodox," and that behind it is a conception of life as fundamentally negative as his own. In either case the silence of the Master will be construed as equivalent to denial and revolt.

This is the fate which has befallen Buddha. Because he said nothing about God he is held—by the "orthodox" as well as by the "unbeliever"—to have "denied the divine." Because he said little about the "Self," and because that little was mainly negative, 1 he is held to have denied the Ego. And he is credited with all the consequences of these tremendous denials. He who on principle kept silence about what is, ultimate is supposed to have elaborated a complete system of negatively ultimate thought.

There is nothing in the history of human thought more dramatic or more significant than the silence of Buddha. Let us try to fathom its depths. That there is a deep spiritual meaning, that there was a deep spiritual conviction, at the heart of it can scarcely be doubted. It was not from indifference that Buddha, of all men, became and remained to the end an apparent agnostic. And, apart from indifference, though there may be silence about "great matters," there can be no agnosticism (in the sense of metaphysical neutrality) in the thinker's inner life. A state of perfect mental equilibrium is incompatible with living interest in the deeper problems of existence. The silence of Buddha seems to have been the deliberate fulfilment of a self-imposed vow. At any rate there was a strong purpose behind it; and that purpose must have been the outcome, not of philosophical indifference, but of some master theory of things.

The more closely I study the stories in which Buddha answers the overcurious with silence and gives his reasons for doing so, and the more freely I surrender myself to the subtle influence of their atmosphere, the stronger does my conviction become that Buddha kept silence, when metaphysical questions were discussed, not because he had nothing to say about great matters, but because he had far too much, because he was overwhelmed by the flood of his own mighty thoughts, and because the channels of expression which the riddle-mongers of his day invited him to use were both too narrow and too shallow to give his soul relief. As it is on the plane of spiritual emotion, so it is on the plane of spiritual thought. "Silence," says one of Shakespeare's characters,

"is the perfectest herald of joy:

I were but little happy if I could say how much."

The babbling river, as another poet reminds us, is overwhelmed and silenced by the flow of the tide-wave from the unfathomed sea. This simile has the beauty of truth. The mind that is visited by world-encompassing waves of thought (or of emotion) has more to say than words can express, or than other minds can receive. There are, indeed, some gifted souls for whom the channel of poetry provides an overflow (rather than an outflow) for their flooding thoughts. For the rest of us (as Buddha saw clearly) there is but one available outlet,—that of action, conduct, life; and life will have a stronger purpose and a larger scope when silence is behind it than when its motive force is a flux of words. So eloquent and so significant is Buddha's own silence, that it seems at last, when one becomes familiar with it, to give a clearer insight into the secrets of his soul than any formulated confession of words could ever have done.

Let us now hear the reasons which Buddha himself (or those who spoke in his name) gave for his silence. Let us study the three stories which Dr. Oldenberg has selected as indicative of his attitude towards the questions with which the thinkers of his day perplexed themselves. The first runs thus:

"Then the wandering monk Vacchagotta went to where the Exalted One was staying. When he had come near him, he saluted him. When saluting him, he had interchanged friendly words with him, he sat down beside him. Sitting beside him the wandering monk Vacchagotta spake to the Exalted One, saying: 'How does the matter stand, venerable Gautama, is there the Ego?'

"'When he said this, the Exalted One was silent.

"'How then, venerable Gautama, is there not the Ego?'

"And still the Exalted One maintained silence. Then the wandering monk Vacchagotta rose from his seat and went away.

"But the venerable ananda, when the wandering monk Vacchagotta had gone to a distance, soon said to the Exalted One:

"'Wherefore, sire, has the Exalted One not given an answer to the questions put by the wandering monk Vacchagotta?'

"'If I, ananda, when the wandering monk Vacchagotta asked me: "Is there the Ego?" had answered: "The Ego is," then that, ananda, would have confirmed the doctrine of the Samanas and Brahmanas who believe in permanence. If I, ananda, when the wandering monk Vacchagotta asked me: "Is there not the Ego?" had answered: "The Ego is not," then that, ananda, would have confirmed the doctrine of the Samanas and Brahmanas who believe in annihilation. If I, ananda, when the wandering monk Vacchagotta asked me: "Is there the Ego?" had answered: "The Ego is," would that have served my end, ananda, by producing in him the knowledge: all existences are non-Ego?'

"'That it would not, sire.'

"'But if I, ananda, when the wandering monk Vacchagotta asked me: "Is there not the Ego?" had answered: "The Ego is not," then that, ananda, would only have caused the wandering monk Vacchagotta to be thrown from one bewilderment into another: "My Ego, did it not exist before? but now it exists no longer!"'"

In this story Buddha gives two reasons for refusing to answer Vacchagotta's question. He is asked to answer Yes or No. Whichever answer he may give, some school of metaphysicians is sure to claim him as its own. And whichever answer he may give, he is sure to bewilder Vacchagotta.

That Buddha had no patience with the metaphysicians is made clear by this and by other stories. He had many quarrels with them. He objected to them for playing with words, with the result that on the one hand they drew people away from the main business of life and on the other hand profaned by the inadequacy of their symbols the deep mysteries which they professed to explore. He objected to the misconception of knowledge, of truth, of reality, which underlay their shallow dualism, and made it possible for them to assume that all the problems of existence could be brought to the issue of a simple Yes or a simple No. Above all, he deplored the loss of temper which the very futility of their wordy wrangling rendered inevitable,—the loss of charity, the loss of serenity, the loss of self-control, the loss of all the qualities which he had called upon men to cultivate. "The theory that the world is eternal, the theory that the world is infinite, the theory that the soul and the body are identical"—of each of these and of all kindred theories he says the same thing—"this theory is a jungle, a wilderness, a puppet show, a writhing and a fetter, and is coupled with misery, ruin, despair and agony and does not tend to aversion, absence of passion, cessation, quiescence, knowledge, supreme wisdom and Nirvana."

But we shall the better understand his antipathy to the metaphysicians if we consider the second of his reasons for remaining silent,—his fear of either misleading or bewildering Vacchagotta. Dr. Oldenberg thinks that in giving this reason he came very near to saying that there was no Ego, and that it was only regard for Vacchagotta's susceptibilities which kept him silent. This criticism is, I think, based on a misconception of Buddha's mental attitude.

Buddha saw clearly enough that the answer to Vacchagotta's question, as to all similar questions, was "Yes and No,"—"Yes" from this point of view, "No" from that. The words that are ascribed to him—words which may well have been his—suggest that some such thoughts as these were passing through his mind: "The Ego is real beyond all reality, but I cannot hope to make Vacchagotta understand this. If I tell him that the Ego is, he will assume that I mean by the word what he does, and so be led astray. If, foreseeing this, I tell him that the body is not the Ego, the sensations are not the Ego, the consciousness is not the Ego, and so forth,—if, in my desire to bring home to him the transcendent reality of the Ego, I refuse to allow him to identify it with any of those things which he has been accustomed to regard as real,—he will come to the conclusion that there is no Ego, that the word is an empty name.

If, on the other hand, I tell him that, as he understands the word, there is no Ego, that the sense of individuality, of separateness, which seems to him to be of the essence of the sense of self, is delusive (separateness being the very negation of true selfhood), he will be equally bewildered. In either case he will feel that he has been living in a dream. What can I do, then, but keep silent?

Had Buddha shared Dr. Paul Carus' fundamental antipathy to the Ego—to the whole idea of selfhood—he would, I think, without hesitation have answered the monk's question with an uncompromising No; for metaphysical atomism, like every other development of materialism, is very easy to explain, the strength of materialism lying in this, that it is the precise system of thought which the average man, who had forgotten his mother's teaching and silenced the questionings of his heart, would—if he took to thinking—construct for himself. Had Buddha believed in the Ego, as the pious Christian believes in it, as a something (to use Dr. Rhys Davids' words) "which flies out away from the body" and retains its individuality for all time, he would have answered the monk's question with an unqualified "Yes"; for he would have known that the monk's conception of the Ego coincided with, or at any rate approximated to, his own.

That he said neither "Yes" or "No" suggests that he neither believed in the Ego, as the pious Christian believes in it, nor disbelieved in it, as the votary of the "religion of science" disbelieves in it; and leaves us free to conjecture that his conception of the Ego, whatever form it may have taken, transcended the range of ordinary thought and would not suffer itself to be translated into intelligible speech.

The second story has been thus epitomized for us by Dr. Oldenberg:

"The venerable Malukya comes to the Master, and expresses his astonishment that the Master's discourse leaves a series of the very most important and deepest questions unanswered. Is the world eternal or is it limited by bounds of time? Does the Perfect Buddha live on beyond death? Does the Perfect One not live on beyond death? It pleases me not, says the monk, that all this shall remain unanswered and I do not think it right; therefore I am come to the Master to interrogate him about these doubts. May it please Buddha to answer them if he can. 'But when anyone does not understand a matter and does not know it, then a straightforward man says: I do not understand that, I do not know that.'

"We see: the question of the Nirvana is brought before Buddha by that monk as directly and definitely as could ever be possible. And what answers Buddha? He says in his Socratic fashion, not without a touch of irony, 'What have I said to thee before now, Malukyaputta? Have I said, Come, Malukyaputta, and be my disciple; I shall teach thee whether the world is everlasting or not everlasting, whether the world is finite or infinite, whether the vital faculty is identical with the body or separate from it, whether the Perfect One lives on after death or does not live on, or whether the Perfect One lives on and at the same time does not live on after death, or whether he neither lives on nor does not live on?'

"'That thou hast not said, Sire.'

"'Or hast thou,' Buddha goes on, 'said to me: I shall be thy disciple, declare unto me, whether the world is everlasting or not everlasting, and so on?'

"This also must Malukya answer in the negative.

"'If a man,' Buddha proceeds, 'were struck by a poisoned arrow, and his friends and relatives called in a skilful physician, what if the wounded man said: "I shall not allow my wound to be treated until I know who the man is by whom I have been wounded, whether he is a noble, a Brahman, a Vaicya, a Cudra"—or if he said: "I shall not allow my wound to be treated until I know what they call the man who has wounded me, and of what family he is, whether he is tall or small or of middle stature, and how his weapon was made with which he has struck me." What would the end of the case be? The man would die of his wound.'

"Why has Buddha not taught his disciples, whether the world is finite or infinite, whether the saint lives on beyond death or not? Because the knowledge of these things does not conduct to progress in holiness, because it does not contribute to peace and enlightenment. What contributes to peace and enlightenment, Buddha has taught his own: the truth of suffering, the truth of the origin of suffering, the truth of the path to the cessation of suffering. 'Therefore, Malukyaputta, whatsoever has not been revealed by me, let that remain unrevealed, and what has been revealed, let it be revealed.'"

In this story Buddha claims to have taught his disciples all that they need to know and can be made to understand. More than this he cannot and will not teach them. He may know more about the deeper realities of existence than he chooses to reveal.

Malukya suggests that he should make open confession of his ignorance, but he makes no response to this. His reason for keeping silent is that, if men are to wait till Malukya's questions have been adequately answered, they will have to wait for ever, and meanwhile the main concerns of life—the pursuit of peace and enlightenment, the practice of self-control, the cultivation of sympathy—will be forgotten and neglected. The average man may either ask the "Doctors" to answer those great questions for him, or he may try to answer them for himself. The result will be the same in either case. The questions will never be answered; the Path will never be entered; and, what is worse, the evil passions which are generated by verbal controversy will poison the springs of spiritual life.

When we read this dialogue we seem to have travelled far from the Indian idea that knowledge of reality is the first condition of "salvation." But, in truth, we have never really quitted it. The metaphysical path to knowledge was one which Buddha looked upon with distrust and aversion; but knowledge itself—the knowledge which has its counterpart in inward enlightenment, the knowledge of reality which makes for peace and deliverance—was the very goal to which the Path was intended to lead.

The truth of things, as Buddha conceived of it, could not be set forth in a series of formulas, for (to go no further) the laws of language would make that impossible; but it could be lived up to and lived in to: and so he bade men control their passions and desires, and cultivate kindness and goodwill, that the consequent growth of their souls might be rewarded by the expansion of their consciousness and the deepening of their insight, till it became possible for them to know (in the truest sense of the word) the fleeting from the abiding, the phantasmal from the real.

The propositions which Malukya challenged Buddha to answer had but little meaning for him. This we may take for granted. But he might conceivably have waived them aside, and tried to disclose to his disciples the inner faith of his own heart.

That he made no attempt to do so does not prove that there was no master theory of things behind his formal teaching. When we read the words "whatsoever has not been revealed by me let that remain unrevealed," we cannot but feel that what "remained unrevealed" was something well worth revealing. What the silence of Buddha does prove, or at least suggest, is that the creed of his heart was too deep for words,—that the realities which it sought to encompass and co-ordinate far transcended the normal range of human thought.

What the first story left us free to conjecture, the second has suggested to us as a plausible hypothesis,—namely, that Buddha's silence was the outcome, not of the hollowness of his creed, but of the very abundance of his spiritual faith. The third story falls into line with the first and second, but brings us nearer to the same conclusion.

"King Pasenadi of Kosala, we are told, on one occasion on a journey between his two chief towns, Saketa and Savatthi, fell in with the nun Khema, a female disciple of Buddha, renowned for her wisdom. The King paid his respects to her, and inquired of her concerning the sacred doctrine.

"'Venerable lady,' asked the King, 'does the Perfect One exist after death?'

"'The Exalted One, O great King, has not declared: the Perfect One exists after death.'

"'Then does the Perfect One not exist after death, venerable lady?'

"'This also, O great King, the Exalted One has not declared: the Perfect One does not exist after death.'

"'Thus, venerable lady, the Perfect One does exist after death, and at the same time does not exist after death?—thus, venerable lady, the Perfect One neither exists after death, nor does he not exist?'

"The answer is still the same: the Exalted One has not revealed it....

"The King is astonished. 'What is the reason, venerable lady, what is the ground, on which the Exalted One has not revealed this?'

"'Permit me,' answers the nun, 'now to ask thee a question, O great King, and do thou answer me as the case seems to thee to stand. How thinks thou, O great King, hast thou an accountant, or a mint-master, or a treasurer, who could count the sands of the Ganges, who could say: there are there so many grains of sand, or so many hundreds, or thousands, or hundreds of thousands of grains of sand?'

"'No, venerable lady, I have not.'

"'Or hast thou an accountant, a mint-master, or a treasurer, who could measure the water in the great ocean, who could say: there are therein so many measures of water, or so many hundreds, or thousands, or hundreds of thousands of measures of water?'

"'No, venerable lady, I have not.'

"'And why not? The great ocean is deep, immeasurable, unfathomable. So also, O great King, if the existence of the

Perfect One be measured by the predicates of corporeal form: these predicates of the corporeal form are abolished in the Perfect One, their root is severed, they are hewn away like a palm tree and laid aside, so that they cannot germinate again in the future. Released, O great King, is the Perfect One from this, that his being should be gauged by the measure of the corporeal world: he is deep, immeasurable, unfathomable as the great ocean. "The Perfect One exists after death," this is not apposite; "the Perfect One does not exist after death," this also is not apposite; "the Perfect One at once exists and does not exist after death," this also is not apposite; "the Perfect One neither does nor does not exist after death," this also is not apposite.'

"But Pasenadi, the King of Kosala, received the nun Khema's discourse with satisfaction and approbation, rose from his seat, bowed reverently before Khema, the nun, turned and went away."

Supreme reality—the ideal object of all high thinking, of all knowledge, of all wisdom—is here symbolized by the Perfect One's existence. And that existence, we are told, is "deep, unfathomable, immeasurable as the great ocean." "When such a reason," says Dr. Oldenberg, "is assigned for the waiving of the question as to whether the Perfect One lives for ever, is not this very giving of a reason itself an answer? And is not this answer a Yes?

No being in the ordinary sense, but still assuredly not a non-being; a sublime positive, of which thought has no idea, for which language has no expression, which beams out to meet the cravings of the thirsty for immortality in that same splendour of which the apostle says: 'Eye hath not seen, nor ear heard, neither have entered into the heart of man, the things which God hath prepared for them that love Him.'"

The nun Khema had caught the spirit of her Master's teaching. The explanation that she gave of his teaching harmonizes so well with those which he himself is reported to have given, when challenged with probing questions by Vacchagotta and Malukya, that we must needs regard it as at least provisionally true. Buddha kept silent because his heart was overfull, because he had too much to say.

What other explanations of his silence can be given?

Three, and three only, suggest themselves to my mind.

The first is that he was a pure and consistent agnostic, an indifferentist not only in the presence of the wrangling dogmatists, but also in the depths of his own soul. Had he been this, had he been what no man is who feels and thinks deeply, he would have told his disciples that he regarded all the statements and all the solutions of the ultimate problems with equal indifference, and in telling them this would have explained and justified his silence.

The second is that his own attitude towards great matters was one of helpless bewilderment. Had it been this, had the light of his clear and authoritative teaching been the reflection of an impenetrable fog of doubt, he would have openly said so, for such a confession would have added force and weight to his contention that men must win deliverance, not by trying to guess metaphysical riddles, but by walking in the Path.

Thus the bare fact of Buddha's silence makes the first and the second explanations of it untenable.

The third is that he was a negative dogmatist, who refrained, for fear of scandalizing his disciples and paralyzing their spiritual energies, from openly formulating his sweeping negations. This is the hypothesis which Dr. Rhys Davids, Dr. Paul Carus, and others are disposed to accept. I have already given my reasons for rejecting the first part of it. I will now consider the second.

Had Buddha been a negative dogmatist, would he have refrained from formulating his nihilistic creed? I think not. So sincere was he and so deeply in earnest, that he would have kept nothing back from his disciples—this we may assume at the outset—which it would have been possible for him to communicate to them.

Now it happens that a creed whose formulæ are all negations is, of all creeds, the easiest to expound; and the fact that

Buddha made no attempt to expound his creed is therefore a convincing proof that the faith of his heart was not the "religion of science." When he expounded his scheme of life, he gave such reasons as he could for inviting men to adopt it. That he kept other reasons in reserve can scarcely be doubted. Had these occult reasons admitted of being stated, he would surely have stated them. That he would have played the opportunist in a matter of more than life and death, that he would have kept silence about the master problems of human thought when it was possible and even easy for him to set forth his solution of them, is to my mind incredible.

The question which confronts us admits of being discussed on other than a priori grounds. There are stories which bear on it. Just before he died Buddha is reported to have said, "I have preached the truth without making any distinction between exoteric and esoteric doctrine; for in respect of the truth, ananda, the Tathagata has no such thing as the closed fist of a teacher who keeps some things back." The inference which Dr. Rhys Davids draws from these words—that there is nothing esoteric in Buddhism—is not warranted by the premises, and is inconsistent with Dr. Rhys Davids' own contention that, in his reply to the two young Brahmins who asked him to show them the way to union with God, Buddha "adopted the opportunist position" and gave his sanction to beliefs which in his heart of hearts he disowned. There is always, in the nature of things, something esoteric in the faith of a man who has thought deeply and sincerely.

There are many thoughts which he cannot communicate—the intervening barriers are insuperable—to the rank and file of mankind. There are some thoughts which he cannot communicate even to those who are in close sympathy with his general attitude towards the deepest of all problems. There are a few thoughts which he is compelled to keep back even from those whose inner life is very near and dear to his own. And, behind and beyond all these, there are movements of his own inner being which will probably some day shape themselves into thoughts, but which meanwhile remain—unformulated and unformulable—below the threshold of his own conscious life. When Buddha told ananda that he had kept nothing back from his disciples, he was doubtless contrasting in his mind his own methods with those of the Brahmanic teachers of his day,—teachers who kept everything back from their disciples, who sought to regulate the lives of the people down to the minutest details of conduct, yet gave no reason for what they prescribed, and so crushed down the spiritual life of India under the deadly burden of an apparently meaningless ceremonialism. And he doubtless meant that he had told his disciples everything which it was possible for him to disclose to them. More than that he did not mean: or the stories of his silence are all untrue.

But whatever his words to ananda may have meant, it is certain that he who spoke them was not an opportunist: it is certain that, if he had been in possession of a creed as clear, as intelligible, and as easy to formulate as the (so-called) "religion of science," he would have disclosed it to all who came to him for guidance. Dr. Rhys Davids makes no attempt to harmonize the ultra-candour of the man who claimed to have kept nothing back from his disciples, with the shiftiness of the man who kept back from the two young Brahmins, while he responded to their demand for spiritual guidance, his disbelief in the fundamental dogma of their creed.

But the attempt deserves to be made. There is surely a mean between the complacent opportunism which allows a man to simulate complete sympathy with beliefs which he has long outgrown, and the aggressive candour which makes him blurt out, or try to blurt out, whatever is in his mind, with the result that he misleads and deceives his neighbour in the sacred name of Truth. "Ilyades choses," says Joubert, *"que l'homme ne peut connaitre que vaguement: les grands esprits se contentent d'en avoir des notions vagues; mais cela ne suffit point aux esprits vulgaires. Il faut, pour leur repos, qu'ils se forgent ou qu'on leur offre des idees fixes et determinees sur les objets meme où toute precision est erreur. Ces esprits communs n'ont point d'ailes; ils ne peuvent se soutenir dans rien de ce qui n'est que de l'espace; il leur faut des points d'appui, des fables, des mensonges, des idoles.*

Mentez leur donc, et ne les trompez pas." It is certainly better to "lie" to men than to "deceive" them. But Buddha did not lie to the "esprits vulgaires" of his day. He kept silence in their presence.

Having rejected as untenable three plausible explanations of Buddha's silence, we are left face to face with the only theory which takes account both of the fact of his silence and of the reasons which he gave for it,—the theory that he had a creed of his own, a creed which went to the root of all great matters, but which, in some sort, bound him to silence. Such a creed was, as it happens, already in existence. The deeply spiritual philosophy which had inspired the authors of the Upanishads was, in its essence, esoteric.

The conception of God—the Supreme Reality—as, on the one hand, the soul or inner life of the Universe, and, on the other hand, the true self of each individual man, is one in the presence of which thought becomes an impertinence and speech a profanation. The feelings which arise in the soul in response—if there happens to be any response—to an idea which is at once overpoweringly vast and elusively subtle, do not suffer themselves to be systematized or formulated, but pass in an instant, in the first pulsation of their mighty movement, far beyond the limits of any tabulated creed. This the sages of India instinctively felt, and feeling this they "let their words be few." Even in the Upanishads, which were composed, not for the world at large but for an inner circle of sages and recluses, the language used is that of paradox and negation. That in which all their thinking centred—the Divine in man—was not to them an object of scientific curiosity, a being whose nature could be exhaustively analyzed or whose attributes could be set forth in a series of formulae.

They habitually spoke of him as "That." They shrank from applying any name to him which might suggest either that he was a member of a class, or that he had a distinct individuality of his own. If they predicated anything of him, they at once predicated its opposite. He is swifter than the mind, yet he moves not: he is far and near: he is at once innermost and outermost: and so forth. The moment of apprehension, as thought strives to grasp him, is also the moment of discomfiture and recoil. Speech, thought, sight, hearing,—each of these in turn is made possible by him, and therefore each in turn fails to reach him. He is beyond sight, beyond speech, beyond mind, beyond the known, beyond the unknown. He is veiled from thought by the excess of his own inward light. Dwelling at the heart of man, as the "unbeholden essence" of all things,—gathering into his infinite inwardness all the outermost boundaries of the Universe,—he is at once too subtle to be grasped by any effort of mental analysis, and too vast to be encompassed by any flight of imaginative thought. "He thinks of it, for whom it passes thought; who thinks of it doth never know it."

Men who had to use such language as this within the narrow limits of an esoteric circle, had no choice but to become silent when those limits were passed. For "those who understand," the language of paradox and negation has a meaning; but paradoxes bewilder the uninitiated, and the language of negation is apt to be mistaken for the language of denial and revolt. This, then, was the tremendous problem that confronted the sages of the Upanishads.

Possessed with a spiritual idea, so deeply, so inexhaustibly true that, if it could but be assimilated by the heart of man, it would in the fullness of time "redeem the world,"—they were debarred, on the one hand by the fundamental laws of thought and language, on the other hand by the very depth and truth of their cherished idea, from revealing it—as an idea—to mankind. How, then, were they to bring it home to the hearts and lives of their fellow-men? The ceremonial solution of the problem, which they adopted as a counsel of despair, proved to be no solution; and the problem remained unsolved till Buddha himself solved it—whether consciously or unconsciously, is the question that now confronts us—by transferring it to the plane of practical life.

That Buddha's ethical scheme was a practical interpretation, an exposition in terms of human conduct and human life, of the paramount idea of the Upanishads, I have already attempted to show. Was the coincidence—at every vital point—between the scheme and the idea an accident, or was it deliberately planned? That the latter is by many degrees the more reasonable hypothesis, is too obvious to need demonstration. If we hesitate to adopt it, the reason is that Buddha, though he worked out the idea, as a principle of action, with consistent thoroughness and consummate skill, not only made no attempt to expound it, but even turned back, on the threshold of their inquiry, all who sought to go behind the scheme to the philosophy that it embodied. But this difficulty will vanish when we remind ourselves that if Buddha, who made it his life's work to preach the gospel of deliverance to all men, had accepted the paramount idea of the Upanishads and made it his own, he would have been bound by the very strength and depth of his faith in it to wall it round with inviolable silence.

Link by link, the chain of proof has been forged which connects the inmost soul of Buddha with the spiritual idealism of ancient India. It is true that, in such a matter as this, demonstration is not to be looked for; but it is also true that each new link adds strength and elasticity to the chain as a whole. The theory that Buddha was at heart a spiritual idealist has received confirmation from many quarters. The last of the arguments that support it—the last and not the least weighty—is that it, and it alone, accounts for and justifies his silence.

10

Literature of Nepal

Nepali Literature refers to the literature of Nepal written in the Nepali language. The Nepali language has been the national language of Nepal since 1958. The Nepali language has also been recognized as a "major Indian literary language" by theSahitya Akademi, India's National Academy of Letters.

The Nepali language evolved from Sanskrit and it is difficult to exactly date the history of Nepali literature since most early scholars wrote in Sanskrit. It is however possible to roughly divide Nepali literature into five periods.

Pre-Bhanubhakta Era

It is thought that Nepali literature has existed in verbal folklore for the past hundreds of years; however there exists no evidence of a written literary work before theBhanubhakta. Before Bhanubhakta, writing was done in Sanskrit, and because it was a language accessible by high-caste Brahmins only at that time, many Nepali people were not involved in literature. A few scholars have argued that poet Suwananda Daas was the first literary figure in the history of Modern Nepal.

Bhanubhakta Era

Nepali speakers honor Bhanubhakta as the "Adikavi" (literally meaning 'first poet') of the Nepali language. Bhanubhakta's most important contribution to Nepali literature is probably his translation of the holy Ramayana into Nepali language. He wrote the Ramayana in metric form, using the same form as Sanskrit scholars. Besides translating theRamayana, Bhanubhakta also wrote original poems on a diverse range of subjects: from advocacy of family morals to satires of bureaucracy and poor conditions of prisoners.

Early 20th century

Motiram Bhatta (1923–1953) revived the legacy of Bhanubhakta and publicized the contributions of the latter. Motiram played such a fundamental role in the legacy of Bhanubhakta that some allege that Bhanubhakta was just a fabrication of Motiram's mind.

1960-1991

The Pre-Revolution Era was a very prolific time for creative writing despite the lack of freedom of expression, during the period the independent magazine "Sharada" was the only printed medium available for publication of Nepali literature.

Short stories by Laxmi Prasad Devkota, Guru Prasad Mainali and Bishweshwar Prasad Koirala has become recognized as of tremendous importance.

It is arguably the most significant period for the development of Nepali literature.

Plays like the influential "Muna Madan" by Laxmi Prasad Devkota tells the tales of human lives: the story is about a man who in order to gain money leaves his wife and goes abroad and tragically dies when he returns. However the story also portrays the life of the wife who suffered greatly without her husband. Other stories by Bishweshwar Prasad Koirala introduced psychology into literature, e.g. "Teen Ghumti", "Doshi Chasma", "Narendra Dai", etc.

This regime produced several prominent poets like Laxmi Prasad Devkota, Gopal Prasad Rimal, Siddhicharan Shrestha, Bhim Nidhi Tiwari and Balakrishna Sama. Later Period several poets come into light during one Panchayat regime. Indra Bahadur Rai, Parijat, Bhupi Sherchan, Madhav Prasad Ghimire, Bairagi Kainla, Krishna Bhakta Shrestha, Praijat, Madan Regmi, Dwarika Shrestha, Mohan Koirala, Upendra Shrestha,

Ishwore Ballab and Tulasi Diwas and Krishnabhushan Bal can be named in this regard.

Nepalese Civil War 1996-2006

Post-Revolution Era

There are many modern Nepali authors who have been active in writing groundbreaking, innovative Nepali literature in the era after the Democracy Revolution of 1991 and continuing into the present day, e.g. Khagendra Sangraula, Shailendra Sakar, Yuyutsu Sharma, Bimal Nibha, Nayan Raj Pandey, Narayan Wagle, Mahananda Poudyal, Toya Gurung, Durba Chandra Gautam, Roshan Thapa, Saru Bhakta, etc.

Among the younger generation poets the names of Sarada Sharma, Ramesh Kshitij, Nawa Raj Subba, Suman Pokhrel, Homraj Acharya, Netra Atom, Raj Kumar Bania, Vivash Basti, Bimal Bhoikaje, Gayatri Bist, Buddhi Sagar Chepain, R. M. Dangol, Prateek Dhakal, Padam Gautam, Jyoti Jungle, Amog Kafle, Khadga Sen Oli, Sudip Pakhrin, Ramesh Paudel, Biplov Prateek, Hom Parbag, Vyakul Pathak, Khumnarayan Poudel, Saran Rai, Vishnu Rai, Rasa, Shyam Rimal, Promod Snehi, Chunky Shrestha, Rajendra Shrestha, Prakash Silwal, Prahlas Sindulee, Lal Gopal Subedi, Bimala Tumkhewa, Tanka Uprety, and Gyanendra Vivash can be cited.

Nepali speakers are rapidly migrating around the globe and many books of Nepali literature are published from different corners of the world. Diasporic literature has developed the new ways of thinking and new branch in the Nepali literature.

NEPAL BHASA LITERATURE

Nepal Bhasa literature refers to literature in Nepal Bhasa. The language has the fourth oldest literature among the Sino-Tibetan languages (the first, second and third being Chinese, Tibetan and Burmese respectively).

The earliest known document in Nepal Bhasa is called "The Palmleaf from Uku Bahal" which dates from 1114 AD during the Thakuri period. The earliest dated stone inscription in

Nepal Bhasa is dated Nepal Sambat 293 (1173 AD). From the 14th century onwards, an overwhelming number of stone inscriptions in the Kathmandu Valley, where they are an ubiquitous element at heritage sites, are in Nepal Bhasa.

The first books appeared in the 14th century.

- *Haremakhala*, a medical manual written in 1374
- *Naradsmriti* a law book written in 1380
- *Amarkosh*, a Sanskrit-Nepal Bhasa dictionary written in 1381
- *Gopalraj Vamshavali*, a history of Nepal written in 1389

The first story book is *Tantrakhyan* (1518), and the first one-act play is *Ekadashi Brata* (1633) written by King Sidhhi Narsingh Malla.

Nepal Bhasa literature can be broadly divided into four periods.

- Classical Period (1505–1847)
- Dark Period (1847–1909)
- Renaissance Period (1909–1941)
- Modern Period (1941 onwards)

Classical Period

This was a golden age of cultural development and art and architecture in Nepal Mandala besides being a prolific period for Nepal Bhasa literature. The literary genres prevalent during this era consist of chronicles, epics, stories, scientific manuals mainly dealing with astrology and medicine, didactic poems and drama.

The kings and queens of the Malla dynasty were keen lyricists and playwrights. Dance dramas written at the time continue to be performed during annual festivals. King Mahindra Malla (reigned 1560–1574) is regarded as the first Nepal Bhasa poet. Other notable poets among the Malla kings include Siddhi Narsingh Malla (1619-1669), Pratap Malla, Ranjit Malla and Jaya Prakash Malla. Siddhi Narsingh Malla was the first Nepal Bhasa playwright. He wrote a one-act play entitled

Ekadashibrata in 1633 based on a Hindu story. His most famous work is *Katti Pyakhan* (1641) which is shown annually at Patan Durbar Square.

The queens Riddhi Laxmi (1680–1687), considered to be Nepal's first woman poet, Jaya Laxmi and Bhuvan Laxmi were also prominent songwriters. Among the public, Jagat Keshari (1678) of Banepa in the east of the Kathmandu Valley is celebrated for a hymn dedicated to Goddess Chandeswari.

In the later part of the Classical Period, Rajendra Bikram among the Shah kings is famed for writing *Mahasatwa Pakhyan* (1831), a play based on a Buddhist story. Pundit Sundarananda (circa 1793–1833) is known for his epics while Amritananda, besides composing poetry, wrote a grammar of Nepal Bhasa (1831).

Dark Period

After the Gorkha conquest of Nepal in 1768 and the advent of the Shah dynasty, the Nepali language, formerly known as Khaskura or Gorkhali, began edging out Nepal Bhasa.

Overt suppression was started by the Rana dynasty (1846–1951). In 1906, official documents written in Nepal Bhasa were declared illegal. The use of the language for business and literary purposes was forbidden. Books were confiscated and writers were jailed. As a result, not only literary creations but also writing for general purposes almost ceased; and the distance between the spoken and the written language began to widen.

A small number of hymns and religious stories were produced during this period. Notable writers of the era were Swami Abhayananda (younger brother of famed prime ministerBhimsen Thapa), Hari Bhakta Mathema, Man Bahadur Joshi and Bir Bahadur Malla.

Renaissance Period

During this period, a new generation of writers emerged who asserted themselves by producing literary works defying government restrictions. The renaissance aimed to restore Nepal Bhasa's lost glory and stimulate creative literature. The activities of this period laid the foundation for the future course of the language. The Nepal Bhasa movement dates from this period.

The renaissance also marked the advent of private printing presses and the end of handwritten books. In 1909, Nisthananda Bajracharya published the first printed book in Nepal Bhasa, *Ek Bishanti Prajnaparamita*, a Buddhist text. Another major change was the adoption ofDevanagari script to write the language instead of Nepal alphabets because of the availability of Devanagari printing type. In 1913, Siddhidas Mahaju composed *Siddhi Ramayana*, a Nepal Bhasa version of the Hindu epic.

Jagat Sundar Malla worked to promote education. In 1925, Dharmaditya Dharmacharya published *Buddha Dharma wa Nepal Bhasa*, the first ever magazine in Nepal Bhasa, from Kolkata, India.

Authors also worked to standardize the grammar and spelling, and new literary styles and genres were embraced. A grammar of the language, the first in modern times, was published in 1928.

The most important figures of this era were:

- Nisthananda Bajracharya
- Siddhidas Mahaju
- Jagat Sundar Malla
- Yogbir Singh Kansakar
- Shukraraj Shastri
- Dharmaditya Dharmacharya

These writers spearheaded the revival of the language. Among the leaders of the renaissance, Bajracharya, Mahaju, Malla and Kansakar are honored as the Four Pillars of Nepal Bhasa.

Modern Period

The 1940s marked the beginning of the modern period in Nepal Bhasa literature. During this period, new genres like short stories, poems, essays, novels and plays also emerged.

The Jail Years

The years 1941–1945 are known as the jail years for the large number of authors who were imprisoned for their literary or political activities. They were a productive period and resulted in an outpouring of works.

Chittadhar Hridaya, Siddhicharan Shrestha and Phatte Bahadur Singh were among the prominent writers of the period who were jailed for their writings. While in prison, Hridaya produced his greatest work *Sugata Saurabha*, an epic poem on the life of the Buddha. Shrestha wrote a collection of poems entitled *Seeswan* ("Wax Flower", published in 1948) among other works.

Singh (1902-1983) was sentenced to life imprisonment for editing and publishing an anthology of poems by various poets entitled *Nepali Bihar*. He had the book printed in Bettiah, India in 1939 and shipped to Nepal. After half of the print run had been sold, the rest of the copies were confiscated; and the contributors along with Singh were put in prison. Singh is best known as the founder of *Nepal Bhasa Patrika*, the first daily newspaper in Nepal Bhasa which began publication in Kathmandu in 1955. He was the editor and publisher.

Poets like Kedar Man Vyathit and Dharma Ratna Yami, who had been jailed on political charges, began writing in Nepal Bhasa too during their time in prison.

Revival of Theravada

Theravada Buddhist monks were especially influential in developing Nepal Bhasa literature. The resurgence of Nepal Bhasa coincided with the revival of Theravada Buddhism in Nepal, which the rulers disliked equally. From 1930, when the first yellow-robed monks appeared on the streets of Kathmandu since the 14th century, the number of their followers rapidly swelled, and books began to be published to educate them.

Braving official harassment, the monks produced a steady stream of books on Buddhism from India and greatly enriched the corpus of religious literature. Among the prominent authors of this period were Bauddha Rishi Mahapragya, Amritananda Mahasthavir, Dhammalok Mahasthavir, Pragyananda Mahasthavir and Aniruddha Mahathera.

In 1944, the Ranas exiled eight monks for refusing to stop teaching Buddhism and writing in Nepal Bhasa. They went to Sarnath, India and formed an organization named Dharmodaya Sabha.

In 1947, the association launched a monthly magazine titled *Dharmodaya* fromKalimpong. Besides providing an opportunity for the growing number of writers, it had a major effect on standardizing the language. In 1946, the monks were allowed to return, and religious writing in Nepal Bhasa was permitted to be published after being censored.

Post Democracy

The overthrow of the Ranas in 1951 and move towards democracy brought a freer environment to writers. The 1950s saw a surge in literary activity and the appearance of new authors.

Baikuntha Prasad Lacoul belongs to the end of the renaissance and the beginning of the modern period. He is credited with introducing Western romanticism in Nepal Bhasa poetry.

Moti Laxmi Upasika (1909–1997) was the first poetess and short story writer in the modern period.

Satya Mohan Joshi (born 1920) is a poet, historian and cultural expert. The epic *Jaya Prakash* (published in 1955) about the last Malla king of Kathmandu, and *Aranikoya Swet Chaitya* (published in 1984) about the Nepalese artist Araniko who went to China in the 13th century, are two of his many notable works.

Ramapati Raj Sharma (born 1931) is a poet whose works draw inspiration from nature. Madan Mohan Mishra (1931–2013) is known for his epic poetry and satire. His *Gajiguluya Mhagasay Pashupatinath*, published in 1975, is one of his most loved works.

Ṙ. R. N. "Syasya" (1932–2002) was the pen name of Rebati Ramanananda Shrestha Vaidya. Syasya belongs to the young generation of writers that emerged in the 1950s. His early works include *Malakha* ("Dragon", a collection of poems, published in 1955), *Kapan* ("Rainbow", short stories, 1956) and *Uphoswan* ("Blue Lotus", story, 1956).

Narayan Devi (born 1935) is a poetess whose poetry deals with women's empowerment and social discrimination.

Durga Lal Shrestha (born 1937) is a prolific, versatile and popular poet and songwriter. His works range from a collection of children's poems and songs entitled *Chiniyamha Kisicha* ("Sugar Elephant") to romantic and progressive compositions that have earned him the epithet of People's Poet.

Girija Prasad Joshi (1939–1987) was a poet whose works encompass romantic to progressive poetry.

Panchayat Era

In 1960, parliament was abolished and the Panchayat system was established. Under the system'e one-language policy, Nepal Bhasa suffered another period of suppression. In 1965, the language was banned from being broadcast over Radio Nepal. The removal of Nepal Bhasa from Nepal's only radio station sparked a protest movement which became known as the Movement of 1965 ("Bais Salya Andolan").

As part of the protests, weekly literary meets were held at street squares and public courtyards for more than a year. Inspired by the literary activity, a host of new and young writers emerged. Poets Buddha Sayami, Nati Bajra Bajracharya, Shree Krishna Anu and Janak Newa and novelist Ratna Bahadur Sayami are some of the figures brought up by the protests.

They introduced fresh literary styles and extended the bounds of Nepal Bhasa literature. The 1965 Movement was thus a very productive period. Birat Nepal Bhasa Sahitya Sammelan Guthi (Grand Nepal Bhasa Literary Conference Trust), formed in 1962 in Bhaktapur, and Nepal Bhasa Manka

Khala, founded in 1979 in Kathmandu, are some of the prominent organizations that emerged during this period to promote literature and struggle for language rights.

Today

Nepal Bhasa literature has a niche readership. Poetry, short stories, essays, novels, travelogues, biographies and religious discourses are the popular genres. A number of literary magazines are published. Translations of Nepal Bhasa literature in English and Nepali appear frequently. Literary organizations hold regular public recitals.

Outside Nepal Mandala

Poets based outside Nepal Mandala have also promoted Nepal Bhasa. Among them, Ganesh Lal Shrestha of Hetauda composed songs and gave music recitals during festivals in the 1940s and 1950s. In Pokhara, the first Grand Nepal Bhasa Literary Conference was held from 17-18 December 1975.

Literary Genres

- Dramas are traditionally performed on open "dabu" (platform) built at temple squares and major intersections. Most of the traditional dramas are related to deities and demons. Masked characters are central to such dramas. Music forms an important part of drama. Most of them are narrated with the help of songs sung at intervals. The theme of most dramas is to create social well-being with morals illustrating the rise, turbulence and fall of evil. There are fixed dates in the Nepal Sambat (Nepal Era) calendar for performance of specific plays. Most dramas are performed by specific Guthis.
- Poetry writing constituted a pompous part of medieval Malla aristocracy. Many of the kings were well renowned poets. Epic poetry is very popular. Sitala Maju, which describes the expulsion of children from Kathmandu in the early 19th century, Ji Waya La Lachhi Maduni,

about a luckless Tibet trader, and Silu, about an ill-fated pilgrimage to Gosaikunda, are among the well-known ballads. Siddhidas Mahaju and Chittadhar Hridaya are two great poets of the modern period.

- Stories ranging from the origin of the Kathmandu Valley to its temples and important monuments have been passed down verbally in Nepal Bhasa. Very few of them were in written form initially. However, with an increase in literacy rate and an awareness amongst the people, those stories have been penned down. Stories on other topics have also taken root.
- Novel writing has increased with the progressive increase in literacy after the modernization of Nepal. Restriction of the knowledge of alphabets to a certain caste of society during the medieval era reduced the viability of leisure reading among the masses.
- History literature in Nepal Bhasa dates from the Malla era. Stone inscriptions were placed in important places to commemorate important events. Mention of family lines of the person instilling the inscription is also found in many cases.
- Philosophy is one of the subjects of Siddhidas Mahaju's writings who has produced a number of works related to the norms of society.
- Legal literature formulated during the reign of Jayastithi Malla formulated a major part of the norm of Newar society.

11

Democracy and Civil Society in the Himalayas

CIVIL SOCIETY

Although there are many variants of the concept, civil society is made up of "some combination of networks of legal protection, voluntary associations, and forms of independent public expression".

A well-developed civil society potentially influences government in two ways. It enhances political responsiveness by aggregating and expressing the wishes of the public through a wealth of non-governmental forms of association, and it safeguards public freedom by limiting the government's ability to impose arbitrary rule by force.

Civil society can be defined as the site where society enters into a relationship with the state: "The values of civil society are those of political participation, state accountability and public politics...

The institutions of civil society are associational and representative forums, a free press and social associations. The inhabitant of this sphere is the citizen." Based on rights, rule of law, freedom and citizenship, civil society becomes the place for a critical rational discourse. It is a precondition for the existence of democracy and a property of democratic states and societies.

But the existence of civil society alone is not enough.

An inactive civil society leads to unresponsive states, while only a politically self-conscious civil society imposes limits upon state power. If the political practices of a self-conscious civil society transgress the boundaries of the state sponsored political discourse, a crisis of legitimacy of the state results. Politics is about the dialogues and contestations that society has with the state. The site at which these encounters take place is civil society.

Civil society has historically been associated with attempts to control the state and subject state practices to critical evaluation. Civil society cannot ask for a democratic state if it is itself undemocratic, and a democratic state requires a democratic society.

Civil society can in one sense be identified with democratization and liberalization, but it is a far more comprehensive and deeper concept than democracy. Democratic practices have often been reduced to rituals and staged political events, such as elections, parliamentary representation and plebiscites which are meant to reaffirm the legitimacy of the state. The concept of civil society, on the other hand, embraces an entire range of assumptions, values and institutions, such as political, social and civil rights, the rule of law, representative institutions, a public sphere and a plurality of associations, which are preconditions of democracy.

Conceptions of state and society

The conception of the modern nation state is of European origin. Every civilization has its own conception and tradition of state. But the modern nation state, as it is defined by the West, has become the only accepted form of nation state in world politics.

The idea of sovereignty, too, in the way as it has been derived from ancient Greek and Roman law, has become international law. With the French revolution of 1789 the European sovereign state turned into a nation state. Its legitimation was based on the principle of people's sovereignty.

This type of nation state became a European institution during the 19th century and a world institution in the course of the 20th century. This globalization has, on the one hand, been the culmination of European expansion, and, on the other hand, the beginning of de-colonization.

But in many regions of the world, e.g. in Africa and Asia, this globalized type of state has neither a material nor a cultural basis. As a consequence, many civilizations have been looking for indigenous, local pre-modern and, thus, pre-global traditions of state. Different kinds of religious fundamentalism are the best examples for this development.

The nation state with its internal and external sovereignty arose from the European bourgeois society and their values of a democratic political order. In its globalised form, this kind of society is called civil society today. This means that 'civil society' is a term to describe the separation of state and society, but it also accentuates the separation of state and religion. In this form is civil society an integral part of a democratic nation state.

The transfer of the western model of nation state upon non-western civilizations has been part of the process of colonization. These states did not become nation states in the course of a long process of development. Their foundation is neither democratic nor are they entities based on civil society.

Samuel Huntington underlines that the nation state according to its historical definition is a democratic state. But most non-western nation states are not based on democratic societies with people conscious of citizenship. Instead, these states are dominated by diverse ethnic identities often competing with each other. They fit more into global forms of civilizations than into a nation state order. On the other hand, is the civil society as the basis of a democratic nation state not defined by ethnicity. But this does not mean that the nation state necessarily has an ethnically homogeneous society. Moreover, a nation state is the result of a consensus on norms and values of a unified community. Constitutional patriotism does not depend upon ethnicity but on the democratic values and norms of the constitution. In non-western nominal nation states identity is mainly based on ethnicity with corresponding conflicts. The particular we-groups experience the state as an imposed and suppressing apparatus of force they cannot identify with. In such states local forces often gain the upper hand against the central authority, since there is no political community that can integrate the different ethnic, cultural and religious groups.

It is a reality of present times that all states, substantial as well as nominal nation states, are systematically related to each other within the current international community. This may lead to the impression that modern history has become a common world history. But this vague and fictive conception of a common world history mostly excludes the history conceptions of local cultures and regional civilizations. Especially in parts of the non-western world we meet ethnically defined local cultures which politically group themselves to civilizations. Culture is always a local social aspect, while civilization is culturally overlapping. This means that both are neither synonymous nor identical.

What Huntington calls 'clash of civilizations' is not an international cultural war. It is more the upheaval of local cultures politically grouped into civilizations against global structures and universally accepted norms and values. Part of this struggle is the opposition against the secular nation state that has not grown from indigenous soil but has been implanted from outside.

The clash or war of civilizations is a struggle against the international order of nation states, against the world order. It is a process of de-westernization. The western world order has first been conceptualized after the Treaty of Westphalia that ended the Thirty Years War in 1648. In the course of the next 300 years the Europeans managed to implant this system upon the whole world.

The nation states of Africa and Asia are thin political surface structures. Under these structures they are conglomerates of multiethnic populations and diverse local cultures that are only formally superseded by the territorial national structures. The latter are the connecting links between the local structures and the global ones.

Globalization produces socio-economic, socio-political and socio-cultural structures into which ethnicity and local cultures are incorporated. But global civilization as a consequence of the process of globalization is not able to integrate the ethnic or we-groups and their local cultures. Only individuals can be integrated. The local cultures become regional civilizations in their area of origin and revolt against the conception of a global civilization. They see the nation state as a western intrigue, as a strategy of *divide et impera* to suppress non-western civilizations.

The de-colonization of the world was at the same time a phase of acculturation: non-western elites educated in the west tended to follow the European conception of nation state and other western achievements. Their demand for a nation state of their own was an effective ideological weapon against European colonialism. In recent years we can observe an opposite trend. The westernized elites of Asian and African states may have originally appeared as secular and modernizing elites, but they now turn into supporters of movements based on religious fundamentalism. They reject their own western education and often aggressively distance themselves from the west. Religious fundamentalism provides the necessary ideology for this revolt of de-westernization. It opposes the nation state and aims at the restoration of the lost unity of civilization.

The western nation state never took roots in non-western cultures. Values of local cultures are nowadays revitalized to fight against the implanted European nation state. This revitalization of local cultures supports at the same time the revival of ethnic connections. The state may become aligned to a civilization based on a special kind of religion, but this civilization is split into numerous groups with different ethnicity and local culture. Civilizations are uniting local cultures on the outside, while ethnicity can be the cause for conflicts between the local cultures.

Applied upon Nepal we have the following situation. Nepal is a multiethnic state as defined by the constitution, i.e. there are great a number of ethnic communities living on the state territory of Nepal. These groups are not civil societies in the western sense of a community independent of the democratic state. Instead, we find ethnic sub-communities, which oppose the authority of the current nation state they cannot identify with.

If you take the term *civil society* independent of its modern western environment then you can also apply it to Nepal's different ethnic groups. They are independent of the political structure of the nation state they formally belong to, but towards which they refuse their substancial integration.

On the nation state level there does not exist a civil society in the modern sense with a community system or at least a common identification with such kind of system.

Models of identity have been implanted by the ruling elites, but they often collide with ethnic affiliations. Thus, if you want to talk about pre-modern civilizations and their local cultures, you have to considerate the concept of ethnicity, since ethnic and religious identities are of greater importance than the artificially implanted nation state identity.

Nepal's ethnic communities, as all ethnic societies, are confronted with the modern global civilization. This leads to a kind of interaction between the local ethnic cultures and their global environment. This interaction takes place within the framework of the nominal nation state. Intellectual state leaders construct idealized identities in order to minimize tensions. This is in the case of Nepal, for example, the constitutional identification with Hindu symbols and values, or the policy of separation from Christian religion or Indian secularism, or the analysis of the society along the conceptions of communist ideologies also derived from the west.

But all this is only externally. Inside, the subordinate ethnic and religious identities are of greater importance. But also the conflict between the different ethnic groups and the nation state only reflects the opposition of local cultures against an institution derived from another civilization.

Ethnicity, nation state and sub systems

The times of de-colonization became a new era of nationalism. At present, we are in a new phase with a shifting of interests from nation building to ethnicity. National consciousness is replaced by ethnic identity. Ethnicity has become a source for conflicts both within the nation state and within regional interstate relations.

Thus ethnicity has become the focus of anthropologists as well as political scientists working on international relations. While anthropologists and ethno-sociologists turn their attention to ethnicity as expression of a local culture, political scientists are trying to analyse ethnicity from the perspective of world, regional or national politics.

In Nepal, being a non-western state, the nation state has not grown out of the indigenous soil, but it has been artificially transplanted. That's why I would like to call it a nominal nation state. Sections of Nepali society, or better to say special Nepali elites, came into contact to modern political thinking based on the conception of the western nation state in the 1930s and especially 1940s. The modern state of Nepal that developed after the successful overthrow of the Ranas in 1950/1 cannot be called a nation state in the western sense, since it did not overcome its ethnic diversity. In modern western nation states, sub-national and ethnic communities have been integrated into a common civil society. They have totally lost their original meanings. Thus, ethnic diversity can be called a pre-nation state phenomenon. Each nation as a modern formation has her own ethnic origin. Anthony Smith speaks in this context of the "ethnic origin of nations".

Nominal nation states like Nepal are missing this common civil society. There is no modern community with national loyalties and patterns of identity based on citizenship, that have replaced the original sectarian ethnic bonds. There does not exist the consciousness of a citizenship that compensates ethnic loyalties and identities. When Nepal's ruling elites defined the state in the constitution of 1990, then they could not break away from the civilization and culture they had been born into. If they talk about the modern nation state Nepal, then many ethnic groups, the so-called depressed castes and the Muslims of the country cannot identify with this conception. Imported western institutions of democracy and symbols like the national flag or the national anthem cannot conceal from the different ethnic groups that there is still no common nation behind this facade. The existing sub-national and sub-ethnic cleavages within the nominal nation state Nepal cannot be removed under the present conditions.

One has to ask if modernization in the sense of a simple transfer of the European model of nation state can help to break up the solidarity within the ethnic we-groups in the interest of the common nation Nepal. The nation state newly defined in 1990 has so far not been able to assimilate the different ethnic groups.

The roots of ethnicity originate from the socially produced and steadily changing foursome of common myths, oral tradition, values and symbols. Nations are neither in the pre-modern sense original and unchangeable nor are they totally modern. They have maintained their ethnic origins even in modern industrialized societies. But there, national bonds have replaced the erstwhile local communal identifications and have thus created a common basis for a local culture on the national level. The modern media of communication further help to promote the process of integration and cultural assimilation. The nominal nation state Nepal with her non-western forms of civilization is not based on a democratic community defined as a communication community.

The nominal nation state does not have a historical experience of her own. Its sovereignty is nominal, not historically grown. In Nepal, even nine years ago sovereignty was still vested in the monarch. The new pattern of state has been transferred from outside. It lacks the necessary institutional infrastructure as well as the accepted legitimacy. Such an artificially constructed state is hardly able to cope with conflicts. In one and the same such state there do exist several ethnic collectives competing for power, all of which having their own culturally given identity. The politization of this ethnic diversity finally leads to a struggle for supremacy within the state.

In each ethnic community there are patron client relations. The patron – often a powerful person in a state position with access to resources – uses his position to gain an advantage to his/her ethnic we-group.

This leads to distribution struggles. The institutionally weak nation state in non-western civilizations is not only lacking a non-ethnic community with a substantial consensus but also the political culture that defines the terms of the competition for the regulation of ethnic conflicts on power and resources. State power is not shared between the different groups, but it is monopolized by one single group.

The ideology of Nepali nationalism is not likely to regulate ethnic conflicts and to manage the ethno-politics in a democratic manner. A democratic solution would be power-sharing. But how can an institutionally weak state like Nepal develop such mechanisms of democratic government?

Sovereignty and the institutionalized political order of a non-ethnic community are substantial principles of a nation state. Ethnic conflicts are typical for political orders that lack these principles. In a really modern state, the citizens feel part of a political community and not of an ethnic one. The political culture of such a state is characterized by norms and values that have been internalized by the whole population. Each group articulates its interests in the public and discusses it with other groups in a peaceful manner. Even events in the Nepali parliament have proved, that Nepal has not reached this level, yet.

To feel as a member of a political community in the sense of citizenship is not an abstract idea, but it demands a really existing structural basis. This feeling must be common to all sections of society independent of ethnic, religious or political orientation. The consciousness of such a political community is the basis for the internalization of a higher identity, which is necessary to overcome pre-modern forms of affiliation.

And this is precisely what only nominal nation states like Nepal are missing. Outwardly, are all political states in the possession of nation state sovereignty, but they are missing it internally in the sense of democratic sovereignty. And this is the crisis of nominal nation states. In most of the nominal nation states, political power is not democratically shared by the members and groups of the political community, but it is monopolized by an ethnic or ethno-religious clientele as a sub-community. Ethnic tensions are boosted, since there is no culture of democratic power sharing.

The Himalayan situation

The following remarks are part of some fundamental ideas concerning my current research project. The purpose of this project is to test some explanatory hypotheses on democratization and development of civil society in multiethnic environment taking the central Himalayas, especially Nepal and Bhutan but also Sikkim and Darjeeling, as an example. All these states or regions have in common that they are inhabited by a large variety of population groups belonging to three main stocks: Tibeto-Mongolian, Indo-Aryan and Austro-Asiatic. The general questions to be explained are as follows: Are there common trends and problems in implementing democracy? Does the social and cultural variety hinder broad scale participation of population? In which way can democracy promote the development of civil society? Why do even states or regions with a longer democratic history still have problems in achieving higher levels of governance? Is the trend to violence, radicalism and separatism the result of shortcomings in implementing democracy and participation?

The Himalaya is neither a geographical nor a social and cultural border line. As the main rivers rise north of the Himalayan chain and later break through the mountains in deep gorges, the area has always been open to infiltration by population groups from the north. So, from the social point of view the Himalaya and its foothills have been a meeting place of different races, cultures, languages, religions and ideologies.

Racially we meet Tibeto-Mongolian peoples side by side with Indo-Arian Groups. In recent years, anthropological research has brought to light a lot of information about the history of immigration of many of the Himalayan peoples. In addition the growing ethnic consciousness has led to some kind of self-identification of many groups on the basis of racial, linguistic, religious and cultural features.

Culturally, the Himalaya is an area where different worlds are meeting. One of the main characteristics of every culture is the language spoken by its representatives. The multitude of languages can hardly be greater than in the Himalayan region, where we find Indo-European, Sino-Tibetan and Tibeto-Burman languages. Even linguistically closely related languages are of such a variety that they are hardly intelligible among each other.

Similar to the situation of the languages is that of the religions. Hinduism, Buddhism, animism and shamanism are the traditional religions of the Himalayan peoples, showing a lot of syncretistic tendencies. In the course of history they have been joined by foreign religions like Islam and Christianity with their missionary foundation; the latter, too, play an important role in the current processes of social change and political formation.

In addition, events and developments in the adjacent northern and southern regions often have caused waves of migration into the area under discussion, where they have influenced the distribution of political, social and economic power in a decisive way.

Political influences and processes of transformation

In quite recent times the Himalayan region has been the meeting place of two different political ideologies, both of whom being the product of western industrial nations: democracy in its western form as it is practised in all South Asian countries today, except in Bhutan, and the communist ideology in its Soviet and Chinese variations. The development of the modern nation states of the region must be seen against the background of confrontation of these western ideologies with the traditional elements of power distribution and participation.

But the ethnic and cultural diversity of the region sometimes conceals common structures. The Hindu state Nepal for example seems to have little in common with the Buddhist state Bhutan. But when you look more closely you will find a lot of historical or structural parallels. In both states the power is in the hands of elite minorities who immigrated, or at least claim to have immigrated, in relatively late historical times. These elites have made their own culture the foundation of their state ideology, which is defended against every kind of attack from inside their state boundaries. In recent times the elites of both states feel endangered by the dawning of the modern western ideology of democracy. The supporters of this democratization are interior forces like disadvantaged ethnic elites, but also the modern state of India with its type of state order closely related to western democracies, and with her efforts for security along her northern border.

Today Nepal and Bhutan are on different stages of a similar process. Both states faced very cautious experiments with democracy in the 1950s, in the case of Bhutan also in the 1960s, followed by a return to traditional forms of politics, when democratic institutions were only used in a hypocritical way. It was only in 1990 that Nepal faced the breakthrough of democratic ideas and the constitutional confinement of traditional forces. Bhutan has not done this step, yet, where so far only disadvantaged groups of population have called for democracy. In Nepal the process of democratization has mainly been carried by special circles of the traditional ruling elite, while in Bhutan the Ngalung elite has so far not participated in this process.

The development of the small Himalayan state of Sikkim, situated between Nepal and Bhutan, has been a little bit different. Similar to its neighbouring countries, Sikkim had been under the political control of a minority elite, in this case Tibetans who had immigrated some centuries ago and reigned the country according to their Tibetan-Buddhist tradition of kingship. But different from Nepal and Bhutan, Sikkim had been a British protectorate since 1860 and had become open to Indian influences. As a result, the country faced an immense pressure for democratization when India became independent in 1947. The forces behind this process were the Nepalis, Sikkim's most numerous population group, but also the Rongs (Lepchas) and Tsongs (indigenous groups of Limbus and Magars). India supported the replacement of the traditional royal system by a democratic one in 1974 and brought about the integration of Sikkim into the Indian Union. But even more than 20 years later it is still under discussion whether this step was right or not, and Sikkim's politics is marked by tensions that have their basis in the multiethnic population of the country. Independent of the Indian annexation, Sikkim's politics of the last two decades is a reflection of the same racial, ethnic and cultural problems, which the young Nepali democracy is confronted with in the 1990s.

Another case is the Darjeeling district of West Bengal, which got special treatment in modern history. After the British forced Sikkim to cede the area in 1835, Darjeeling became a summer resort and later the centre of a flourishing tea industry. Since the middle of the 19th century many people from Eastern Nepal were called in as cheap labourers. This is the reason why today Darjeeling's population is mainly of Nepali origin. This ethnic potential has given the politics of the district a special orientation, that differs from the rest of West Bengal. Since the 1980s Darjeeling has faced a militancy similar to that of the North-East Indian states. It culminated in the clash between the government of West Bengal and the Nepali elite of the district with its constructed ethnicity as Gorkhas.

With the exception of Bhutan democratic forms of government have taken the place of traditional ones in all states and regions of the central and eastern Himalaya. But tradition has not been totally superseded. Even the former systems in their final stages had tried to revive and safeguard their tradition by integrating some democratic aspects and institutions. One such example was the Nepali *panchayat* system, that had been sold as an indigenous Nepali system of democracy by its founder, King Mahendra. The introduction of fictitious democratic institutions by the Bhutanese King Jigme Dorji Wangchuk must be seen in a similar context. But in both countries there has not been a radical coup d'état, e.g. the replacement of the traditional monarchy by a republic.

Those forces that have brought democracy have frequently compromised with the traditional forces. So, in Nepal the monarchy that had been absolute according to western political thinking was changed into a constitutional one in very recent times. The persons in power may have changed, but they come from the same ethnic and cultural groups as their predecessors. The reason is that the social hierarchy of the Hindu state that had been fundamental for all kinds of participation in the partyless *panchayat* system is also dominating the thinking and structure of the political parties of the 1990s. An outward characteristic is the retention of the term Hindu state in the constitution by today's democratic elite.

A bit different is the situation in Sikkim, where the integration into the republican state of India in 1974/75 meant the expulsion of the Namgyal monarchy and its ruling elite minority of immigrated Tibetans out of power which had controlled the country for about 300 years. Since then the political parties in power are dominated mainly by Nepalis who immigrated within the last 150 years, but also by the old indigenous groups of Lepchas and Limbus. Typically enough the great Indian national parties have hardly played any role in the past.

The role of ethnic movements

It may be asked in which way the very differentiated aspects of education and political consciousness have influenced this development. The democratization of the Himalayan states has been the consequence of the fast growing political consciousness of ever growing circles of society. Bhutan, the country with the lowest standard of general education, characteristically has the lowest grade of democratization scale.

The great attraction of the most disadvantaged people by radical parties and organizations, that call for a further revolution and the introduction of a republic, is an indication that the process of democratization is also incomplete in countries like Nepal.

The very tradition that has been removed or changed has been the tradition of the ruling elite in the respective countries. Compromises with this tradition, as they are typical even for communist parties like the CPN-UML, necessarily lead to the retention of the traditional power structures.

Thus, in the case of Nepal the political, economic and social domination of the high Hindu castes has been retained irrespective of some kind of democratization. The disregard of the traditions of the other peoples of the country has in the same way survived the system change of 1990. The disadvantaged groups in a state democratized in this way have only the chance of subordinate participation by adaptation and Hinduization.

In Sikkim the situation is different. The integration into the republican Indian state meant a total break with the tradition of the elite ruling before.

With the constitutional exclusion of religion and culture from politics, the Tibetan-Buddhist Bhutia elite lost any chance to save their former supremacy in a democratized form of government. The numerically dominating Nepali population within the political parties of Sikkim gives the impression that the changes of 1974/75 have given way to another form of ethnic and cultural domination. But Sikkim's Nepalis are of a similar ethnic, linguistic and religious divergence as the society in neighbouring Nepal. This became obvious in the mid 1990s when Nar Bahadur Bhandari, a Nepali Bahun who had dominated the politics of Sikkim for 15 years, was driven from power by ethnic Nepalis.

Democratic ideas and the formation of civil society

Successful ethnic movements that have brought a greater power sharing in countries like Sikkim, but also in the North-East Indian states, lead to the question, if the western democracy can be a form of government, that is appropriate to replace the traditional systems and to solve the numerous conflicts in the multiethnic and multicultural states of the central and eastern Himalayas.

With a western democracy, some kind of "foreign" tradition is replacing the "indigenous" one of the ruling elite. The latter usually hinders an equal participation of social groups other than the ruling one.

This means that the western democracy could be a positive foundation for at least a theoretically broad-based participation of population. The western democracy uses political parties via which persons are elected into special functions or bodies by the people for a definitive period of time. These political parties are tied to common principles of organization and state mechanism, but they, at the same time, represent different approaches of social and economic order.

The very special problem of transferring western democratic types of state lies within the multiethnicity being so characteristic for the countries of the central and eastern Himalayas.

In Germany like in many other Western European nations, ethnic boundaries and differences have become fluid. In the course of centuries the European states have developed a more a less single national identity, which is bound to territory and language, and to a lesser degree also to culture and religion. But in spite of these established identities even Western European Countries are confronted with tensions that even escalate sometimes.

There is no democratic country in the western world that has nearly as many ethnic groups, cultures and religions as the Himalayan states. So one has to ask the question how far western models can be transferred to these countries. King

Mahendra, for example, justified his coup d'état of 1960 arguing that the western kind of democracy had proved unsuitable for Nepal.

The political system introduced by him afterwards was based on the tradition of those population groups, to whom also the royal Shah family belonged. But this royal system failed as well, and again it was replaced by a western type of democracy in 1990.

The Nepali system of government practised in the 1950s as well as the later *panchayat* system were lacking in openness for the multicultural set-up of the country's society. But even though the democracy introduced in 1990 has similar starting points, the situation is different because of the growing political consciousness of the disadvantaged population groups and because of the guarantee of fundamental rights by the new constitution. Today the state meets demands that would have been nipped in the bud during *panchayat* times, but now they lead to open discussions.

The way of democratization introduced in Nepal can lead towards two directions. The current democratic system did not supersede the tradition of the ruling elite, but instead incorporated this tradition.

This means in practice that members of those population groups, which before constituted the ruling elite of the former *panchayat* system, today decide the politics of the political parties. It depends upon them, if they are willing to reduce the dominance of their own tradition and so make possible the integration of other population groups into the nation. Their instruments at hand are the political parties.

The constitution of 1990 prohibits the recognition of parties which have been formed on the basis of religion, community, caste, tribe or region. But the same constitution continues to orientate the state according to the tradition of the high Hindu castes of the *pahad*, Nepal's hill area, only. If this basic foundation is not corrected, the state may go another way that might not have been in the mind of many of those people who fought for democracy in 1990. The special feature of this second way is the accentuation of the respective traditions of the different population groups of the country. The repeated demands for autonomous regions based on ethnicity are a first indication for such kind of development. The North-East Indian states have set a good example for this.

So western democracy does not automatically solve the numerous problems of the Himalayan states mainly based on social conflicts. But different from the tradition of a dominating elite, democracy can lead to a solution, if those responsible finally make up their minds and separate politics and culture. In view of the great importance of tradition among the peoples of the Himalayan area it will always remain a question of tolerance, if conflicts can be avoided or solved.

12

Environmental Issues in Nepal

Environmental issues in Nepal are numerous environmental problems. Sedimentation and discharge of industrial effluents are prominent sources of water pollution, and the burning of wood for fuel is a significant source of indoor air pollution and respiratory problems. Vehicular and industrial emissions increasingly have contributed to air pollution in urban areas.

Deforestation and land degradation appear to affect a far greater proportion of the population and have the worst consequences for economic growth and individuals' livelihoods. Forest loss has contributed to floods, soil erosion, and stagnant agricultural output. Estimates suggest that from 1966 to 2000 forest cover declined from 45 to 29 percent of the total land area. Often cited causes of deforestation include population growth, high fuelwood consumption, infrastructure projects, and conversion of forests into grazing- and cropland. According to government estimates, 1.5 million tons of soil nutrients are lost annually, and by 2002 approximately 5 percent of agricultural holdings had been rendered uncultivable as a result of soil erosion and flooding.

Land degradation is attributed to population growth, improper use of agro-chemicals, and overly intensive use of landholdings that are too small to provide most households with sufficient food. Since the late 1980s, government policies have attempted to address these numerous and related problems, but policies often are hampered by lack of funding, insufficient understanding of Nepal's mountain ecosystems, bureaucratic inefficiency, and sometimes contentious relations between the central government and local communities. Main Threats and Development Pressures There are several threats and development pressures to the biodiversity of Nepal, caused by the cumulative effects of socio-economic status, ecological degradation and political instability (MFSC, 2000). A major threat factor is represented by the Nepalese human population. According to the 1991 population census, the total population of Nepal was around 18.5 million and the population in the year 2000 was estimated at 22 million (MFSC, 2000). More than half (53 per cent) of this population lies under the absolute poverty line and is about to double in the next 26 years (MoPE (a), 2000).

Poverty has causal effects on population and vice versa, which contributes to environmental deterioration. Fast growth of the population caused an increase in demand for fuel wood, timber, fodder and land to grow more food (MFSC, 2000). Non-timber forest products are threatened by deforestation, habitat degradation and unsustainable harvesting. Major threats to some protected areas are grazing all year around, poaching for high value products, illegal timber harvesting and unsustainable tourism. Rangelands are suffering from an enormous grazing pressure and wetland biodiversity is threatened by encroachment of wetland habitat, unsustainable harvesting of wetland resources, industrial pollution, agricultural run-off, the introduction of exotic and invasive species into wetland ecosystems, and siltation. Mountain biodiversity is suffering due to ecological fragility and instability of high mountain environments, deforestation, poor management of natural resources, and inappropriate farming practices (MFSC, 2000). Agrobiodiversity is under threat due to use of high yielding varieties, destruction of natural habitat, overgrazing, land fragmentation, commercialisation of agriculture and the extension of modern highyielding varieties, indiscriminate use of pesticides, population growth and urbanisation, and changes in farmer's priorities (MFSC, 2000). More factors for loss of biodiversity include landslide and soil erosion, pollution, fire, overgrazing, introduction of alien species, illegal trade, hunting and smuggling

CLIMATE

Altitudinal Belts

Nepal's latitude is about the same as that of Florida, however with elevations ranging from less than 100 meters (300 ft) to over 8,000 meters (26,000 ft) and precipitation from 160 millimeters (6 in) to over 5,000 millimeters (16 ft) the country has eight climate zones from tropical to perpetual snow.

The tropical zone below 1,000 meters (3,300 ft) experiences frost less than once per decade. It can be subdivided into lower tropical (below 300 meters or 1,000 ft.) with 18% of the nation's land area) and upper (18% of land area) tropical zones. The best mangoes and well as papaya and banana are largely confined to the lower zone. Other fruit such as litchee, jackfruit, citrus and mangoes of lower quality grow in the upper tropical zone as well. Winter crops include grains and vegetables typically grown in temperate climates. The Outer Terai is virtually all in the lower tropical zone. Inner Terai valleys span both tropical zones. The Sivalik Hills are mostly upper tropical. Tropical climate zones extend far up river valleys across the Middle Hills and even into the Mountain regions.

The subtropical climate zone from 1,000 to 2,000 meters (3,300 to 6,600 ft) occupies 22% of Nepal's land area and is the most prevalent climate of the Middle Hills above river valleys. It experiences frost up to 53 days per year, however this varies greatly with elevation, proximity to high mountains and terrain either draining or ponding cold air drainage. Crops include rice, maize, millet, wheat, potato, stone fruits and citrus.

The great majority of Nepal's population occupies the tropical and subtropical climate zones. In the Middle Hills, upper-caste Hindus are concentrated in tropical valleys which are well suited for rice cultivation while *Janajati* ethnic groups mostly live above in the subtropical zone and grow other grains more than rice.

The Temperate climate zone from 2,000 to 3,000 meters (6,600 to 9,800 ft) occupies 12% of Nepal's land area and has up to 153 annual days of frost. It is encountered in higher parts of the Middle Hills and throughout much of the Mountain region. Crops include cold-tolerant rice, maize, wheat, barley, potato, apple, walnut, peach, various cole, amaranthus and buckwheat.

The Subalpine zone from 3,000 to 4,000 meters (9,800 to 13,100 ft) occupies 9% of Nepal's land area, mainly in the Mountain and Himalayan regions. It has permanent settlements in the Himalaya, but further south it is only seasonally occupied as pasture for sheep, goats, yak and hybrids in warmer months. There are up to 229 annual days of frost here. Crops include barley, potato, cabbage, cauliflower, amaranthus, buckwheat and apple. Medicinal plants are gathered. The Alpine zone from 4,000 to 5,000 meters (13,100 to 16,400 ft) occupies 8% of the country's land area. There are a few permanent settlements above 4,000 meters. There is virtually no plant cultivation although medicinal herbs are gathered. Sheep, goats, yaks and hybrids are pastured in warmer months.

Above 5,000 meters the climate becomes Nival and there is no human habitation or even seasonal use.

Arid and semi-arid land in the rainshadow of high ranges have a Transhimalayan climate. Population density is very low. Cultivation and husbandry conform to subalpine and alpine patterns but depend on snowmelt and streams for irrigation. Precipitation generally decreases from east to west with increasing distance from the Bay of Bengal, source of the summer monsoon. Eastern Nepal gets about 2,500 mm (100 in) annually; the Kathmandu area about 1,400 mm (55 in) and western Nepal about 1,000 mm (40 in). This pattern is modified by adabiatic effects as rising air masses cool and drop their moisture content on windward slopes, then warm up as they descend so relative humidity drops. Annual precipitation reaches 5,500 mm (18 ft) on windward slopes in the *Annapurna* Himalaya beyond a relatively low stretch of the *Mahabharat Range*. In rainshadows beyond the high mountains, annual precipitation drops as low as 160 mm (6 in).

Seasons

The year is divided into a wet season from June to September—as summer warmth over Inner Asia creates a low pressure zone that draws in moist air from the Indian Ocean—and a dry season from October to June as cold temperatures in the vast interior creates a high pressure zone causing dry air to flow outward. April and May are months of intense water stress when cumulative effects of the long dry season are exacerbated by temperatures rising over 40 °C (104 °F) in the tropical climate belt. Seasonal drought further intensifies in the *Siwaliks* hills consisting of poorly consolidated, coarse, permeable sediments that do not retain water, so hillsides are often covered with drought-tolerant scrub forest. In fact much of Nepal's native vegetation adapted to withstand drought, but less so at higher elevations where cooler temperatures mean less water stress.

The summer monsoon may be preceded by a buildup of thunderstorm activity that provides water for rice seedbeds. Sustained rain on average arrives in mid-June as rising temperatures over Inner Asia creates a low pressure zone that draws in moist air from the Indian Ocean, but this can vary up to a month. Significant failure of monsoon rains historically meant drought and famine while above-normal rains still cause flooding and landslides with losses in human lives, farmland and buildings.

The monsoon also complicates transportation with roads and trails washing out while unpaved roads and airstrips may become unusable and cloud cover reduces safety margins for aviation. Rains diminish in September and generally end by mid-October, ushering in generally cool, clear, and dry weather, as well as the most relaxed and jovial period in Nepal. By this time, the harvest is completed and people are in a festive mood. The two biggest and most important Hindu festivals—*Dashain* and *Tihar* (*Dipawali*)—arrive during this period, about one month apart. The post monsoon season lasts until about December.

After the post monsoon comes the winter monsoon, a strong north easterly flow marked by occasional, short rainfalls in the lowlands and plains and snowfalls in the high-altitude areas. In this season the Himalayas function as a barrier to cold air masses from Inner Asia, so southern Nepal and northern India have warmer winters than would otherwise be the case. April and May are dry and hot, especially below 1,200 meters (4,000 ft) where afternoon temperatures may exceed 40 °C (104 °F).

Environment

The dramatic changes in elevation along this transect result in a variety of biomes, from tropical savannas along the Indian border, to subtropical broadleaf and coniferous forests in the hills, to temperate broadleaf and coniferous forests on the slopes of the Himalaya, to montane grasslands and shrublands, and finally rock and ice at the highest elevations.

This corresponds to the Terai-Duar savanna and grasslands ecoregion.

Subtropical forests dominate the lower elevations of the Hill Region. They form a mosaic running east-west across Nepal, with Himalayan subtropical broadleaf forests between 500 and 1,000 meters (1,600 and 3,300 ft) and Himalayan subtropical pine forests between 1,000 and 2,000 meters (3,300 and 6,600 ft). At higher elevations, to 3,000 meters (10,000 ft), are found temperate broadleaf forests: eastern Himalayan broadleaf forests to the east of the Gandaki River and western Himalayan broadleaf forests to the west.

The native forests of the Mountain Region change from east to west as precipitation decreases. They can be broadly classified by their relation to the Gandaki River. From 3,000 to 4,000 meters (10,000 to 13,000 ft) are the eastern and western Himalayan subalpine conifer forests. To 5,500 meters (18,000 ft) are the eastern and western Himalayan alpine shrub and meadows.

ENVIRONMENTAL CONCERNS

Natural hazards

Earthquakes, severe thunderstorms, flooding, landslides, drought, and famine depending on the timing, intensity, and duration of the summer monsoons

Environment - current issues

Deforestation (overuse of wood for fuel and lack of alternatives); contaminated water (with human and animal wastes, agricultural runoff, and industrial effluents); wildlife conservation; vehicular emissions

Environment - international agreements

- Party to: Biodiversity, Climate Change, Climate Change-Kyoto Protocol, Desertification, Endangered Species, Hazardous Wastes, Law of the Sea, Ozone Layer Protection, Tropical Timber 83, Tropical Timber 94, Wetlands
- Signed, but not ratified: Marine Life Conservation
- Existing and proposed dams, barrages and canals for flood control, irrigation and hydroelectric generation

Geography - note

Landlocked; strategic location between China and India; contains eight of world's 10 highest peaks, including Mount Everest and Kanachenjunga – the world's tallest and third tallest – on the borders with China and India respectively

River systems

Nepal has three categories of rivers. The largest systems -— from east to west *Koshi*, *Gandaki/Narayani*, *Karnali/Goghra* and *Mahakali*—originate in multiple tributaries rising in or beyond the high Himalaya that maintain substantial flows from snowmelt through the hot, droughty spring before the summer monsoon. These tributaries cross the highest mountains in deep gorges, flow south through the Middle Hills, then join in candelabra-like configuration before crossing the

Mahabharat Range and emerging onto the plains where they have deposited *megafans* exceeding 10,000 km^2 (4,000 sq mi) area.

The Koshi is also called *Sapta Koshi* for its seven Himalayan tributaries in eastern Nepal: *Indrawati, Sun Koshi, Tama Koshi, Dudh Koshi, Liku, Arun,* and *Tamur*. The Arun rises in Tibet some 150 kilometres (100 mi) beyond Nepal's northern border. A tributary of the Sun Koshi, Bhote Koshi also rises in Tibet and is followed by the Arniko Highwayconnecting Kathmandu and Lhasa.

The *Gandaki/Narayani* has seven Himalayan tributaries in the center of the country: *Daraudi, Seti Gandaki, Madi, Kali, Marsyandi, Budhi,* and *Trisuli* also called *Sapta Gandaki.* The *Kali Gandaki* rises on the edge of the Tibetan Plateau and flows through the semi-independent Kingdom of Mustang, then between the 8,000 meter *Dhaulagiri* and*Annapurna* ranges in the world's deepest valley. The Trisuli rises north of the international border inside Tibet. After the seven upper tributaries join, the river becomes the*Narayani* inside Nepal and is joined by the *(East) Rapti* from Chitwan Valley. Crossing into India, its name changes to *Gandak*.

The *Karnali* drains western Nepal, with the *Bheri* and *Seti* as major tributaries. The upper Bheri drains Dolpo, a remote valley beyond the Dhaulagiri Himalaya with traditional Tibetan cultural affinities. The upper Karnali rises inside Tibet near sacred *Lake Manasarovar* and *Mount Kailash*. The area around these features is the hydrographic nexus ofSouth Asia since it holds the sources of the Indus and its major tributary the *Sutlej*, the Karnali—a Ganges tributary—and the *Yarlung Tsangpo/Brahmaputra.* It is the center of the universe according to traditional cosmography. The *Mahakali* or *Kali* along the Nepal-India border on the west joins the Karnali in India, where the river is known as *Goghra*or *Ghaghara*.

Second category rivers rise in the Middle Hills and *Mahabharat Range*, from east to west the *Mechi, Kankai* and *Kamala* south of the Kosi; the *Bagmati* that drains Kathmandu Valley between the Kosi and Gandaki systems, then the *West*

Rapti and the *Babai* between the Gandaki and Karnali systems. Without glacial sources, annual flow regimes in these rivers are more variable although limited flow persists through the dry season.

Third category rivers rise in the outermost *Siwalik* foothills and are mostly seasonal.

None of these river systems support significant commercial navigation. Instead, deep gorges create obstacles to establishing transport and communication networks and de-fragmenting the economy. Foot-trails are still primary transportation routes in many hill districts.

River management

Rivers in all three categories are capable of causing serious floods. Koshi River in the first category caused a major flood in August 2008 in *Bihar* state, India after breaking through a poorly maintained embankment just inside Nepal. The West Rapti in the second category is called *Gorakhpur's Sorrow* for its history of urban flooding. Third category Terai rivers are associated with flash floods. Since uplift and erosion are more or less in equilibrium in the Himalaya, at least where the climate is humid, rapid uplift must be balanced out by annual increments of millions tonnes of sediments washing down from the mountains; then on the plains settling out of suspension on vast alluvial fans over which rivers meander and change course at least every few decades, causing some experts to question whether manmade embankments can contain the problem of flooding. Traditional *Mithila* culture along the lower Koshi in Nepal and Bihar celebrated the river as the giver of life for its fertile alluvial soil, yet also the taker of life through its catastrophic floods.

Large reservoirs in the Middle Hills may be able to capture peak flows and mitigate downstream flooding, to store surplus monsoon flows for dry season irrigation and to generate electricity. Water for irrigation is especially compelling because the Indian Terai is suspected to have entered a *food bubble* where dry season crops are dependent on water from tubewells that in the aggregate are unsustainably "mining" groundwater. Depletion of acquifers without building upstream dams as a sustainable alternative water source could precipitate a Malthusian catastrophe in India's food insecure states Uttar Pradesh and Bihar, with over 300 million combined population. With India already experiencing a Naxalite–Maoist insurgency in Bihar, Jharkhand and Andra Pradesh, Nepalese reluctance to agree to water projects could even seem an existential threat to India.

As Nepal builds barrages to divert more water for irrigation during the dry season preceding the summer monsoon, there is less for downstream users in Bangladesh and India's Bihar and Uttar Pradesh states. The best solution could be building large upstream reservoirs, to capture and store surplus flows during summer monsoon as well as providing flood control benefits to Bangladesh and India. Then water sharing agreements could allocate a portion of the stored water to be left to flow into India during the following dry season.

Nevertheless, building dams in Nepal is controversial for several reasons. First, the region is seismically active. Dam failures caused by earthquakes could cause tremendous death and destruction downstream, particularly on the densely populated Gangetic Plain. Second, global warming has led to the formation of glacial lakes dammed by unstable moraines. Sudden failures of these moraines can cause floods with cascading failures of manmade structures downstream. Third, sedimentation rates in the Himalaya are extremely high, leading to rapid loss of storage capacity as sediments accumulate behind dams. Fourth, there are complicated questions of cross-border equity in how India and Nepal would share costs and benefits that have proven difficult to resolve in the context of frequent acrimony between the two countries.

13

Boundary of Nepal

The Himalayan Kingdom of Nepal lies between two big countries, China and India on its north and South. It is elongated on the east and the west. Since the last two hundred years the frontier of Nepal is surrounded on its south, east and west by India and on the north by China. History is evidence that at one time the boundary of Nepal was extended towards Tista River on the East; to Kangara across Sutlej River in the west; to the confluence of Ganga and Jamuna Rivers to the south; and to Shigatshe and Tashilhunpo Gomba (monastery) across the Himalayas in the north. In the course of time, at one time the western border was limited to Sutlej in the west to the mid-plains of the Ganges in the south; and it had touched the present day Bangladesh on the east. But because of time, situation and the activities of the past, the borderline of the Tista and Sutlej constricted to Mechi River on the east to Mahakali river on the west, and to watershed of the Himalayan Range on the north, and to the Siwalik range and the plains of the Tarai on the South.

The northern borderline of Nepal has been fixed at watershed of the Himalayan Range by the Nepal-China Boundary Protocol of 20 January 1963. Although the Sugauli Treaty of 4 March 1816 and Supplementary Treaties have tried to fix Nepal's borderline on the east, south and west on the above-mentioned boundaries, because of border encroachments, claims and counter-claims, intrusions and controversies it has not been finalized yet. After the demarcation of the border points with India is completed, the process of Nepal-India Boundary Protocol should be finalized formally and the delineation of the Nepal-India border should be ascertained according to the protocol. While the northern border has so many Himalayan peaks, and the borderline passes through the high peaks, mountains, passes, *deuralis* (terminal points of up mountain), gorges and the pasturelands, the southern borderline runs through fertile plains, jungles and rivers. On the east there is the Mechi River and the watershed of Singhalila Range, hills and hillocks stand as the border line, and the Mahakali River runs through the whole borderline on the west. No matter what the historical perspective of the Nepalese frontier was, the Kingdom of Nepal is bounded by a perimeter of 3,222.88 kilometers (including the disputed areas) Of this 1,414.88 km lies on the borderline with China and the remaining 1,808 km length along with the Indian border. Of the Nepalese border touching India, 1,213 km consists of land border and the remaining 595 kilometers is river boundary. There are 60 big and small rivers and rivulets which demarcate the border between Nepal and India. Of them the most important are the Mechi on the east and Mahakali on the west. The Mechi River forms 80 kilometers of the borderline, and similarly the Mahakali forms 230 km, Rapti 20 km, Ghongi 15 km, Rapti 6 km and the others form 244 kilometers of the borderline.

The perimeter of the greater Nepal extending from Tista on the east to Sutlej on the west was 4,079 line kilometres, east-west length as 1,373 kilometers and its area was 204,917 square kilometers. It was even bigger when the country's boundaries had extended from Tista on the east to Kangara on the West and to the confluence of the river Ganges and Yamuna on the south with the total perimeter stretching to 5,119 line kilometers, east-west length as 1,415 km and the total area as 267,575 square kilometers. But the modern Nepal has an encircled boundary line of 3,222.88 kilometers covering an area of 147,181 square kilometers.

The geographical position of the country lies between at 80^0 04' to 88^0 12' east longitude, and from 26^0 22' to $30^0$27' north latitude, with a length of 885 kilometer from east to west and a mean width of up to 193 kilometers from north to south. The lowest part of the country lies 57.3 meters above the mean sea level at Mushaharniya of Dhanusha district, and the highest part is the world's highest mountain Mt. Everest at 8,850 meters. Nepal's nearest point to the sea is 500 kilometers from the eastern border. Physiographically, Nepal can be divided into five regions. The southern plain covers 14 per cent of the total area, the Siwalik region with low hills and hillocks covers 13 per cent, the middle mountains cover 30 per cent, the high mountain region covers 20 per cent and the high Himalayan region covers 23 per cent of the total area. Of the Himalayan region 14 per cent are perennially under the cover of snow.

The sudden rise of altitude from south to north leading to drastic differences in climate, vegetation, animal habitat and human life-style and dresses of the people is the characteristic of the Nepalese topography. As a result during the same season of the year it is sweltering hot in some places while it is shivering cold in some others.

In the context of land use, 18.0 per cent of the total land is covered by settlement, 18.0 per cent by snow and water, 13.4 per cent is pasture land, 37.6 per cent is forest, 12.3 per cent is rocky, steep slopes, fallow or used for other purposes, and 0.7 per cent of the land is covered by human settlement and roads. The population of Nepal is 23.2 million and 14.2 per cent of them live in urban area with nine per cent of the total population estimated to be homeless. The literacy rate is 53.7 per cent and the per capita GDP is US$ 220 and 38 percent of the entire population are under poverty line.

For the administrative purposes the country is divided into 5 development regions, 14 zones, 75 districts, 58 municipalities and 3,913 Village Development Committees (VDCs). Each district, for the purpose of development, is normally divided into 9 areas; and the municipalities into 11 to 35 Wards and each VDC into 9 Wards. For the election purpose the country is divided into 205 election constituencies. Twenty-six districts of the country are bordered with India and 15 others with

China. Within the country, inhabited by four ethnic communities and 36 castes, there are various internal boundaries such as geographical and geological constructions, administrative and political units, and other border lines for social development and land use pattern. While the demarcation and the erection of border pillars on the Nepal-China border line and the third phase of periodic supervision and maintenance of the border pillars have been completed. But with India even the preliminary demarcation of the border, as delineated by the Sugauli Treaty of 1816 and other supplementary treaties, that started 22 years ago is yet to be completed. The work of demarcation of boundary line with India has neither stopped nor been completed. The border line which has entanglements in so many places often tries to find solutions but it entangles itself again and again. However, the boundary business with India will surely be completed one day in future, since it has been already completed with China. And in such way, encirclement of the international boundary line of the Kingdom of Nepal with two neighbouring countries will be completed in a safe and secure manner.

BORDER AREA PROBLEMS IN THE INDO-NEPAL

The border areas of the countries particularly belonging to South Asia are vested with problems (Pattanaik and Singh, 2005). The illegal flow of people, goods and money violets the border (Kearney, 1993). Securing the border against its violation is a major function of the post-colonial state in South Asia (Samadhar, 1999)

India has international border with six countries such as Pakistan, China, Nepal, Bhutan, Myanmar and Bangladesh. Nearly 17 states of the Indian union mark a border with neighbouring countries. Sensitized to the fact that border areas are less developed as compared to the mainland, the Government of India launched the Border Area Development Programme (BADP) during the Seventh Five Year Plan (1985-90) for the comprehensive development of the border areas. Presently, the BADP covers 345 blocks of 94 districts belonging to 17 states.

Altogether, the international Border of India is 15,126 kilometer length, comprising an approximate population of 40 million spread over an are of 2,40,500 square Kilometers.

Uttar Pradesh is geographically, historically, socially, culturally and demographically an important state of Indian Union. The state is bounded by Haryana, Delhi and Rajasthan in the west; Madhya Pradesh in the south and Bihar in the east. Its northern frontiers are adjoining Nepal. Uttar Pradesh comprises 17 divisions, 70 districts and 299 tehsils (sub-divisions). It is still the largest state of the Indian Union in population having 16.2 percent (2001 Census) of total population.

The bordering districts of Uttar Pradesh touching Nepal border are Pilibhit, Lakhimpur Kheri, Balrampur, Bahraich, Siddharthnagar, Maharajaganj, Deoria, Kushinagar and Shrawasti.

A few border districts of the state are socio-economically much backward as compared to other districts. For example, the male literacy rate of Balrampur district is the lowest in the state, 46.28 percent as compared to the state average 70.23 (2001 census). On the contrary, the female literacy rate of Shrawashti district is the lowest only 18.75 percent as compared to the state average of 42.98 percent.

Because of poverty and lack of employment opportunities as opined by the border area people, there is large scale outmigration of people to different cities i. e. Mumbai, Delhi, Ludhiana, etc. The 2001 Census depicts decline in rural population from 80.33 percent to 79.22 percent in 1991. This is further supported by the figure that these is a slight increae in the population of women from 46.69 percent in 1991 to 47.33 percent in 2001, with corresponding decrease in men's population from 53.31 percent to 52.67 percent.

The study general objective of the study

General objective of the present rapid survey was to assess the implementation of BADP, security concerns, border trade, border tourism and livelihood of the people living in the Indo-Nepal border areas of Uttar Pradesh.

Specific Objectives

1. To assess the various activities undertaken by the state government under BADP;
2. To observe the livelihood of the people living in the villages of the border areas;
3. To find out the security concerns in the Indo-Nepal border;
4. To register the border trade taking place in the Indo-Nepal border; and
5. To point out the need and scope for economic activities and tourism in the border areas.

Methodology

The methodology adopted in the rapid survey is: (I) Focus Group Discussions; (i) Interaction with the agencies, officials and peoples' representatives; and (ii) scanning of secondary data on BADP. The personnel involved in the discussion during field survey are as follows:

1. Chief Development Officers
2. District Statistical Officers
3. Block Development Officers
4. Sasastra Sena Bal (SSB): Assistant Commandants and Inspectors
5. Village Pradhans and opinion leaders

The study team visited 16 villages of nine blocks of seven districts i. e. Pilibhit, Lakhimpur (Kheri), Bahariach, Shrawasti, Sidharthnagar, Balrampur and Maharajganj. All these villages are situated in the corridor of Indo-Nepal borderline and within 15 km. of the borderline. An attempt was made to visit the nearest village to the border.

Impact of Border Area Development Programme

The various activities/infrastructure developed with the help of BADP are road, irrigation, health, education, energy, diary, horticulture and security. However, it is observed that the condition of border roads at many places particularly within

15 kilometer from borderline are in very bad condition and theiroperation and maintenance is poor.

The Laxmipuria village of block Sirsia of district Sarwasti has no pacca link road and also do not have electricity connection since independence. People of these villages feel alienated. Similarly, the migrant population of village Ramnagaria in Purampura block of district Pilibhit also do not have electricity facility. Because of lack of communication (surface transport) facility, villages nearer to the boarder are facing a lot difficulties.

Although schools are opened under BADP, they are not optimally functioning because of lack of teachers. There are no vocational educational institutions opened in the border areas under BADP for the skill education of youth. The expenditure of BADP funds in different heads of developmental activities.

Infrastructure Development in Border Areas

As opined by the district officials, earlier only villages situated within 10 kilometers away from the borderline were considered as border villages. However, according to recent notification of the state government all the villages in a developmental border block are being considered as border villages. This declaration of all villages in the border block as border area village has diluted the focus on real border area problems. It was observed during the field survey that many villages situated within 10 to 15km. of borderline lack following basic infrastructure facilities.

(i) Concrete Border Road

(ii) Electricity

(iii) Health Centre with doctor facility

(iv) Safe Drinking Water

(v) Sanitation

(vi) Irrigation facility

The border areas of the districts are concentrated with Scheduled Castes, Scheduled Tribes, and economically weaker

Muslim minorities population. For example in the village Ram Nagara Panchayat of block Puranpur of district Pilibhit, 16 villages were predominated with Nab Sudra (Scheduled Castes) Bangladeshi migrant rehabilitated during 1967. Besides, this cluster also consists of migrant Sikh population (economically weaker) and migrant Eastern UP population. Many villages of this panchayat have been affected by the changing river basin of Sarada river, flowing from the Nepal. The households of these villages are staying in kachha houses devoid of basic amenities. They are in the constant fear that the weak embarkment of the water reservoir of Sarada river, if bursted, would completely washed out their villages. People of these villages live in complete darkness and are devoid of electricity facilities. According to Block Development Officer, the growing population among these migrant populations (particularly Bangladeshi migrants) is a concern for us to provide basic amenities to these villages. The drinking water of many border area villages is contaminated with iron, which cause diseases like jaundice and cancer and people are dying every year by these diseases. More than 95 percent of deliveries are occurring in home without aseptic delivery facilities and trained personnel.

The people of village Kealpur of block Nawabganj opined that for referral health care services they are going to Nepal. Lack of referral health care centres especially for women is a gloomy feature of health care system in these critical areas. More than 90 percent of people residing in the border area villages are receiving treatment from the Jholechaps (quacks) doctors. Many hand-pumps constructed by the government have become defunct. The maternal mortality and infant mortality is a regular feature in these border area villages. Generally speaking, women are deprived of their right to reproductive health care services.

Although panchayat is active, yet they are not being consulted by the block officials for planning and implementation of developmental activities in the villages. Because of traditional believes and values, women Pradhans (panchayat head) do not take part actively in the panchayat affairs. The panchayat although aware about the needs of their community, yet because of lack of empowerment (financial) are unable to do need-based development and well-being of the community.

The people of border area villages earn their livelihood through agriculture and daily wage labour. Because of lack of assured employment, many youths in the border area villages are migrating to cities like Delhi and Mumbai for job. Those who are staying in villages are disguised unemployment in the agriculture sector. There are no vocational educations for youths and most of them are unskilled labourer and not fit for skilled jobs. In a few places as opined by SSB, unemployed youths are engaged in illegal trade of fertilizers, pulses and even narcotics.

The literacy status among the Muslims residing in the border villages is low and astoundingly low (less than two percent) among Muslim women. The two main aspects of educational backwardness of backward Muslim minorities in border area villages are: Poor educational infrastructure and lack of teachers in the schools. Many schools are managed by a single teacher sometimes with additional Sikhya Sahayaks. This has resulted in non-enrolment and dropout of children from the schools.

The education of many Muslim girl ends in Mosques and Madrasas. If properly motivated and substantiated with presence of teachers in the school, many Muslim community leaders opined that girl child education would improve.

More than 70 percent of families living in the border area villages have martial relation and kiths and kins in bordering villages of Nepal. One of such examples, the people of Laxanpuria village of Nepal offer Namaz in the Rosanpuria village of India (block Sirsia of district Sarawasthi). The marriages are even taking place and it is an ongoing feature as admitted by the people of the border villages of both Nepal and India and also opined by the security forces deployed in the border.

There are no registered village level institutions such as Youth Clubs and Mahila Mandals in border villages. In a few village SHGs are formed but they are in paper only and are not engaged in any gainful self-employment activities. On the whole, there is a general lack of community level institutions and activities. There is no concrete programme for women empowerment.

The centrally sponsored schemes although implemented in border areas, yet they are not adequate compared to the conditions of border area people. The drying up of 50 percent of tube well, anomalies in BPL families distribution, 90 percent of population using open field for defecation and out migration of youths to Mumbai and Delhi for employment, needs a critical thinking of implementation of these schemes in border area villages. Moreover, in border area villages of Rupedia of district Balrampur, 30 to 40 percent of youths are working in the industrial area of Nepal. In the same vein many people during their critical conditions are receiving health care services from Nepal. It is pertinent to note here that many points of border areas of Nepal are well-developed as compared to India.

DELINEATION OF NEPAL-CHINA BOUNDARY, PROBLEM AND SOLUTION OF DEMARCATION

The border areas between Nepal and China represent one of the least known areas of the world. The first regular survey of Nepal was conducted by the Survey of India in 1926-27 and that resulted in the actual demarcation of Nepal-India boundary with 10yard no man's land on either side of the land boundary. However, the demarcation of Nepal-China boundary was made through a survey from a much lower altitude. The topographical survey of 1956-58, which covered the whole of Nepal, was also conducted by the Survey of India. But this survey also could not properly delineate the boundary between Nepal and China because of the lack of proper and sophisticated instruments and equipment as well as the trained personnel to conduct survey in the high altitudes and rugged terrain. Because of the strategic importance of the Himalayas and boundary dispute between India and China as far back as 1950, when India insisted on Mc Mahon line as Sino-Indian boundary which was rejected by China. India did not provide topographical maps for a large section of the Nepal Himalayas as the aerial photographs of these regions had been damaged. When boundary talks between Nepal and China were initiated for a Boundary Agreement on March 21, 1960, its basis was the maps submitted by both countries. However, these maps were not based on proper surveys. The boundaries were drawn on sketch maps, or represented simply by a boundary line on plain paper or cloth. In order to solve the dispute resulting from such unscientific maps, the Joint Boundary Commission was constituted to survey the entire length of Nepal-China boundary as well as to resolve the territorial dispute through on-the-spot visit and assessment of the problem.

The acceptance of traditional customary boundary by both sides was the major reason for conclusion of a border agreement on as October 5, 1961. Nepal and China established diplomatic relations for the first time on August 1, 1955, that is, six years after the establishment of the People's Republic of China in 1949, and four years after the installation of democracy in Nepal in 1951. In the Agreement designed to maintain friendly relations between the People's Republic of China and the Kingdom of Nepal and in the Agreement on trade between the Tibetan Autonomous Region of China and Nepal the customary movement of people and goods along the border has been accepted..

It is to be noted that the survey for the delineation of Nepal-China boundary in 1960-61 had to be carried out with several constraints. Firstly, the survey had to be carried out from lower altitude and there was no aerial survey. Secondly, the instruments and equipment for the survey, manpower as well as proper training for high altitude survey were completely lacking. Moreover, in the absence of on-the-spot survey of high altitude areas, the drawing of the boundary line through the survey was done by recording actual location of important peaks and then drawing boundary line tentatively between the two surveyed peaks. This mainly accounts for change in position and alignment of Nepal-China boundary between 1961 and 1982 as well as change in the total length of boundary between

1961 and 1982. A glance at the maps of 1961 and 1982 shows a major change in Humla and Mustang. The 1982 boundary maps had been prepared through ground survey on higher altitude than in 1961 and was supported by aerial survey and satellite imageries. As compared to 1961, the length of Nepal-China boundary in 1982 increased to 303 kilometres and the area has increased by 1.876 sq. km. for Nepal.

The Nepal-China border extends along the whole length of northern border of Nepal and the starting and ending point of Nepal-China boundary is the tri-junction of the boundary between Nepal, China and India. However, because of the Sino-Indian boundary dispute as well as Nepal-India dispute over the Kalapani on the source of the Mahakali River, the demarcation started 5 kilometers ahead of the tri-junction in the west and 5 kilometres behind the tri-junction in the east. There is no man-made boundary demarcation on land as indicated in the boundary treaty maps, except for the boundary pillars. Along the whole length of Nepal China boundary, there are 79 boundary pillars, only as against more than 1000 boundary pillars along Nepal India border with 10 yards no-man, land on either side of Nepal India boundary. Under the protocol signed and exchanged between Nepal and China on January 20,1963, the contracting parties agreed to maintain and adopt necessary measures to prevent the removal, damage or destruction of boundary pillars as far as possible, to prevent the boundary rivers from changing their course and to make a joint inspection of the entire boundary every five years. Accordingly, in 1979 a new agreement was signed between the two countries after detailed mapping and demarcation of the boundary.

CHINA'S INROADS INTO NEPAL: INDIA'S CONCERNS

The political crisis that triggered off in Nepal with Prime Minster Prachanda's resignation yet again indicates not only the trials and tribulations of a fledgling democratic process but also points to the geopolitical vulnerability of the country sandwiched as it is between the two Asian giants. While India considers Nepal a part of its sphere of influence, it is increasingly being challenged by China's inroads into Nepal. In fact, the growing Nepal-China nexus should be seen in the context of India-China power competition in Asia. Essentially Nepal facilitates China's security interests in the South Asian region. This can be clearly glimpsed from Chinese ambassador, Zheng Xianglin's statement delivered at the Council of World Affairs in August 2008 that "Nepal is situated in a favourable geographical position in South Asia, and a passage linking China and South Asia."

Nepal constitutes an important element of China's South Asia policy. One may recall Mao Zedong's five finger policy in which Nepal constituted one of the five fingers along with Ladakh, Bhutan, Sikkim and Arunachal Pradesh. The five fingers were essentially meant to serve as a 'new buffer' zone between India and China after the 'old buffer' (Tibet) came under China's sovereign control in 1951. With growing tensions in Tibet, particularly after the March 2008 uprising, China's conception of Nepal as a new buffer acquired particular significance. Its policy towards Nepal came to be driven by the need to curb the clandestine activities of some 20,000 Tibetan refugees (the second largest Tibetan refugee community in the world) in Nepal. Consequently, China has been increasingly playing a significant role in determining the future shape of Nepali politics. During each of the high-level meetings China has extracted assurances from Nepal that it adheres to the one-China principle, acknowledges Tibet as an inalienable part of China, and will ensure that no anti-China activity is allowed on its soil. Underscored in China's South Asia policy is the strategy to marginalize India's influence in Nepal. Marginalizing India would allow China not only to dominate South Asia but also provide easy access to Nepal's roughly 83,000 megawatts of hydroelectric potential.

It is interesting to note that China pronounces its foreign policy towards Nepal in a manner which presents not only a benign image of itself but which also helps assuage Nepal's fears of a domineering India. For instance, the December 2008 Yang Jiechi's assurance to protect Nepal's "sovereignty and independence" not only strengthened Beijing's diplomacy but also sought to obviate India's influence. News reports from Nepal even go further to suggest that "China intended to develop relations with Nepal in a way that would serve as a role model for bilateral ties between big and small countries." China has, in fact, laid down a four-fold policy to strengthen its bilateral relations with Nepal: "First, accommodate each other's political concern. Second, enhance the economic cooperation on the basis of mutual benefit. Third, boost people-to-people and cultural exchanges. Fourth, strengthen the coordination and cooperation in international and regional affairs."

Apart from stating a clear policy towards Nepal, China has been systematically pursuing a multi-dimensional engagement with Nepal. There has been a flurry of visits between China and Nepal in recent times. According to one news report, about 38 Chinese delegations visited Nepal in 2008 alone. China has been cultivating ties with not only the Communist Party of Nepal-Maoist (CPN-M) but also with the Communist Party of Nepal-United Marxist-Leninist (CPN-UML) and the Madhesi People's Rights Forum. Lately, China has begun taking interest in Terai politics. There are reports of a high level Chinese delegation visiting the General Convention of the Madhesi People's Rights Forum in early 2009. In April 2009, a CPN-UML delegation led by Jhala Nath Khanal visited Beijing when China had impressed upon the delegation that it wants "a new kind of relationship" with Nepal.

Besides high level visits, China's inroads into Nepal are being greatly facilitated by the systematic promotion of China Study Centers (CSCs) which are completely funded by China. The number of CSCs in Nepal has increased in recent times. According to the CSC website, there are ten local branches located in Butwal, Banepa, Sankhuwasabha, Pokhara, Biratnagar, Morang, Sunsari, Chitwan, Nepalgunj and Lumbini, besides the central organization of the CSC-Nepal in Kathmandu. According to Bhim Prasad Bhurtel, the executive director of the Nepal South Asia Centre, Kathmandu, "33 China Study Centres have been established in southern Nepal adjoining the Indian border." He also mentions that China Radio International has launched a local FM radio station in Kathmandu with the purpose of bringing China closer to Nepal. Besides CSCs, a Nepal-China Mutual Cooperation Society (NCMCS), funded by the Chinese Embassy in Nepal, was established in March 2005. The primary aim of NCMCS is to strengthen diplomatic relations between the two countries as well as to disseminate an image of a friendly China as opposed to hegemonic India. Besides, there are other associations like the Nepal-China Executives Council in Kathmandu, the Nepal-China Friendship Association in Lumbini and the Nepal-China Youth Friendship Association in Pokhara. Further, to promote bilateral cooperation and exchanges the Nepal-China bilateral consultation mechanism was constituted in 1996. Such multi-layered engagement enabled China to not only strengthen its diplomacy in the region but also project a benign and cooperative image. It may be noted that India does not have such multi-layered levels of contact and lacks innovative ways (cultural or diplomatic) of reaching out to the Nepali government and people. In fact, similar culture and traditions in Nepal create a kind of extended cultural zone for India and often therefore many of the natural linkages that exist between India and Nepal are taken for granted.

China's proactive policy in Nepal can also be discerned from the military assistance it has been providing. On December 7, 2008 during a meeting in Kathmandu between Nepal Defence Minister Ram Bahadur Thapa and the deputy commander of China's People Liberation Army, Lieutenant General Ma Xiaotian, China pledged to provide US $2.6 million as military assistance for Nepal's security sector. Earlier in September 2008, China had announced military aid worth $ 1.3 million, the first such assistance to the Maoist government in Nepal. It may be recalled that in 2006 China had provided clandestine military assistance to the Maoists in a bid to placate them. In recent times, Beijing has shown keen support for the Maoist governments' proposal to integrate some 19,000 Maoist guerrillas with the Nepal Army.

As part of economic assistance, ahead of Prachanda's now-cancelled second visit to China, China had announced a doubling of aid to Nepal amounting to $21.94 million. To attract Chinese investment in Nepal, on April 7, 2009, the Nepal-China Executives Council (NCEC) and the Chinese People's Association for Friendship with Foreign Countries (CPAFFC) signed a MoU. The trade volume between the two countries currently stands at $401 million with China selling goods worth about $386 million, and Nepal exporting a mere $15 million.

To bridge the trade deficit, China has agreed in April 2009 to provide duty free access to 497 Nepali goods in the Chinese market. There are also proposals for a second South Asian Countries Commodity Fair to be held from 6 to 10th June 2009 at Kunming where 40 Nepali enterprises are slated to participate with 30 stalls. China is the third largest country to provide FDI to Nepal, India and the US being the first and second, respectively.

Also, not to forget, China's initiative in building a road link between Lhasa and Khasa, a border town located some 80 kilometres north of Kathmandu. China has also accepted Nepal's proposal in April 2009 to open up two more custom points in addition to the existing five. China is also building a 65 km second road link, the Syafrubesi-Rasuwagadi road, which is the shortest route from Tibet to Kathmandu. As part of promoting Nepal's hydro-power projects, in 2008, China's Assistant Minister for Foreign Affairs, He Yafei, pledged to provide Nepal a loan of $125 million for Upper Trishuli 3 'A' and $62 million for Upper Trishuli 3 'B'. The plants would start operating from 2012.

There has thus evolved a multi-layered engagement between China and Nepal, causing considerable concern in the Indian establishment. Even if Prachanda's statement is to be believed that "not a single (Chinese) delegation came to Nepal on my invitation," it nonetheless does not rule out China's growing inroads into Nepal. China's growing ties with Nepal undoubtedly supports its wider South Asia policy, much to the concern of India.

More importantly, China's strategic interest has been facilitated by the rise of the Maoists in Nepal. In fact, the January 2008 speech of Prachanda which got leaked has fuelled India's concern about the possibility of Nepal inching towards a Maoist dictatorship. Indeed, ideological similarity with Communist China lends suspicion to the growing affinity between the two countries.

Unlike Royal Nepal, the Maoists under Prachanda have shown in no ambiguous terms their strategic goal of reducing dependence on India and increasing ties with China.

In this context, it is worth noting the draft proposal for a China-Nepal friendship treaty submitted on February 27, 2009 by the visiting Chinese delegation to Nepal led by Assistant Chinese Foreign Minister Liu Jieyi.

The official reason provided was the need for a fresh treaty to meet the changing political environment in Nepal after the Maoists came to power. For Nepal, signing a treaty with China on the lines of the 1950 India-Nepal treaty undoubtedly curtails India's special relations with Nepal. At the same time, by pledging to overhaul the 1950 treaty with India on the ground that it "does not represent the aspirations of the Nepalese people anymore" Maoist Nepal clearly seeks to reduce India's influence in Nepal. Prachanda's May 09, 2009 interview to the Times of India in which he asked, "Why should Nepal seek India's consent on its security?" seems to hint at the Maoist's search for independent foreign policy. And on the other hand are reports about China pledging support for Prachanda's decision to sack the army chief when India was trying hard to prevent it.

In sum, observing the growing trends of Nepal-China ties, it may be argued that Nepal under the Maoist government has been clearly seeking closer ties with China at the cost of India and is far from pursuing a policy of equidistance. Further, Nepal's geo-political location coupled with China's proactive South Asia policy has clearly accentuated the security dilemma in the region. At this juncture, when Nepal is in turmoil, a great deal of foreign policy dexterity is required on the part of the Indian establishment to preserve its influence in South Asia and at the same time ensure a democratic Nepal that would deter China's inroads into Nepal.

BORDER ECONOMIC ZONE (BEA)/BORDER FOCAL POINT (BFP) DEVELOPMENT

A few points in the Indo-Nepal border in Uttar Pradesh have scope for economic activities, reason being that many border points in the adjacent Nepal side have industrial town where young people from bordering villages from India are going for work. The similar kind of Border Economic Zone (BEZ) would not only promote trade between India and Nepal but also provide employment opportunity to the impoverished people in the border. The village panchayats are willing to share their panchayat land for such activities. Two such points are:

Rupedia in the district Sarwasti having communication link with Delhi, Himachal Pradesh and Uttaranchal. In the opposite side of Nepal, there is a well developed industrial area. Youth from India are working in that industrial town of Nepal. According to the opinion of six village panchayat pradhans, the Economic Zone with activities most suitable in the opinion of local people for the area are:

(a) Plastic Industry
(b) Ply wood
(c) Glass
(d) Iron and steal

Aligarwha of Sidharthnagar district also can be developed as a Border Economic Zone (BEA). It will promote both economic activity and border tourism and trade and businesses between India and Nepal.

Similar other important points must be identified and environmental friendly Mini Border Economic Zone should be established in these focal points.

INSECURE BORDER MANAGEMENT OF NEPAL

Nepal is situated between two emerging Asian giants, China and India. The frontier of Nepal is surrounded on its south, east and west by India and on the north by China. China has expanded its economic market almost all over the world against the background of its emerging political scenario. And India is attaining economic prosperity in South Asia by enhancing its global political image. Historically, Nepal was elongated 1,415 km east to west from Tista to Kangra with an area of 267,575 sq. km. But it was shrunk to Mechi and Mahakali, after the Treaty of Sugauli on 4 March 1816 and subsequent Boundary Treaties of 11 December 1816 and 1 November 1860 with British East India Company. As a result, present Nepal's territory has been limited to an area of 147,181 sq. km having 885 km east-west length.

Nepal has a regulated border management system with China, whereas there is an open border between Nepal and India. This paper analyzes how Nepal's open border with India is faced with external threats due to cross border terrorism. It further analyzes the implications of open border system in order to maintain law and order, peace and security not only in both the nations but also in other countries of South Asia. Besides, it describes what border management strategies are available between the two countries and how they are working in practice. It also emphasizes that the existing border management system needs some change to prevent cross border terrorism.

THERE IS NO TREATY TO MAKE THE BORDER OPEN

There is no such treaty/agreement or memorandum to keep the border open between two countries. Even Nepal-India Peace and Friendship Treaty of 31 July 1950 does not have the provision for open border system.

Article-VII of the treaty says: "The government of India and Nepal agree to grant, on reciprocal basis, to the nationals of one country in the territories of the other the same privileges in the matter of residence, ownership of property, participation in trade and commerce, movement and privileges of a similar nature."

But there is no mention of the open border between two countries. It only suggests that the border management system must be reciprocated by both the countries. What it means is that if open or regulated system is enacted by one country, the same system should be implemented by the other on the basis of reciprocity.

If we examine some regulations, there is no mention of open border system. Passport Regulations-1952 says: "In case of the Nepalese residing for long or permanently settled down in any foreign country want to visit Katmandu, they will require to have the permit issued from the concerned District/City Magistrate or Passport issued by the Embassies or Consulates of Nepal in the respective country or from the Alainchikothi (as Consulate Office of Nepal) in Patna, India."

In the same way, the Sample of Rahadani/Permit-April 1862 says: "Nepalese to go out of Katmandu Valley and Nepal to Nepal via India should require to obtain Rahadani/Permit from Rahadani Goswara (Office) or Gadhi/Gaunda." There was also arrangement to provide permanent passport paying Nepali Rupees Five for one year to the general people, who come and go through Gadhi and by aero-plane from 14 April 1952.

On the other hand, if we make a study on the existing Immigration Act-1992, even the Indian nationals should produce visa to enter Nepal. Article-3 (1) of the Act says: "No foreigners are entitled to enter into the Kingdom of Nepal and reside in Nepal without having passport and visa." In this connection, the question arises: who are the foreigners?

Immigration Regulations-1992 (Second Amendment-2002), Article 2(B) defines: "Foreigner means any person, not being the citizen of Nepal at present, as it must be understood." In the regulations, no special provision has been made for Indian nationals.

It indicates that the regulated border system should also be followed for the Indian nationals. If there was some memorandum or agreement to maintain open border system between two countries, the Immigration Act and Regulations would not have been issued in this manner.

Next, Article-7 of Nepal-India Joint Press Statement-23 March 2000 reads: "The two Prime Ministers agreed on the need to prevent the misuse of the open border by terrorists, criminals and other undesirable elements and directed that co-operation in this regard be enhanced. Discussions on the management of the border would continue in the Joint Working Group on Border Management between the two Home Secretaries."

This scribe had published an article in a daily newspaper on the regulation of border. In response to this article, Sanjaya Verma, Counselor of Indian Embassy, Katmandu wrote in the Letter to the Editor column of the same daily supporting this scribe that "Open border between two countries is not mentioned in any of the articles of 1950 Nepal-India Treaty.

Open border is an emblem of most intimate friendship that has existed between both countries from ancient time to this date."9 So all these facts reveal that there is no black and white document on the prevalence of open border system between Nepal and India.

How the border is made open

There may be a query as to how the open border system prevailed between two countries. The answer may be, it prevailed only on the basis of mutual understanding, good neighbourly relations, religious sentiment, the same topography, social similarities, and family relationship.

The next factor may be political. There was a very close contact among high-ranking political leaders of both nations. While Nepalese leaders had participated actively in the independence movement of India, Indian leaders also contributed to establish democracy in Nepal. And the open border made the movement of political leaders and bureaucrats of India and Nepal easy to shuttle back and forth without any interrogation or check in the border.

The third factor is the social one. Socially, Nepalese boys are the sons-in-law of Indian nationals and Indian girls are the daughters-in-law of the Nepalese, mostly those who reside in the frontier. As a consequence, Indian and Nepalese parents are Samdhi (parents of daughter-in-law) to each other. So the border was made open socially for frequent visits to the kith and kin on either side of the frontier. The administration did not obstruct them in practice.

Implications of open border system

There are positive and negative implications of open border system between Nepal and India. Negative implication outnumbers the positive one in the Nepalese context. Convenience in movement and travel, strengthening mutual ties, quick emergency response and assistance, competitive frontier market, supply of labour etc. are positive features. But there are many other negative aspects of insecure open border system.

This may be cross-border terrorism, transaction of illegal arms and ammunitions, encroachment of border and no-man's land, effect on peace and security, trans-border crime, theft and robbery, girls and women trafficking, narcotic drug trafficking, kidnapping of individuals, illegal migration, smuggling of goods and machinery, leakage in revenue collection and anti-social activities.

The terrorist and Maoist rebels have gained benefits from the open border. They have misused it for the transaction of illegal arms and ammunitions. But the common people of Nepal and India fear insecurity for their life and property. Maoists and unwanted elements create terror in Nepalese frontier time and often.

They attack mainly government offices, set fire to them and loot the bank. Some of them have been killed during fighting. Those who manage to escape flee on the other side of the porous border with no restriction and take shelter there. In the same way those who are wounded and injured, cross the open border easily, with blood leaking from their bodies. They get treatment in the hospitals of Indian frontier. When they recover and get recharged, they go again to create terror and horror in Nepal. In such a fashion Indo-Nepal porous border has been made insecure and misused.

On the other side, not only the Indian and Nepali nationals cross the porous border without any restriction, but these days some Pakistani, Bangladeshi, Sri Lankan and even Afgan and Iranian nationals infiltrate into Nepalese territory, misusing the open border to some extent. Their similar face, attire, posture and behaviour resemble the Nepalese and Indian nationals. Some of the Pakistani, Iranian, and Myanmar infiltrators are seeking asylum in mostly western nations through United Nations High Commissioner for Refugees (UNHCR) office in Katmandu. In one sense, the porous border has helped to initiate rebellion activity in both nations to some extent. So Indo-Nepal open border management system is going to be difficult for the common people of both countries.

THE EVOLUTION OF NEPAL'S INTERNATIONAL BOUNDARY WITH CHINA AND INDIA

Like most of the countries of the world, the existence of Nepal had been recognised even before the international boundaries had been fully and finally established. Mention of Nepal is found in the ancient history of both China and India. Nepal-China boundary is as old as the history of the two countries, but in contrast to the very ancient cultural, social, political and economic relations, Nepal-India boundary has a comparatively recent origin and its present boundary demarcation and delimitation took place after the Anglo-Nepal War of 1814-16.

In contrast to Nepal's boundary with India on three sides: west, south and east, the boundary between Nepal and China lies in the north only. However, the demarcation of Nepal-China boundary had been a problem in the past, because more than 90 percent of the frontiers run through high altitudes with rocks and snow, glaciers and ice fields which are entirely uninhabited. Both countries have respected and continue to respect the existing traditional and customary boundary line and have lived in amity. No remarkable or noticeable territorial dispute has existed between Nepal and China. The few territorial disputes that existed were over rival claims for the settlements of Kimathanka in the Sankhuwasabha and Taplejung districts, the area adjoining the border of Rasuwa, and Nara Nangla of Humla district with the origin of dispute dating back to 1815, 1818 and 1834 respectively.:These disputes were resolved by the Nepal-China Joint Boundary Commission on October 5, 1961.

The ruggedness of Nepal-China boundary is clearly revealed by its length which is 1415 kilometres, while Nepal-India boundary which runs along three sides of Nepal is only 1850 kilometres, 465 kilometres longer than Nepal-China boundary. The 1415 kilometre length of Nepal-China boundary is based on measurement in the maps. If the actual measurement is made on the ground along the slopes and ridges of the mountains, the length of the boundary will be more than that indicated by the measurement in the maps. So far as Nepal-India boundary is concerned, the mountainous portions of the boundary lie in Sikkim State and Darjeeling district of West Bengal State in the east, while rest of the boundary runs along the plains in the south and along the Mahakali River in the west.

The Delineation and Demarcation of Nepal-India Boundary

Prior to the domination of India by the British East India Company, both Nepal and India were divided into petty kingdoms and principalities. As such, very little information is available regarding the extent of border as well as border disputes between Nepal and India. The British East India Company had already started the colonisation, expansion and consolidation of Indian states and principalities through invasion, and was planning to invade Nepal after the death of King Prithvinarayan Shah. The plea for invading Nepal was their false claim over the control of Butawal, which in reality belonged to Nepal. The Anglo-Nepal War of 1814 and the subsequent treaty of peace signed between Nepal and the East India Company on December 8, 1816 resulted in the delimitation and delineation of Nepal-India border. The Mahakali River formed the western boundary, while the Mechi formed the boundary in the east along with ridges in the Darjeeling hills and Sikkim. Accordingly, Nepal had to forsake the areas lying to the west of the Mahakali River and the areas lying to the east of the Mechi River including the return of the territory of the Rajah of Sikkim occupied by Nepal. The East India Company delineated and demarcated the southern boundary on its own. But no demarcation was made for the Tarai region lying between the Mahakali River and the Arrah Nala, which was ceded to the British India in 1816.

Moreover, the entire western Tarai was almost covered with dense forests, and, at the same time, there was no physical basis to discern the northern limit of Tarai. Nepal and India had a dispute over this ill-defined and ill-demarcated boundary. Prime Minister Jung Bahadur spent the last two decades of his rule in solving these problems. In his lifetime, he settled all the problems affecting the boundary between Nepal and India, because he was apprehensive that in the future such problems might lead to friction between the two states.

A straight line between the two pillars was drawn for the demarcation of the border in the forest areas, while demarcation in the cultivated land was made on the basis of village boundaries on the principle of mutual give and take. Major disputes and problems arose in the case of river boundary due to erratic changes in the river courses in the Tarai region. In recognition of assistance of Nepalese army in quelling the 1857 mutiny in Lucknow, and because of the fact that the western Tarai, which was ceded to India under the Treaty of 1816, was retrocede to Nepal, the Boundary Commissions of the two Governments met in North Oudh at Bhagura Tal in February 1860 to survey and demarcate the boundary.

After the completion of the survey and demarcation, the King of Nepal and the British Resident signed a formal treaty on November 1, 1860. Even after that, the dispute over the river boundary between Mondia Ghat to Bunbasa along the Mahakali (Sharada) river arose immediately after the treaty and was resolved in December 1864. Nepal made the claim over the Dudhawa Range up to the foot of the hills, while the British insisted on the Range watershed forming the boundary and the area along the Southern slopes of the watershed belonging to India. The Agreement endorsing the claim of Nepal was ratified on June 7, 1875. For the Nepalese territory of 2800 acres ceded to India for the construction of the Sharada Barrage in the early 1900s, a total of 4000 acres in Taratal area to the south of Bardia district was given to Nepal. Later, the survey and review of the territory ceded to India by Nepal revealed that an excess of 31 acres had gone to India. India had agreed to compensate for that area, but it has not yet materialised.

The actual scientific demarcation of Nepal-India boundary started during the topographical survey of the whole of Nepal carried out by the Survey of India in 1926-27. As the survey was carried out from the lower altitudes in the mountain areas in the north, it failed to delineate Nepal-China boundary in the north. This survey produced topographical maps for Nepal indicating Nepal-India boundary including the location and number of each boundary pillar together with topographical details of the Indian side in the maps as well. The scale of topographical maps was 1 inch to 4 miles. The topographical survey of 1955-58 conducted again by the Survey of India provided more detailed survey of Nepal both through aerial and ground surveys and resulted in the publication of maps to the scale of 1 inch to a mile. This map also indicated the boundary line and boundary pillars with their respective numbers.

However, the Indian territory across Nepal-India boundary was left blank. One notable fact about the topographical maps of Nepal and Bhutan is that the Surveyor General of both was Brigadier General Gambir Singh, and in the case of the topographical maps of Bhutan, details across the India Bhutan border on both sides have been shown. The absence of landmarks onon the topographical maps on the Indian side across the Nepal India border has been the major reson behind the encroachment of Nepalese territories across the border. Since the demarcation of Nepal India border after the Treaty of Sugauli, there has been tremendous change in the landscape on either sides of the border with tremendous change in man made features as compared to the natural landscapes. There has been no attempt so far to up date the boundary treaty maps according to these changes. In case of the Nepal China boundary, the boundary treaty maps contain detailed land features both natural and man-made features on either sides of the border and provided basis for the adjustment of the border to its original position if some discrepancies occurred due to natural or man made causes. It is due to this fact that since the signing of the boundary protocol between Nepal and China since 1961, there has not been any problem regarding the boundary between Nepal and China.

There has been several delays in making available the topographical maps by Survey of India to Nepal..It took more than 25 years to secure the topographical maps of Nepal as they were provided on piecemeal basis. The Survey of India has not make available 17 sheets of which 12 sheets pertain to Nepal India barder area including that of the Kalapani, and 5 sheets pertaining to the Nepal China border. Under the Sugauli Treaty, Nepal withdrew from all the territory it had occupied in Sikkim as Nepal had no formal treaty with Sikkim regarding Nepal-Sikkim boundary. The British East India Company, under the Treaty of Titaliya on 10 February 1871 with the Government of Sikkim restored the territory ceded by Nepal. A Sunnud dated 7 April 1817 regarding the granting of the territory to the Rajah of Sikkim stated:

"The honourable East India Company, in consideration of the services performed by the Hill tribes under the control of the Rajah of Sikkim, and of the attachment shown to him to the interest of the British Government, grants to the Sikkimputtee Rajah, his heirs and successors all that portion of low land situated eastward of the Meitchie River, and westward of the Maha Nuddee, formerly Possessed by the Rajah of Nepaul, but ceded to the Honourable East India Company by the Treaty of Segoulee, to be held by the Sikkimputtee Rajah as a feudatory, or as acknowledging the supremacy of the British Government over the said lands, subject to the following conditions." Moreover, there has not been any formal treaty between Nepal and India on Nepal-Sikkim Boundary after the independence of India, and even after the annexation of Sikkim with India in 1975. It is to be noted that Nepal has not yet formally recognised the annexation of Sikkim by India,. and, at the same time, India has not sought recognition from Nepal.

Before the independence of India, there existed a system of regular survey and supervision of Nepal-India boundary jointly conducted by the officials of both countries every year to oversee and find out encroachment, if any, on the boundary, ill-defined boundary, missing and broken as well as displaced boundary pillars with the objective to fix and place them in their original position. Accordingly, while Nepal has been entrusted to look after the pillars having odd number, India looks after the pillars having even number. After the independence of India, no joint boundary survey has been conducted until the formation of a Joint Boundary Commission in 1981 with the composition of six boundary survey teams.

Delay in the formation of a Joint Boundary Commission resulted in several boundary disputes, which remain unresolved, because the activities of the Commission are going on at a very slow pace. There is provision for two meetings of the Joint Boundary Commission every year. Twenty years have elapsed since the formation of the Commission in 1981 and accordingly, there should have been 36 meetings up to 1999, but so far only 22 meetings have been convened.

Boundary survey of almost all the districts bordering India has been completed except for Darchula, Dadeldhura and Kanchanpur as well as the border with Sikkim state of India. Moreover, there have been several cases of encroachment on and tampering with the boundary markers and damage, destruction and removal of boundary pillars in the areas already surveyed by the joint boundary teams. As a result, there exist several cases of boundary disputes with resulting claims and counter claims. There are reportedly 8 disputed areas along the Nepal India border with a total of six along the rivers of the Mahakali, the Narayani/Gandak (Susta) and the Mechi and the other two are in Pasupatinagar and Thori.

There are several areas along the Nepal-India border where no man's land has been encroached on both sides. According to Mr. Buddhi Narayan Shrestha, the former Director General of the Department of Survey of Nepal, there are 53 disputed and encroached areas along the Nepal-India boundary. However, the All Nepal Free Students' Union affiliated with the Nepal Communist Party (Marxist and Leninist) has indicated 61 disputed areas along the Nepal-India boundary. Out of the 26 districts of Nepal bordering India, the map indicates 22 districts having encroachment (problem) and the only 4 remaining districts having no boundary problem are Baitadi, Bara, Mahottari and Dhanusha. The map also indicates boundary problems in the districts bordering the Sikkim State of India. Recently, it has been made mandatory by the both governments to their district authorities on both sides of the Nepal India border to provide information on the status of their respective border in other to oversee and prevent encroachment and damage to the boundary.

The Nepal-India Open Border

Before the signing of the Sugauli Treaty between Nepal and India and subsequent demarcation of the Nepal India boundary, there existed free and unrestricted movement of people of Nepal and India across the border. It was almost impossible to control and regulate the movement of people along more than 1400 kilometres long border. Nevertheless, the main thoroughfare existed for social relations, cultural exchanges (pilgrimages, festivities, fairs, etc.) and trade and commerce and they constituted the major road junctions and places for levying customs duties. Nepal-India border is unique in the world in the sense that people of both the countries can cross it from any point, despite the existence of border checkposts at several locations. The number of check posts meant for carrying out bilateral trade is 22. However, only at six transit points out of them, the movement was permitted to nationals of third countries, who require entry and exit visa to cross the border. As the whole length of the border except police does not patrol the checkposts or paramilitary or military forces of either country, illegal movement of goods and people is a common feature on both sides of the India-Nepal border.

It is not known how the system of free movement of people on either side of the border continued even after the delineation and demarcation of Nepal-India border after 1816. Prior to the 1814 war, the movement of people of both countries was allowed, but they were not allowed to purchase land and settle in the Tarai. Nevertheless, Nepal has been the land of shelter for the refugees fleeing due to the fear from powerful enemies. The Lichhavis, the Mallas and the Shakyas who existed before the birth of Lord Buddha, took refugee in the Tarai and the Valleys of the Himalayas when their lands were usurped by Ajatasatru. Similarly, during the Muslim invasions of India, the Mallas and the Shahs are reported to have taken refuge in Nepal. The growing domination of India the British East India Company prompted the rulers of Nepal to restrict the movement of Indians into Nepal. Moreover, the Tarai could not be brought under cultivation through immigrants from India, because they were neither permitted to purchase land nor entitled to have tenancy rights. Thus the large tracts of the Tarai were covered by dense forests and infested with malaria. The cattle herders of adjoining Indian territories of Champaran and other districts used to graze cattle annually for four months (October to January) by paying duty. Duty was levied on buffaloes and cows were exempted from the levy. Similarly, the agreement on Dudhawa Range specially preserved the right of the Indian nationals to come to the hills for bankas (a type of grass) by paying revenue. Prior to 1789, the Nepal Government established bazaars on the border of Nepal and India for regulating trade and decided that trade could be conducted at these points only. This hampered the freedom of trade, as the British (Indian) merchants had to cross the border and enter into the Nepalese bazaars, and return with whatever they could not sell. Anyone entering Nepal, particularly the Kathmandu Valley and other places in the Tarai in general, prior to the restoration of Oudh Tarai to Nepal in 1860, had to get rahadani or visa from the district governor. This was relaxed during the festival of Shivaratri and after the festival the combing up operation was done to expel all those who had come to attend the festival. This system continued even after the installation of democracy in 1951 until the opening of the Tribhuvan Rajpath in late 1950s.

The Treaty of 1860 and the Nepal India Open Border

In recognition of the supply of Nepalese army at the disposal of the British East India Company to quell the Sepoy Mutiny, the Treaty of 1 November 1860 signed between India and Nepal restored the territory ceded to India under the 1816 Treaty of Suguali. Prime Minister Jung Bahadur tried to develop the Far Western Tarai restored to Nepal by the British as his family property. In order to develop it he made provision in the first legal code of the country formulated during his time, in which foreigners were entitled to purchase and sell land in the Tarai. He even invited the businessmen, traders and the landlords from India. This led to the large scale immigration of Indians into the Tarai for reclamation of forests, for agriculture and for trade and commerce. In the eastern Tarai the Yadav community exploited this opportunity and their significant number is an instance in point. Some of them had even settled in these places before that. Moreover, in the historical past after the draining away of the Kathmandu Valley lake, some of the cow herders from the south settled in Nepal and are said to have established the Gopalbanshi Dynasty. Before the conquest of the Kathmandu Valley by King Prithvinarayan Shah, the culture and economy of the Valley was so rich that it not only attracted people from outside, but also assumed the role of a melting pot, wherein the in-migrants to the valley coming from both the south and north adopted the Newari culture and language.

The British Government kept the Nepal-India border open primarily for two purposes. The first was to maintain unrestricted migration of the Nepalese hill people to India and to procure them for recruitment in the Indian army. Recruitment of the Nepalese in the British army was very difficult up to the period of Prime Minister Ranodip Singh, because the Government of Nepal was in principle against the recruitment of its people in a foreign army. The clandestine and secret operations adopted by the British to get Nepal hill people in the Indian army were disliked by the Nepalese government which took strong measures to discourage the practice. Some of the Gorkhas serving in the Indian army on their return home on leave were even put to death and the property of those serving the Indian army was confiscated. Sensing the harassment meted to families of the Gorkhas in the Indian army by the Nepalese government and to make the recruitment easier, the British Government encouraged migration of the Gorkhas from Nepal with their families and established Gorkha settlements in the hills of India, such as Bhagsu, Bakloh, Almora, Darjeeling, Deharadun, Shillong, etc. It was only during the period of Prime Minister Bir Shumsher that the Nepalese government freely allowed enlistment of Nepalese in the Indian army.

The second important factor for maintaining open border by the British was to have easy and free access of British and Indian manufactured goods into Nepal as well as to Tibet wherein Nepal was the only easy and accessible route from India before the discovery of Chumbi Valley route from Sikkim.. Moreover, the British wanted to have secure and easy supply of raw materials from Nepal into India such as timber and forest produce, herbs and medicinal plants, hides and skins, etc.

The large scale involvement of men from the hills of Nepal in the World War I led to the shortage of able-bodied youths, particularly the Magars and the Gurungs, resulting in drastic decline in agriculture activities and shortage of foodgrains in the hills. More than 200,000 Nepalese took part in the war with a casualty of 20,000 men or one in every 10. In recognition of this assistance the British government gave Nepal an annual gift of Rs. 100,000 in perpetuity and the amount was increased to Rs. 200,000 after World War II. Most of those who were retired and released from war duty after the war, instead of coming back to Nepal, stayed in India where they could get employment in police and para-military services, security services in factories, offices as well as as domestic servants in Indian cities where they were in great demand for their honesty, loyalty and hard work. In recognition of the contribution of Nepal during World War I, the Treaty of Friendship between Great Britain and Nepal signed at Kathmandu on 21 December 1923 recognised Nepal as a sovereign independent country, and this treaty erased from the Nepalese mind the apprehension of invasion by the British. In order to meet the foodgrains need of the country and to resettle the landless, Prime Minister Chandra Shumsher initiated the development of the Tarai. On the one hand, the clearing of the forests in the Tarai provided agricultural lands and on the other hand, the sal tree that was felled provided much needed timber to be used as sleepers for the expansion of Indian railways. Due to the fear of malaria and unbearable heat of the Tarai, the hill people were reluctant to move to the Tarai and the programme rather benefited the immigrants from India. Moreover, development programmes of the Tarai during the period of Chandra Shumsher like railways linking Amlekhganj to Raxaul and Janakpur to Jayanagar, Chandra canal etc attracted more immigrants from India. Chandra Shumsher abolished slavery in 1926 and the emancipated slaves were resettled in Bicha Khori and which was named as Amlekhgunj, town of emancipation. The freed slaves provided the labour for the construction of railway from Raxaul to Amlekhgunj.

Industrialisation and Development in the Tarai

There has been significant contribution of the Indian technical manpower and skilled immigrants to the industrialisation of the Tarai. During the period of Prime Minister Juddha Shumsher, a lot of industries were established in Biratnagar, Birganj and other areas of the Tarai in the process of industrialisation in the Tarai. Industries were established in jute, cotton and textile, matches, plywood and bobbin, pulses, rice, flour, oil, etc.

The skilled, semi-skilled and unskilled labour for these industries came from India. Those living in the Tarai who had enough land to till for livelihood were not in need of employment outside agriculture, while people from the hill areas, who lacked technical and industrial skills were reluctant to move down to the hot, humid and malarial Tarai and were more inclined to migrate to India for employment. Thus employment opportunities generated by industrialisation in the Tarai benefited and attracted the Indian immigrants. This trend is still continuing. After the Great Earthquake of 1934, a new modern township around New Road was created in the Kathmandu city with new buildings and shopping lines; local businessmen of Kathmandu and businesmen from India were invited to open up shops. The Marwaris some of whom have been settling before earthquake and the other Indian business communities established shops at New Road and in and around Indrachowk, while the original inhabitants who were displaced as a result of the creation of New Road were resettled in Naya Bazar, the are a between Paknajol and Balaju in Kathmandu.

Bibliography

Adhikari, Krishna Kant. *Nepal under Jang Bahadur, 1846-1877.* Kathmandu: Buku, 1984.

Ashok K. : *The Royal Nepal Army : Meeting the Maoist Challenge,* Rupa, Delhi, 2005.

Cheek, Timothy: *Mao Zedong and China's Revolutions: A Brief History with Documents.* Boston: Bedford/St. Martin's, 2002.

Conway, G. 1992. *Sustainable Rural Livelihoods: Practical Concepts for 21st Century.* Sussex: Institute of Development Studies.

Debray, Regis. *Revolution in the Revolution.* New York: Grove Press, Inc., 1993.

Dhanalaxmi, Ravuri. *British Attitude to Nepal's Relations with Tibet and China, 1814-1914.* Chandigarh, India: Bahri, 1981.

Dhanalaxmi, Ravuri. *British Attitude to Nepal's Relations with Tibet and China, 1814-1914.* Chandigarh, India: Bahri, 1981.

Dietmar Rothermund. *A History of India.* Totowa, New Jersey: Barnes and Noble, 1986.

Ellis, F. 2000. *Rural Livelihoods and Diversity in Developing Countries.* New York: Oxford University Press.

Gaige, Frederick H. *Regionalism and National Unity in Nepal.* Berkeley: University of California Press, 1975.

Gao, Mobo: *The Battle for China's Past: Mao and the Cultural Revolution,* London, Pluto Press, 2008.

Jain, M.S. *Emergence of a New Aristocracy in Nepal, 1837-58.* Agra, India: Sri Ram Mehar, 1972.

Kapuria, R.S. *The Indian Rupee: A Study in Retrospect and Prospect.* Bombay: Vora, 1967.

Kay, Geoffrey: *Development and Underdevelopment: A Marxist Analysis,* London, Macmillan, 1975.

Kulke, Hermann, and Dietmar Rothermund. *A History of India.* Totowa, New Jersey: Barnes and Noble, 1986.

Kumar, Satish. *Rana Polity in Nepal: Origin and Growth.* New York: Asia, 1967.

Misra, Shashi P. *B.P. Koirala: A Case Study in Third World Democratic Leadership*. Bhubaneswar, India: Konark, 1985.

Muni, S.D. : *Maoist Insurgency in Nepal : The Challenge and the Response,* Rupa, Delhi, 2004.

Parmanand. *The Nepali Congress since Its Inception: A Critical Assessment.* Delhi: B.R. Publishing, 1982.

Pemble, John. *The Invasion of Nepal: John Company at War*. Oxford: Oxford University Press, 1971.

Rose, Leo E., and Margaret W. Fisher. *The Politics of Nepal: Persistence and Change in an Asian Monarchy*. Ithaca: Cornell University Press, 1970.

Schurmann, Franz: *Ideology and Organization in Communist Nepal.* Berkeley: University of California Press, 1971.

Sharma, P. 1989. *Urbanization in Nepal.* Hawaii: East-West Population Institute.

Sijapati, Li, : *A Kingdom Under Siege : Nepal's Maoist Insurgency, 1996 to 2003,* The Printhouse, Delhi, 2003.

Spear, Percival. *A History of India.* New York: Penguin Books, 1981.

Stuart R. Schram: *The Political Thought of Mao Tse-Tung.* New York: Praeger, 1969.

Thapa, Deepak and Bandita Sijapati: *A Kingdom Under Siege : Nepal's Maoist Insurgency, 1996 to 2003,* The Printhouse, Delhi, 2003.

Thapar, Romila. *A History of India.* New York: Penguin, 1966.

Tilouine, Marie Lecomte : *Hindu Kingship, Ethnic Revival, and Maoist Rebellion in Nepal*, Oxford University Press, Delhi, 2009.

Tse-tung Mao: *Mao and the Nepali Revolution.* London: Oxford University Press, 1965.

Tyagi, Sushila. *Indo-Nepalese Relations, 1858-1914.* Delhi: D.K. Publishing, 1974.

Uddhab P : *Maoist Movement in Nepal: A Sociological Perspective,* Adroit, Delhi, 2007.

Upreti, B C : *Maoists in Nepal : From Insurgency to Political Mainstream*, Kalpaz Pub, Delhi, 2008.

Index

D

E

F

G

H

I

S

T

V

W

❑❑❑